Library Education and
Professional Issues

HANDBOOKS FOR LIBRARY MANAGEMENT

Administration, Personnel, Buildings and Equipment
Acquisitions, Collection Development, and Collection Use
Reference Services and Library Instruction
Cataloging and Catalogs
Circulation, Interlibrary Loan, Patron Use, and Collection Maintenance
Library Education and Professional Issues

Library Education and Professional Issues
A Handbook for Library Management

David F. Kohl

Foreword by Kathleen M. Heim

ABC·CLIO

Santa Barbara, California
Oxford, England

*This book is Smyth sewn and printed on acid-free paper to
meet library standards.*

Library of Congress Cataloging in Publication Data

Kohl, David F., 1942–
  Library education and professional issues.

  (Handbooks for library management)
  Bibliography: p.
  Includes index.
  1. Library education–Handbooks, manuals, etc.
2. Library science–Vocational guidance–Handbooks,
manuals, etc. 3. Librarians–Employment–Handbooks,
manuals, etc. I. Title. II. Series: Kohl, David F.,
1942–   . Handbooks for library management.
Z668.K58 1985   020'.7   85-15833
ISBN 0-87436-436-1 (v.6)
ISBN 0-87436-399-3 (set)

10 9 8 7 6 5 4 3 2 1

ABC-Clio, Inc.
2040 Alameda Padre Serra, Box 4397
Santa Barbara, California 93103

Clio Press Ltd.
55 St. Thomas Street
Oxford OX1 1JG, England

Manufactured in the United States of America

CONTENTS

1.

Library Education

2.

Professional Issues

FOREWORD

Since my days as a doctoral student, I have longed for a source that would isolate variables explored in quantitative library research. I have spent countless hours tracking articles that looked, from the terms under which they were indexed, as if they would supply information I needed, only to find that they only vaguely addressed my topic or that the findings reported were insubstantial. At last, with this final volume of Dr. David Kohl's *Handbook for Library Management*, a reference tool has been developed that will enable researchers to identify statistically valid studies in dozens of areas at the level of individual variables.

While Dr. Kohl's intent is to assist managers and decision-makers who need information quickly, he has also done a significant service for the theoretical base of the profession by analyzing over 800 original studies that meet tests of statistical significance and internal consistency. Scholars as well as managers will find these volumes invaluable for their organization of the results of research findings broken out by discrete variables. Given Dr. Kohl's standards for selection, I anticipate that one measure of the quality of empirical research in our field will be inclusion in this series or its updates.

To some degree it is chilling, given the tons of paper and ink that have been spilled on the topics covered in the *Handbook* series, to see how little research the profession has produced on major topics as disseminated through the journal literature. On the other hand, Dr. Kohl has thrown us a gauntlet and challenged us to initiate research in important areas that will lead to results that can improve librarianship as it is practiced.

In a professional discipline the very purpose of research is a central concern for those who undertake it. Dr. Kohl has demonstrated that all that has been written in our major journals since 1960 can be distilled into fewer than a thousand articles of statistically meaningful findings. His dissection of these articles for presentation of substantive results is a blueprint for future research. Through his analysis the linkage between research and professional practice is clarified and the need for researchers to investigate central problems is made more lucid.

There is a simple analog to medical research called to mind by Dr. Kohl's efforts. A list of illnesses followed by a list of studies providing degree of cures is an obvious indicator to medical researchers of where to place their energies. Similarly, the lists of topics on library issues presented in this series indicate that for many topics there has been a paucity of research. Thus the centrality of a given issue viewed in relationship to the research concerning it often signals that more substantive investigations are needed. The *Handbook* series functions as a guide both to what is known and to what yet needs study to be understood.

The volume at hand is divided into two sections, "Library Education" and "Professional Issues." The first is of immediate and obvious use to librarian educators in search of quantitative data on such areas as curriculum, advanced degrees, faculty evaluation, program rankings, or student attitudes.

At a time when the composition and structure of graduate library education is under scrutiny in the face of changing technologies, this compendium provides easy access to much needed information for planning. For instance, joint degree programs, which seem to be proliferating among schools of library and information science education, are developing in many areas different than those ARL directors deem valuable. According to an annotation in the *Handbook*, over three-fourths of all directors felt that joint degrees are desirable but wanted applicants to earn them in business or computer science. The connection between research on the types of education desired and the types of education being provided does not seem to have been effectively made. In the future it is feasible that reference to the *Handbook* series might alter such dysfunctional behavior.

Oftentimes the studies selected link areas that have eluded the indexer's skill, with the result that more effective use of management data can be obtained. For instance, the scope of faculty publishing as reported in a number of studies completely unrelated to library education supplies a measurement of faculty productivity vis-a-vis areas of subject specialization. Such interconnections are the most valuable aspect of the *Handbook* series.

The second section of this volume, "Professional Issues," is of great importance to all librarians—whether they are supervisors attempting to find successful solutions to affirmative action problems or individuals seeking information for their own professional development. While managers will find it useful to have such issues as career patterns, faculty status, and staff development delineated in concise annotations, I find the importance to the professional contemplating career change just as significant.

The subtopics under "Career Issues" report quantitative findings in 16 different categories subdivided by type of library. Under this rubric an individual with questions about the correct professional decisions for career advancement will find that mobility, increased qualifications (languages, computer expertise), or a second master's degree relate to better placement opportunities. Professional association involvement and publication are also seen to have a positive effect on careers.

Under the topic "Gender Issues," Dr. Kohl has gathered items that contribute to a broader understanding of differential achievement by women and men in the profession. These items are certain to be the subject of close scrutiny as the pay equity movement gains momentum and hard data are required to substantiate recommendations for comparable worth studies.

Considered together the two parts of this volume provide a framework for the occupational sociology of librarianship from entrance to the profession to career development and achievement of goals. They not only provide reliable management information for those whose business is education or staff development, but are a sourcebook for study by individuals seeking guidance in their careers as well. A third group of users of this volume will be those outside of the field who study the professional culture of occupations, require data on pay equity issues, or require statistics on shifting vocational systems.

Since this volume completes Dr. Kohl's ambitious undertaking its appearance will undoubtedly call up the question of updating the project. It is my opinion that yearly *Handbook* updates are certainly in order. The existence of the set will generate an even greater desire on the part of decision-makers to determine policy with all the facts in order. So long as standard abstracting and indexing services continue to assign minimal terms to articles, the need for the *Handbooks* will persist. Until we reach a state of the art where free-text searching is the norm, there will be no substitute for the careful assignation of research findings to key topics developed by Dr. Kohl.

—*Kathleen M. Heim*
Louisiana State University

INTRODUCTION

The *Handbooks for Library Management* have been designed for library managers and decision makers who regularly need information, but who are chronically too short of time to do involved and time-consuming literature searches each time specific, quantitative information is desired. This unusual tool, rather than abstracting complete studies or providing only citations to research, instead presents summaries of individual research findings, grouped by subject. By looking under the appropriate subject heading in the *Handbook*, librarians can find summaries detailing the research findings on that topic. For example, what percentage of reference questions are answered correctly, and does it make a difference whether professional or nonprofessional staff are doing the answering? As a result, helpful information can be found in minutes and without an extensive literature review. Furthermore, if a more complete look at the study is desired, the user is referred to the bibliographic citation number so that the full study can be consulted.

Arrangement

The series consists of six volumes, with each volume covering two or more of the sixteen basic subject areas that divide the volumes into parts. While most of these basic subject divisions reflect such traditional administrative division of library work as administration, circulation, and reference, at least two subject areas go somewhat further. "Library Education" may be of interest, not just to library school administrators, but to faculty and students as well, and "Professional Issues" should be of interest to all career-oriented library professionals. Each basic subject division is further divided by specific subject headings, which are further subdivided by type of library: General (more than one library type), Academic, Public, School, and Special. For example, readers seeking information on book loss rates in academic libraries would consult the basic subject division "Collection Maintenance" and look under the specific subject heading "Loss Rates (Books)," in the "Academic" libraries subdivision. There they would find the summarized results of studies on book loss rates in academic libraries followed by the number referring to the full citation in the Bibliography of Articles.

Each volume in the series follows the same basic pattern: The introduction; a list of the journals surveyed; a detailed table of contents listing all subject headings used in that volume; the research findings arranged by subject; the complete bibliography of articles surveyed for the series with page numbers indicating locations of corresponding research summaries in the text; and an alphabetically arranged author index to the Bibliography of Articles.

The summaries of the research findings also tend to follow a standard format. First the study is briefly described by giving location, date, and, when appropriate, population or survey size and response rate. This information is provided to help users determine the nature, scope, and relevance of the study to their needs. The actual findings, signaled by an italicized *"showed that,"* follow and include, when appropriate, such supporting data as significance level and confidence interval. Information in brackets represents editorial comment, for example "[significance level not given]" or "[remaining cases not accounted for]," while information in parentheses merely represents additional data taken from the article.

The Sample Entries on page xxi identify the elements and illustrate the interrelationships between the subject organization of the volume, research summaries of the text, corresponding article citations in the bibliography, and the author index entries.

Scope

In order to keep the *Handbook* series manageable, a number of scope limitations were necessary. The time period, 1960 through 1983, was selected since it covers the time when quantitative research began to come of age in library research. Only journal literature has been surveyed, because the bulk of quantitative library research is reported in that medium, and because the bulk of editorial and refereeing process required by most journals helps ensure the quality of the research reported. This limitation does ignore a number of important studies reported in monographic form, however, and we hope to cover this area at a later date. Further, only North American journals and research were reviewed since they constitute the main body of quantitative library research reported. Again, this ignores several journals reporting significant library research, particularly journals from Great Britain. We plan to expand our focus and include these in later editions or updates of the *Handbook* series.

Although we generally followed the principle that research good enough to publish was research worth including in the *Handbook* series, several caveats must be stated. First, no research findings with statistical significance exceeding .05 were reported. This follows general Social Science practice and, in recent years, almost universal library research practice. Second, occasional findings, and sometimes whole studies, were not reported in the *Handbook* series when there were serious problems with internal consistency and/or ambiguous and confusing text. At issue here is not the occasional typographical error or arithmetical miscalculation, but those situations where charts and text purportedly presenting the same information differed in substantial and unaccountable ways. Fortunately, such problems were not excessive. And third, as a general rule, only original and supported findings were used in the *Handbook* series. Findings that were reported second-hand, or where the study documentation was reported elsewhere (often the case with doctoral research), were generally not used in the series. Only in those instances when the second-hand data were used to show a pattern or otherwise resulted in new data by their juxtaposition, were such findings reported.

Finally, under the category of unsought limitations, we, like many library users, were not always able to find all the journal articles we needed in the time available to us. However, the excellent holdings and services of the University of Illinois Library Science Library provided us with access to almost all of the journal issues actually published and received by March 1984—a fact that should probably be listed as a record rather than as a limitation.

Acknowledgements

As might be expected, a project of this size required assistance from many quarters. Both the University of Illinois Library Research and Publication Committee and the University of Illinois Research Board provided invaluable assistance in the form of financial support for graduate assistants. The assistants themselves, Becky Rutter, Nicki Varyu, and Bruce Olsen, constituted a dedicated, bright, and hardworking team. The Undergraduate Library staff deserve special thanks for their support and cooperation, as do the Library Science Library staff, who were unfailingly courteous and helpful in making their truly outstanding collection available. The staff at ABC-Clio, particularly Gail Schlachter and Barbara Pope, provided much needed encouragement and good advice, even in the face of several delays and at least one nasty shock. And last, but by no means least, I would like to acknowledge the patience and support of my wife, Marilyn, and my son, Nathaniel, who have given up much in the way of a husband and father so that this *Handbook* series could be completed on schedule.

—David F. Kohl
Urbana, Illinois

SAMPLE ENTRIES

CONTENTS

1. _____

Library Education ◄───────────────────── ──Basic Subject Division
── Specific Subject

Page Number

TEXT

10   LIBRARY EDUCATION ◄

Curriculum—Joint Degree Programs ◄

■ A survey reported in 1983 of directors of Association for Research Libraries ◄── Research Summary
concerning their attitudes toward joint degree programs (resulting in both a
library degree and a degree in some other field) (population surveyed: 111
directors; responding: 93 or 84%) *showed that* only 9 (9.7%) respondents
opposed joint degree programs while 38 (40.9%) felt that "most academic
disciplines" were suitable for joint programs. The 2 disciplines most frequently
mentioned as desirable for joint programs were computer science (47 or 50.3%
respondents) and management or business (47 or 50.3% respondents).   **(803)** ──Number Leading to Article Citation

Ibid. . . . *showed that*, in considering applicants for jobs, directors reported they ◄── Further Summary (Same Article)
would consider the joint degree as follows:

asset	70 (75.3%) respondents
irrelevant	12 (12.9%) respondents
liability	2 (2.2%) respondents
no response	9 (9.7%) respondents

(803) ◄

Citation Number

BIBLIOGRAPHY OF ARTICLES

Author Name
Article Citation
Page Numbers

803 June L. Engle and Elizabeth Futas. "Sexism in Adult Encyclopedias," *RQ* ◄
23:1 (Fall 1983), 29-39. **(10, 11, 91, 92)** ◄

AUTHOR INDEX
TO BIBLIOGRAPHY OF ARTICLES

Number Leading to Article Citation

LIST OF JOURNALS SURVEYED

American Libraries. Chicago: American Library Association, 1970–. Monthly. LC 70-21767. ISSN 0002-9769. (Formerly *ALA Bulletin,* 1907–1969.)

American Society for Information Science. Journal. (JASIS) New York: John Wiley & Sons, 1970–. Bimonthly. LC 75-640174. ISSN 0002-8231. (Formerly *American Documentation,* 1950–1969.)

Canadian Library Journal. Ottawa: Canadian Library Association, 1969–. Bimonthly. LC 77-309891. ISSN 0008-4352. (Formerly *Bulletin,* 1944–March 1960; *Canadian Library,* 1960–1968.)

Catholic Library World. Haverford, PA: Catholic Library Association, 1929–. Monthly. LC 39-41. ISSN 0008-820X.

Collection Building. New York: Schuman, 1978–. Quarterly. LC 78-645190. ISSN 0160-4953.

Collection Management. New York: Haworth Press, 1975–. Quarterly. LC 78-640677. ISSN 0146-2679.

College and Research Libraries. Chicago: American Library Association, 1939–. Bimonthly. LC 42-16492. ISSN 0010-0870.

Drexel Library Quarterly. Philadelphia: Centrum Philadelphia, 1965–. Quarterly. LC 65-9911. ISSN 0012-6160.

Harvard Library Bulletin. Cambridge: Harvard University Library, 1947–. Quarterly. LC 49-1965//R802. ISSN 0017-8136.

International Journal of Legal Information. Camden, NJ: International Association of Law Libraries, 1982–. 6/yr. LC 82-643460. ISSN 0731-1265. (Formerly *Bulletin. International Association of Law Libraries,* 1960–1972; *International Journal of Law Libraries,* 1973–1979.)

International Library Review. London: Academic Press, 1969–. Quarterly. LC 76-10110. ISSN 0020-7837.

Journal of Academic Librarianship. Ann Arbor, MI: Mountainside Publishing, 1975–. Bimonthly. LC 75-647252. ISSN 0099-1333.

Journal of Education for Librarianship. State College, PA: Association of American Library Schools, 1960–. 5/yr. LC 63-24347. ISSN 0022-0604.

Journal of Library Administration. New York: Haworth Press, 1980–. Monthly. LC 80-644826. ISSN 0193-0826.

Journal of Library Automation. Chicago: American Library Association, 1968– . Quarterly. LC 68-6437//R82. ISSN 0022-2240.

Journal of Library History, Philosophy and Comparative Librarianship. Austin, TX: 1966– . Quarterly. LC 65-9989. ISSN 0275-3650. (Formerly *Journal of Library History,* 1966–1975.)

Law Library Journal. Chicago: American Association of Law Libraries, 1908– . Quarterly. LC 41-21688//R6. ISSN 0023-9283.

Library Acquisitions: Practice and Theory. Elmsford, NY: Pergamon Press, 1977– . Quarterly. LC 77-647728. ISSN 0364-6408.

Library Journal. New York: R.R. Bowker, 1876– . Semimonthly, except July–August. LC 76-645271. ISSN 0363-0277.

Library Quarterly. Chicago: University of Chicago, 1931– . Quarterly. LC 32-12448. ISSN 0024-2519.

Library Research. Norwood, NJ: Ablex Publishing, 1979– . Quarterly. LC 79-643718. ISSN 0164-0763.

Library Resources and Technical Services. Chicago: American Library Association, 1957– . Quarterly. LC 59-3198. ISSN 0024-2527. (Formed by the merger of *Serial Slants* and *Journal of Cataloging and Classification.*)

Library Trends. Champaign: University of Illinois at Urbana-Champaign, 1952– . Quarterly. LC 54-62638. ISSN 0024-2594.

Medical Library Association. Bulletin. Chicago: Medical Library Association, 1911– . Quarterly. LC 16-76616. ISSN 0025-7338.

Microform Review. Westport, CT: Meckler Publishing, 1972– . Quarterly. LC 72-620299. ISSN 0002-6530.

Notes. Philadelphia: Music Library Association, 1942– . Quarterly. LC 43-45299//R542. ISSN 0027-4380.

Online. Weston, CT: Online, 1977– . Quarterly. LC 78-640551. ISSN 0416-5422.

Public Libraries. Chicago: American Library Association, 1978– . 4/yr. ISSN 0163-5506. (Formerly *Just Between Ourselves,* 1962–1969; *PLA Newsletter,* 1962–1977.)

RQ. Chicago: American Library Association, 1960– . Quarterly. LC 77-23834. ISSN 0033-7072.

RSR Reference Services Review. Ann Arbor, MI: Perian Press, 1972– . LC 73-642283//R74. ISSN 0090-7324.

School Library Journal. New York: R.R. Bowker, 1954– . Monthly except June and July. LC 77-646483. ISSN 0362-8930.

School Library Media Quarterly. Chicago: American Library Association, 1981– . 4/yr. LC 82-640987. ISSN 0278-4823. (Formerly *School Libraries,* 1951–1972; *School Media Quarterly,* 1972–1980.)

Special Libraries. New York: Special Libraries Association, 1910– . 4/yr. LC 11-25280rev2*. ISSN 0038-6723.

Wilson Library Bulletin. Bronx, NY: H.W. Wilson, 1914– . Monthly except July and August. LC 80-9008(rev.42). ISSN 0043-5651.

1.

Library Education

Accredited Programs

■ A study reported in 1978 of 23 middle managers and 11 administrators in 5 Association of Research Libraries libraries as well as a review of ads for 82 middle managerial positions in academic libraries posted in 1975 *showed that* 43 (52.4%) of the ads listed an ALA-accredited library master's degree as a qualification, 37 (45.1%) listed library master's degree without specifying ALA-accredited, 30 (36.6%) listed second master's degree, 4 (4.9%) listed Ph.D., 1 (1.2%) listed an other professional degree, and 1 stated that a master's degree was not required.   **(423)**

Ibid. . . . *showed that*, of 23 middle managers, 21 (91.3%) had ALA-accredited master's degrees, none had unaccredited library master's degrees, 13 (56.5%) had second master's degrees, 1 (4.3%) had a Ph.D., and 2 (8.7%) had an other professional degree.   **(423)**

Administration

■ A 1977 study of library school assistant deans involving 33 assistant deans at 31 responding schools (out of 33 schools identified as having such a position) *showed that* 25 (76%) were male and 8 (24%) were female.
      (289)

Ibid. . . . *showed that* (multiple responses possible) 24 (73%) had academic library experience, 10 (30%) had public library experience, 10 (30%) had school library experience, 2 (6%) had special library experience, 2 (6%) had information science experience, and 13 (39%) had teaching experience in other fields.   **(289)**

Ibid. . . . *showed that* the 5 most common responsibilities of assistant deans were: admissions (20), scheduling (17), placement (11), general correspondence (11), and editing of catalog, handbooks, etc. (11). All the assistant deans had teaching responsibilities.   **(289)**

Ibid. . . . *showed that* the teaching load for assistant deans was as follows: 1 course (6), 2 courses (14), 3 courses (5), 4 courses (7), and 1 teaches 6 courses.   **(289)**

Ibid. . . . *showed that* 15 (45%) had secretaries of their own (or secretaries over whom they have priority in assigning work), 8 (24%) share the dean's secretary, 7 (21%) use the faculty secretary, 2 use the secretarial pool, and 1 has a graduate assistant.   **(289)**

Ibid. . . . *showed that* the 3 main committees on which assistant deans had regular membership were: curriculum (22), admissions (20), and continuing education (12).   **(289)**

Ibid. . . . *showed that*, of 32 respondents, 20 (61%) had complete freedom to make decisions within all areas of their responsibility, 6 (18%) had freedom to make some decisions, 2 (6%) were rarely involved in the decision-making process, and 5 (15%) had some variation of the above. Further, 17 (54%) were able to act with full authority in the dean's absence, 13 (39%) act only in designated matters in the dean's absence, while 2 (6%) had no authority to act for the dean.   **(289)**

Ibid. . . . *showed that* of 32 respondents, 22 (69%) felt they exercised a leadership role in the library school, 8 (25%) felt they exercised a leadership role to a limited extent, and 2 (6%) felt they did not exercise a leadership role.   **(289)**

Ibid. . . . *showed that* 22 (68%) reported they liked administrative work and wished to continue in their present position while 3 (9%) stated they did not like administrative work and would return to teaching as soon as an opportunity arose. None were interested in returning to library work.
                                                                                                (289)

■ A 1978 survey of full-time faculty in 7 Canadian graduate library schools (population: 81 faculty; survey size: 71 faculty; responding: 59 or 83%) *showed that*, of the 7 library school deans and directors, 5 were male and 2 were female.   **(551)**

Ibid. . . . *showed that* 13 (22.0%) respondents (spread through 4 schools) were involved in extension work. Further, 45 (76%) respondents were involved in academic administration, of which 26 (57.8%) devoted at least 10% of their time to academic administration. 22 (37.3%) respondents reported an involvement in consulting activities.   **(551)**

Admissions

■ A 1974-75 study of university libraries including all Association of Research Libraries libraries (sample size: 92; responding: 72 or 78%) and all library schools with ALA-accredited programs (sample size: not given; responding: 44 or 80%) *showed that*, in Fall 1974, responding library schools reported a total enrollment in the master's program of 9,224 students, of which 125 (1.4%) had subject Ph.D.'s. The total number of subject Ph.D.'s enrolled in the previous 2 years together was 101. **(445)**

■ A study reported in 1978 of students entering the Queens College Graduate Department of Library Science in 1972 and completing the program or withdrawing by Fall 1975 (sample size: 169) *showed that* there was a statistically significant relationship between undergraduate GPA and final graduate library school GPA (significant at the .005 level). Specifically, 63% of those students with UGPAs between 3.35 and 4.0 had GGPAs over 3.76, compared to 29.3% of those with UGPAs under 3.35 who had GGPAs between 3.35 and 4.0. **(291)**

Ibid. . . . *showed that* there was a statistically significant relationship between both verbal and quantitative scores on the Graduate Record Examination and final graduate library school GPA (significant in both cases at the .001 level). Specifically, 39.1% of the students with GREV scores over 600 had GGPAs over 3.76 compared to 12% of the students with GREV scores under 400. Further, 72.2% of those with GREQ scores 600 or better had final graduate library school GPAs of 3.6 or better, while only 65.9% of those with GREQ scores between 400 and 599 had final graduate library school GPAs of 3.6 or better. **(291)**

Ibid. . . . *showed that* comparison of standardized regression coefficients (Betas) revealed that undergraduate GPA was the best predictor of final library school GPA (B = .302), verbal score on the Graduate Record Examination next best (B = .247), and number of years between finishing undergraduate work and beginning library school work (B = .187) (all significant at the .01 level). However, all 3 of the independent variables together only explained 16% of the variance in GGPA. **(291)**

Ibid. . . . *showed that* the equation for predicting final library school GPA was: GGPA = .203 (UGPA) + .00051 (GREV) + .0088 (Interyear) + 2.76 (where Interyear is number of years between finishing undergraduate degree and beginning library school). **(291)**

Ibid. . . . *showed that* an undergraduate GPA 4+ years old (graduating in 1968 or earlier) predicted a higher final library school GPA than the same undergraduate GPA less than 4 years old (graduating after 1968). For example, a pre-1968 3.0 UGPA was the equal of a post-1968 3.6 UGPA. **(291)**

■ A study reported in 1981 of 97 full-time master's degree candidates at the University of Illinois Graduate Library School *showed that* undergraduate GPA was the most strongly correlated variable with Library School graduating GPA. The following variables and their correlation coefficients were: undergraduate GPA, 0.322; score for prior library work, −0.250; Graduate Record quantitative score, 0.241; Graduate Record verbal score, 0.167; score for professional statement, −0.099; and score for recommendations, 0.055 (no significance level given). **(294)**

Ibid. . . . *showed that* taken together the undergraduate GPA, the verbal and quantitative scores from the Graduate Record exams, and the scores derived from the students' application recommendations accounted for 16% of the variance of the graduating GPA from library school (significance level at .005). **(294)**

Ibid. . . . *showed that* the best equation for predicting library school graduating GPA was: GGPA = 2.962 + .671 (UGPA) + .003 (GREV) + .007 (GREQ) + .011 (RECS), where RECS was score derived from application recommendations for library school. **(294)**

Admissions—Medical Library Education Programs

■ A survey reported in 1973 of 16 past and present medical library education programs (8 degree programs; 8 internship programs) *showed that* the 4 most important factors (out of 8) in selecting trainees for the medical library degree programs were:

academic record	8 (100.0%) respondents
statement of interest	6 (75.0%) respondents
recommendations	5 (62.5%) respondents
aptitude tests	5 (62.5%) respondents

while the 4 most important factors (out of 8) in selecting trainees for the medical library internship programs were:

academic record	7 (87.5%) respondents
interviews	5 (62.5%) respondents
personal appearance and personality	4 (50.0%) respondents
subject competency	4 (50.0%) respondents **(694)**

Curriculum—General Issues

■ A 1976 survey of students enrolled at the Graduate Library School at Indiana University (population: 194; responding: 147 or 76%) *showed that* 17% agreed, 38% disagreed, and 45% were uncertain as to whether librarianship lacked theory to give it direction and purpose. Of those already holding an advanced degree, 33% felt that librarianship lacked theory, while only 12% of those without an advanced degree felt that librarianship lacked theory. This was a statistically significant difference (significant at the .05 level). **(293)**

Ibid. . . . *showed that* 35% agreed that librarianship should be more concerned with "why" than "how," 20% disagreed, and 45% were unsure. 42% of the women vs. 16% of the men agreed that librarianship should be more concerned with "why" than "how." This was a statistically significant difference (significant at the .05 level). **(293)**

Ibid. . . . *showed that* 50% of the students agreed that library school courses should stress "how-to-do-it," while 11% disagreed and 39% were uncertain. However, when asked if library schools should prepare students for the immediate tasks of their first job rather than teach principles useful for the future, only 3% agreed, 67% disagreed, and 30% were unsure. **(293)**

■ A survey of the larger employers of librarians in the state of Indiana reported in 1977 and including academic, public, special, and school libraries (31 institutions or systems queried; 30 responding) *showed that* 17 (57%) of the respondents reported that they felt the preparation of present-day graduates was "equal" to that of former graduates; 9 (30%) felt that present graduates had superior preparation to former graduates, and 2 (7%) felt that present-day graduates had preparation "not as good" as former graduates (2 employers did not respond). **(285)**

■ A 1979 survey of members of the ACRL Discussion Group of Personnel Officers (sample size: 45; responding: 30) concerning entry-level requirements for professionals *showed that*, assuming the basic courses have been taken, 6 respondents mentioned courses involving business skills, 5 mentioned courses involving automation/computer networking, 4 mentioned courses involving online reference and/or cataloging, and 2 mentioned courses involving research skills as best preparation for beginning librarians in academic libraries. **(240)**

Ibid. . . . *showed that* for long-term growth the skills respondents mentioned were in the following areas: management skills (10 respondents), computer background (6 respondents), advanced degrees (5 respondents), and depth of subject expertise (5 respondents).   **(240)**

■ A study reported in 1981 of 339 undergraduate and graduate students primarily enrolled as education and library science majors at the University of Iowa and Michigan State University (142 in treatment group; 197 in control group) *showed that* the group exposed to an educational censorship unit were statistically significantly less likely to reject books for a school library collection whose positive book reviews had been arbitrarily assigned a warning indicator signaling that the book might contain objectionable material than the control group.   **(221)**

Ibid. . . . *showed that* the treatment effects were across the board and made no statistically significant differential increase in the number of books with warning indicators selected for older children as compared to younger children.   **(221)**

Curriculum—Acquisitions Courses

■ A 1978 survey of accredited library school programs in North America (population: 64; responding: 27 or 42%) to determine the courses including at least some teaching about acquisitions ("actual procurement of bibliographic items" rather than selection) *showed that* a total of 65 specific courses were identified. The acquisitions element was found in a collection development course in 16 cases, in a technical service course in 8 cases, and in a foundations or introductory course in 3 cases. An acquisitions element was also frequently found in special materials courses such as government documents, serials, media, and rare books.   **(304)**

Curriculum—Cataloging Courses

■ A 1977 survey of the cataloging department heads in the library of each of the universities with American Library Association accredited graduate library programs (survey size: 60 libraries; responding: 42 or 70%) *showed that*, although 39 (93%) respondents reported that the "quest for theory in cataloging" was a worthwhile objective, only 23 (55%) reported that knowing cataloging theory was more important for graduate library students than knowing cataloging techniques (18 or 43% reported that knowing cataloging techniques was more important than knowing cataloging theory, while 1 respondent reported that both were important).
                      (761)

Ibid. . . . *showed that* 37 (88%) agreed with the idea that since the first cataloging course taken by a graduate students was sometimes their only cataloging course it should focus on practical applications. 5 (12%) disagreed. **(761)**

Ibid. . . . *showed that* 26 (62%) respondents felt that the type of course work presently available in most library schools did not adequately prepare students for positions in cataloging. 10 (24%) respondents felt the course work did, 1 (2%) felt both that it did and did not, and 5 (12%) did not respond. **(761)**

Ibid. . . . *showed that* 33 (79%) respondents felt that the actual procedures of university library cataloging did not reflect the way cataloging was taught in library schools. 6 (14%) respondents did think university library cataloging procedures reflected the way cataloging was taught in library schools, 1 (2%) both agreed and disagreed, and 2 (5%) did not respond. **(761)**

Ibid. . . . *showed that* 39 (93%) respondents reported that cooperative cataloging had not lessened the need for cataloging courses in the curriculum while 3 (7%) respondents felt that it had. **(761)**

Curriculum—Information Science Courses

■ A survey reported in 1978 of 54 catalogs (84%) of the 64 accredited library programs in North America as listed in the 1977 *Journal of Education for Librarianship* concerning courses in the 5 areas of information science (library automation, information storage and retrieval, systems analysis, interactive computer systems, and programming) *showed that*:

library automation: 44 (81%) of the schools offered 1 or more courses in this area, while 22 (41%) offered 2 or more courses in this area;

information storage and retrieval: 43 (80%) of the schools offered 1 or more courses in this area, while 18 (33%) offered 2 or more courses;

systems analysis: 26 (48%) of the schools offered 1 or more courses in this area, while 5 (9%) offered 2 or more courses;

interactive computer systems: 15 (28%) of the schools offered 1 or more courses in this area, while 3 (6%) offered 2 or more courses;

and programming: 6 (11%) of the schools offered 1 or more courses in this area, while no schools offered 2 or more courses. **(255)**

Ibid. . . . *showed that,* of all the information science courses offered in all of the schools, the average number of courses offered per school was 3.7 while the median was 3. **(255)**

Ibid. . . . *showed that* 98% of the schools offered 1 course in information science, 54% of the schools offered 4 or less courses in information science, 30% of the schools offered 5 or less courses in information science, and 2% of the schools offered 9 or less courses in information science. **(255)**

Ibid. . . . *showed that,* of the 5 categories of information science courses, the average number of categories per school was 2.5, the median was 2, and the mode (33% of the schools) was 3. **(255)**

Ibid. . . . *showed that,* of the computer languages taught in the programming courses, the 2 most frequently mentioned were PL/1 (mentioned in connection with 4 courses) and query languages (mentioned in connection with 3 courses). **(255)**

Curriculum—Joint Degree Programs

■ A survey reported in 1983 of directors of Association for Research Libraries concerning their attitudes toward joint degree programs (resulting in both a library degree and a degree in some other field) (population surveyed: 111 directors; responding: 93 or 84%) *showed that* only 9 (9.7%) respondents opposed joint degree programs while 38 (40.9%) felt that "most academic disciplines" were suitable for joint programs. The 2 disciplines most frequently mentioned as desirable for joint programs were computer science (47 or 50.3% respondents) and management or business (47 or 50.3% respondents). **(803)**

Ibid. . . . *showed that,* in considering applicants for jobs, directors reported they would consider the joint degree as follows:

asset	70 (75.3%) respondents
irrelevant	12 (12.9%) respondents
liability	2 (2.2%) respondents
no response	9 (9.7%) respondents **(803)**

Ibid. . . . *showed that* the maximum number of semester hours that the joint program should be reduced from the number of hours required for the 2 programs separately was as follows:

no reduction	6 (6.5%)	respondents
6 hours reduction	15 (16.1%)	respondents
8 hours reduction	5 (5.4%)	respondents
9 hours reduction	1 (1.1%)	respondents
10 hours reduction	15 (16.1%)	respondents
12 hours reduction	24 (25.8%)	respondents
16 hours reduction	1 (1.1%)	respondents
no response	26 (28.0%)	respondents **(803)**

Ibid. . . . *showed that* 54 (58.1%) respondents felt that joint graduate degrees were equal to the same degrees earned independently, 27 (29.0%) felt they were not equal, and 12 (12.9%) did not respond.   **(803)**

Ibid. . . . *showed that* directors' responses to hiring job applicants with joint graduate degrees compared to hiring applicants with just the M.L.S. degree were as follows:

6 (6.5%) respondents reported that there would be no preference between the candidates;

65 (69.9%) reported they would be more likely to hire the candidate with the joint degrees, while 2 (2.2%) reported they would be more likely to hire the candidate with the M.L.S. only;

47 (50.5%) reported they would pay more to a candidate with the joint degrees, while 20 (21.5%) reported they would not pay more;

43 (46.2%) reported they felt 2 graduate degrees were desirable for nearly all professional positions, 3 (3.2%) reported that they felt 2 graduate degrees were undesirable for most positions, 54 (58.1%) reported they felt 2 graduate degrees were desirable for specialist positions, and 30 (32.3%) reported they felt 2 graduate degrees were desirable for administrative positions.   **(803)**

Curriculum—Reference Courses

■ A report published in 1976 on a statewide Teletype reference service provided by library school students at the University of Iowa in an advanced reference course, involving 460 questions received in the first 6 months of 1974 from college libraries or public library regional centers, *showed that* 61% of the questions were answered completely successfully, 13% received nearly complete answers, 10% of the answers may have been minimally useful to the patron, and for 16% there were no available answers.   **(146)**

Ibid. . . . *showed that* only 36 (7.8%) of the questions were answered using sources listed in *Reference Books for Small and Medium-Sized Libraries* and that theoretically should not have required referral of the question.
(146)

Curriculum—Relations with the Field

■ A 1979 survey of Canadian librarians in 3 groups (librarians who were or had been executives of a library or library-related associations in Canada; library administrators and department heads in public or academic libraries located within 20 miles of a library school; and library school full-time faculty) concerning the interaction [no time period given] between the library field and library schools (survey size: 120 association librarians, 120 library administrators, and [65] library school faculty; responding: 78 or 65% association librarians, 90 or 75% library administrators, and 43 or 66% library school faculty) *showed that* interaction related to course preparation (e.g., what elements should be included in a course, course assignments, examples from experience, etc.) averaged .8 activities per both groups of practitioners, with the following breakdown:

0 activities per practitioner	54% practitioners
1 activity per practitioner	23% practitioners
2 activities per practitioner	15% practitioners
3 activities per practitioner	8% practitioners **(554)**

Ibid. . . . *showed that* interaction related to degree programs (e.g., serving on an accreditation team, curriculum committee, etc.) was as follows:

54% of the practitioners had volunteered suggestions or recommended topics for the curriculum;

11% had been asked to review a program;

10% had sat on a curriculum or other library school committee;

and 3 respondents had served as members of an accreditation team.
(554)

Ibid. . . . *showed that* interaction with practitioners reported by library school faculty in terms of course planning and presentation was as follows:

> 63% of the instructors consulted with practitioners concerning 3 elements: course elements, course assignments, and illustrations of theory;

> 80% of the instructors consulted with practitioners concerning 2 of the 3 elements listed above. **(554)**

Curriculum—Special Librarianship Courses

■ A study reported in 1976 of the 1974-75 bulletins of 62 ALA-accredited library school programs in North America *showed that* 1 course in special librarianship was offered in 66% of the schools and a further 15% offer 2 courses in this area for a total of 81% of the schools offering 1 or more courses in special librarianship. **(414)**

Ibid. . . . *showed that* 26% of the schools offer formal programs in special librarianship. **(414)**

Ibid. . . . *showed that* the 4 most common areas in which 1 or more courses for special librarianship were taught were: medical/health librarianship (37 or 60% schools), law librarianship (22 or 35% schools), music librarianship (13 or 21% schools), and art librarianship (5 or 8% schools). **(414)**

■ A survey reported in 1983 of 249 special library respondents in 28 major firms (126 of the respondents had a master's degree in library science or the equivalent) *showed that* the 3 library school courses out of 9 ranked by the most respondents as "important' or "very important" were:

> online searching (43% respondents took the course in library school; 83% rated it as "important" or "very important");

> specialized reference (93% respondents took the course in library school; 76% rated it as "important" or "very important");

> general reference (97% respondents took the course in library school; 69% rated it as "important" or "very important"). **(443)**

Ibid. . . . *showed that* the 4 courses that the most respondents with library school degrees wished they had taken were (multiple responses allowed): programming (45 or 35.7% respondents), online searching (37 or 29.4% respondents), computer science (30 or 23.8% respondents), and management and business administration (22 or 17.5% respondents)   **(443)**

Ibid. . . . *showed that* those courses that special librarians rank most highly are not those that academic librarians rank highly. A comparison of course rankings by special librarians and by ARL library directors in terms of importance for subsequent job performance *showed that* the 5 courses that special librarians rank most highly receive only an average rank of 10.2 out of 19 by the ARL librarians.   **(443)**

Deans

■ A 1978 survey of full-time faculty in 7 Canadian graduate library schools (population: 81 faculty; survey size: 71 faculty; responding: 59 or 83%) *showed that*, of the 7 library school deans and directors, 5 were male and 2 were female.   **(551)**

■ A study reported in 1983 investigating the educational and professional qualifications of the 162 individuals holding deanships (excluding acting or interim deans) of ALA-accredited library school programs in North America during the period 1960-81 *showed that* for the whole period women accounted for 39 (24.1%) of the deanships and men for 123 (75.9%) of the deanships. Further, of the 62 library school deans holding office in 1981, 13 (21%) were women and 49 (79%) were men.   **(562)**

Ibid. . . . *showed that* the 29 library education programs in the U.S. that had maintained ALA accreditation throughout the period 1960-81 had 77 deans during this period, including 14 (18.2%) women and 63 (81.8%) men. The 2 Canadian library education programs that had likewise maintained ALA accreditation throughout the 1960-81 period had 9 deans, including 8 (88.9%) women and 1 (11.1%) men.   **(562)**

Ibid. . . . *showed that* the average age at which the 39 women were first appointed dean was 49.7 years while the average age at which the 123 men were first appointed dean was 44.8 years.   **(562)**

Ibid. . . . *showed that* 144 (88.9%) of the deans had a fifth-year (master's level) library degree, including 37 (94.9%) of the women and 107 (87%) of the men. Further, 3 library schools together accounted for 40.3% of the 144 fifth-year degrees awarded deans. These were: Columbia (32 or 22.2% of the fifth-year degrees), University of Illinois (14 or 9.7% of the fifth-year degrees), and University of Michigan (12 or 8.3% or the fifth-year degrees).   **(562)**

Ibid. . . . *showed that* 67 (41.4%) of the deans held subject master's degrees, including 9 (23.1%) women and 58 (47.2%) men.   **(562)**

Ibid. . . . *showed that* 124 (76.5%) of the deans held doctorates, including 24 (61.5%) women and 100 (81.3%) men. The types of doctorates held were as follows:

Ph.D.	15 (38.4%) women;	88 (71.5%) men
D.L.S.	6 (15.4%) women;	7 (5.7%) men
Ed.D.	3 (7.7%) women;	4 (3.3%) men
Des. L.	0 (0.0%) women;	1 (0.8%) men

Further, 78 of the doctorates were in library science, while the remainder were in other subject areas.   **(562)**

Ibid. . . . *showed that*, of the 12 ALA-accredited library schools awarding a total of 77 Ph.D.'s or D.L.S.'s to the deans, the 3 schools awarding the most library science doctorates to this group of deans were: University of Chicago (15 or 19.5% of the library science doctorates), University of Michigan (14 or 18.2% of the library science doctorates), and Columbia (12 or 15.6% of the library science doctorates).   **(562)**

Ibid. . . . *showed that* the average total years of professional experience per library school dean was 17.5 years, including an average of 21.7 years of professional experience per female dean and 16.2 years of professional experience per male dean.   **(562)**

Ibid. . . . *showed that* the average total years of library experience per library school dean was 10.5 years, including an average of 11.3 years per female dean and an average of 10.3 years per male dean.   **(562)**

Ibid. . . . *showed that* 62 (38.3%) library school deans had previously served as faculty members of the same library school to which they were appointed dean, including 24 (61.5%) of the female deans and 38 (30.9%) of the male deans.   **(562)**

Ibid. . . . *showed that* 33 (20.4%) library school deans had had previous library school administrative experience, including 7 (17.9%) women deans and 26 (21.1%) male deans.   **(562)**

Ibid. . . . *showed that* 147 (90.7%) deans had had library experience. A higher proportion of women than men had received most of their library experience in school libraries (12 or 30.8% women; 10 or 8.1% men), while a larger proportion of men than women had received most of their library experience in govermental libraries (2 or 5.1% women; 14 or 11.4% men) and special libraries (no women; 7 or 5.7% men). There was little difference between the proportions of men and women who had received most of their library experience in public libraries (5 or 12.8% women; 17 or 13.8% men) or academic libraries (19 or 48.7% women; 57 or 46.3% men).   **(562)**

Doctoral Education—General Issues

■ An analysis reported in 1974 of 660 library science and library science related dissertations completed between 1925 and 1972 *showed that* overall, for the period 1925-72, 76.95% of the doctorates awarded for library science research were Ph.D.'s, 13.20% were Ed.D.'s, 8.55% were D.L.S.'s, and 1.3% were other.   **(283)**

Ibid. . . . *showed that* 48% of the 435 doctoral recipients who received their degrees between 1953-72 worked in positions or with activities that appeared to be far removed from the scope of their dissertations. The primary exception to this general trend was library school faculty, where 63.3% taught courses that generally coincided with their dissertation topic.
                                                                              (283)

Ibid. . . . *showed that*, of the 435 doctoral recipients who received their degrees between 1953-72, there was no statistically significant relationship between type of degree earned (Ph.D., D.L.S., and Ed.D.) and the type of position held (faculty, academic libraries, public libraries, school libraries, special libraries, other) at the time of the analysis. D.L.S. recipients were as likely as Ph.D. or Ed.D. recipients to teach on library school faculties, while Ph.D. recipients were as likely as D.L.S. or Ed.D. recipients to have jobs in academic libraries, etc.   **(283)**

■ A 1974-75 study of university libraries including all Association of Research Libraries libraries (sample size: 92; responding: 72 or 78%) and all library schools with ALA-accredited programs (sample size: not given; responding: 44 or 80%) *showed that*, in Fall 1974, responding library schools reported a total enrollment in the master's program of 9,224 students, of which 125 (1.4%) had subject Ph.D.'s. The total number of subject Ph.D.'s enrolled in the previous 2 years together was 101.   **(445)**

Ibid. . . . *showed that*, of those Ph.D.'s enrolled in library master's degree programs in the 2 years prior to the study, the major subject areas represented were: history (16.9%), English (16.9%) education (9.6%), languages (7.2%), law (4.8%), and music (3.6%).   **(445)**

Ibid. . . . *showed that* the 13 responding library schools that awarded Ph.D.'s reported 113 Ph.D.'s awarded in the 2 years prior to the survey. Of this 113, 31 did not seek employment, 36 took positions in library administration, and 46 took teaching positions.   **(445)**

■ A survey reported in 1978 of traceable North American librarians who had earned library doctorates in American Library Association accredited programs between 1930 and 1975 (survey size: 568; responding: 403 or 71%) *showed that* 51.3% reported being in library education, 33.8% reported being in the field of library administration, 11.1% reported library research (as distinct from any other categories), and 3.8% reported being in library operations.   **(463)**

Doctoral Education—Dissertation Research

■ A study of the citations in 186 doctoral dissertations of the 190 completed between the years 1969-72 in ALA-accredited library science programs (population: 43,500 citations; sample size: 2,139 citations, providing a sampling error of ±2% at 95% confidence level) *showed that* 917 (42.9%) of the citations were to books, 498 (23.2%) to journals, 457 (21.4%) to unpublished materials (due primarily to the 15% of the dissertations on historical topics), 70 (3.3%) to proceedings, 64 (3%) to annual reports, 59 (2.8%) to dissertations, 43 (2%) to newspapers and magazines, and 31 (1.4%) to reports.   **(633)**

Ibid. . . . *showed that* for all categories of dissertations combined the age of cited work from dissertation date was as follows: 0-5 years (24.2%), 6-10 years (12%), 11-20 years (12.5%), 20+ years (51.3%). The most striking exceptions to this general pattern were dissertations on automation (9% of the dissertations overall), which had 68.2% of their citations in the 0-5 year category, and historical dissertations (28% of the dissertations overall), which had 76.9% of their citations in the 20+ category.   **(633)**

Ibid. . . . *showed that* 88.6% of the citations were to English-language publications, 5.6% were to German-language publications, 0.2% to French-language publications, and the remainder to "other" language publications.   **(633)**

Ibid. . . . *showed that* 1,610 (75.3%) citations were to publications published in the U.S., 240 (11.2%) citations were to foreign, English-language publications, and 289 (13.5%) were to foreign, non-English-language publications.   **(633)**

■ An analysis reported in 1974 of 660 library science and library science related dissertations completed between 1925 and 1972 *showed that* categorizing the 660 dissertations into 1 of 7 research methodologies ("all others" includes theory and experimental design as well) over time revealed the following percentages of total dissertations for the periods 1925-29, 1930-39, 1940-49, 1950-59, 1960-69, 1970-72:

citation analysis:	0	2.00	19.39	10.64	9.65	9.9
operations research:	0	3.33	0	2.50	6.65	16.75
survey research:	33.33	50.66	57.29	33.71	46.23	53.00
historical analysis:	66.67	25.60	23.32	48.15	33.70	14.26
all others:	0	18.41	0	5.00	3.77	6.09

(283)

Ibid. . . . *showed that* there was a statistically significant relationship (significant at the .05 level) between type of doctorate received and research method used for dissertation. The heaviest users of the survey research method were Ed.D. candidates (82.49% compared to 47.25% for D.L.S., 36.86% for Ph.D., and 25.00% for other); the heaviest users of citation analysis were D.L.S. candidates (15.75% compared to 9.50% for Ph.D., 2.26% for Ed.D., and 0% for other); the heaviest users of historical analysis were Ph.D. candidates (33.25% compared to 29.05% for D.L.S., 0.04% for Ed.D., and 0% for other).   **(283)**

Ibid. . . . *showed that* for 262 proposed dissertation topics there was a statistically significant relationship between research method chosen and likelihood of completing the dissertation. Generally the ratio of finishers to nonfinishers was approximately 60% to 40%, but for candidates using survey research methodology the ratio was 66.7% to 33.3%, while for candidates using historical analysis the ratio was 35.4% to 64.6%.   **(283)**

Ibid. . . . *showed that,* for 145 completed dissertations for which the starting date was known, 2.8% were completed in less than 1 year. 31.7% took 1 year, 31.1% took 2 years, 17.5% took 3 years, 11.0% took 4 years, 4.5% took 5 years, and 1.4% took 6+ years. Neither sex of candidate nor research method chosen related in a statistically significant way to completion time.   **(283)**

■ A review reported in 1980 of public library research reported in the 1970s that involved at least 1 person-year of effort (193 studies considered consisting of 90 doctoral dissertations, 40 HEA Title II-B projects, and 63 other reports, monographs, or studies) *showed that*:

> universities were the facilitating agency for 90 dissertations, 21 Title II-B projects, and 16 other projects;
>
> professional associations were the facilitating agency for 4 Title II-B projects;
>
> R and D firms were the facilitating agency for 7 Title II-B projects and 22 other projects;
>
> municipal, state, or regional agencies were the facilitating agency for 8 Title II-B projects and 11 other projects;
>
> and individuals were the facilitating agency for 14 projects.   **(364)**

Ibid. . . . *showed that* the 6 most popular areas for public library research were:

public services	43 projects
user studies	37 projects
management	33 projects
funding	21 projects
cooperation	20 projects
history	20 projects **(364)**

■ A study reported in 1983 of 98 doctoral dissertations in library administration (taken from *Dissertations in Library Science* 1930-80 by C. H. Davis, 1980) *showed that* doctoral dissertations in library administration tended to be supervised by a widely scattered, rather than small core, of individuals. For example, only 1 supervisor oversaw as many as 8 dissertations in library administration, while 34 supervisors oversaw 1 dissertation each, and 14 oversaw 2 dissertations each in library administration.   **(560)**

Ibid. . . . *showed that* research continuinty in the area of library administration was very limited. For example, of the 23 individuals supervising 2 or more doctoral dissertations in library administration:

> 4 of the supervisors had no earned Ph.D.;
>
> of the 19 supervisors who had an earned doctorate, 4 had doctorates in fields or disciplines other than library science;
>
> of the 15 supervisors who had doctorates in library science, only 1 supervisor had a degree in library administration.   **(560)**

Doctoral Education—Major Institutions

■ An analysis reported in 1974 of 660 library science and library science related dissertations completed between 1925 and 1972 *showed that*, while the 660 dissertations came from a total of 68 private and public academic institutions, "three-fifths" of them were written at 6 schools: University of Chicago, University of Michigan, Columbia University, University of Illinois, Case Western Reserve University, and Rutgers University. Between 1925-50 the University of Chicago produced 2/3 of the 100 dissertations written; since the early 1960s Columbia and University of Michigan each produced twice as many dissertations as the University of Chicago.
(283)

■ A study reported in 1983 of 98 doctoral dissertations in library administration (taken from *Dissertations in Library Science* 1930-80 by C. H. Davis, 1980) *showed that* the 3 most productive library schools (out of 18) in this area were:

Florida State	13 (13.3%) dissertations
Indiana	13 (13.3%) dissertations
University of Pittsburgh	11 (11.2%) dissertations

Further, the 3 library schools with the oldest doctoral programs (University of Chicago; University of Illinois, Urbana; and Columbia University) had each only produced 6 doctoral dissertations in the area of library administration, while Indiana's first dissertation in library administration appeared in 1970 and Florida State's first such dissertation appeared in 1972.
(560)

■ A study reported in 1983 investigating the educational and professional qualifications of the 162 individuals holding deanships (excluding acting or interim deans) of ALA-accredited library school programs in North America during the period 1960-81 *showed that*, of the 12 ALA-accredited library schools awarding a total of 77 Ph.D.'s or D.L.S.'s to the deans, the 3 schools awarding the most library science doctorates to this group of deans were: University of Chicago (15 or 19.5% of the library science doctorates), University of Michigan (14 or 18.2% of the library science doctorates), and Columbia (12 or 15.6% of the library science doctorates).
(562)

Doctoral Education—Number of Degrees Awarded

■ An analysis reported in 1974 of 660 library science and library science related dissertations completed between 1925 and 1972 *showed that* there were "three distinct and increasingly active periods of production": 1925-59 with an average of 4.5 dissertations a year, 1960-69 with an average of 24.1 dissertations a year, and 1970-72 with an average of 73.0 dissertations a year. **(283)**

■ A 1974-75 study of university libraries including all Association of Research Libraries libraries (sample size: 92; responding: 72 or 78%) and all library schools with ALA-accredited programs (sample size: not given; responding: 44 or 80%) *showed that* the 13 responding library schools that awarded Ph.D.'s reported 113 Ph.D.'s awarded in the 2 years prior to the survey. Of this 113, 31 did not seek employment, 36 took positions in library administration, and 46 took teaching positions. **(445)**

■ A study reported in 1982 comparing U.S. government projections (taken from *Projections of Educational Statistics*) for the number of graduates from library science degree programs with actual numbers of graduates from such programs *showed that* for all 3 kinds of library degrees the long-term projections were extremely inaccurate and even the shortest-term projections were quite inaccurate except for doctoral candidates. For example:

> in 1979-80, 73 doctoral degrees in library science were actually granted, while the projected number of doctoral degrees for 1979-80 in 1971 was 40, in 1973 was 60, in 1976 was 90, and in 1978 was 80;

> in 1979-80, 5,374 master's degrees in library science were actually granted, while the projected number of master's degrees for 1979-80 in 1971 was 19,280, in 1973 was 10,940, in 1976 was 10,250, and in 1978 was 8,920;

> in 1979-80, 398 bachelor's degrees in library science were actually granted, while the projected number of bachelor's degrees for 1979-80 in 1971 was 1,580, in 1973 was 1,520, in 1976 was 1,410, and in 1978 was 940. **(665)**

Ibid. . . . *showed that* the number of doctoral degrees granted in library science rose from 14 in 1960-61 to a high of 102 in 1972-73 and declined to 73 in 1979-80. **(665)**

■ A study reported in 1983 of data gathered by the Office for Library Personnel Resources on master's and doctoral level degree recipients from ALA-accredited programs during the period 1973-74 through 1980-81 *showed that* the number of master's level graduates dropped from 6,323 in 1973-74 to 3,776 in 1980-81, a decline of 40%. The number of earned doctoral degrees awarded remained fairly constant during that period, ranging (with the exception of 1974-75, when 78 doctoral degrees were awarded) from 46 awarded in 1979-80 to 56 awarded in 1978-79.   **(787)**

Doctoral Education—Women and Minorities

■ An analysis reported in 1974 of 660 library science and library science related dissertations completed between 1925 and 1972 *showed that*, although the absolute number of dissertations in librarianship written by women had increased steadily, the proportion of dissertations written by women had remained relatively unchanged at an average rate of 31.1% in any given year. Annual increases and decreases in the number of dissertations by women were statistically nonsignificant.   **(283)**

Ibid. . . . *showed that* there was no statistically significant relationship between sex and type of degree received, between sex and research method chosen, or betweeen sex and whether the dissertation was completed.   **(283)**

Ibid. . . . *showed that* for 435 doctoral recipients who received their degrees between 1953-72 there was a statistically significant relationship between sex and current type of position held (significant at the .001 level). Specifically, a higher proportion of males (29.3%) than females (14.3%) tended to work in academic libraries, while a higher proportion of females (65.7%) than males (58.1%) tended to join library school faculties. 3.8% of the females vs. 1.4% of the males worked in public libraries, 6.7% of the females vs. 0.5% of the males worked in school libraries, and 1.9% of the females vs. 2.7% of the males worked in special libraries. 7.6% of the females and 8.0% of the males worked in "other" positions.   **(283)**

Ibid. . . . *showed that* for 435 doctoral recipients who received their degrees between 1953-72 there was no statistically significant relationship between sex and mobility. Specifically, comparing location of job to location of school, 17.0% of the females and 9.5% of the males were in the same state, 27.4% of the females and 31.8% of the males were in contiguous states, while 55.6% of the females and 58.7% of the males were "geographically removed."   **(283)**

■ A study reported in 1983 of data gathered by the Office for Library Personnel Resources on master's- and doctoral-level degree recipients from ALA-accredited programs during the period 1973-74 through 1980-81 *showed that* during the 8-year period 436 doctoral degrees were awarded, of which 213 (48.85%) went to females and 223 (51.15%) went to males. Since 1978-79 more females than males received doctoral degrees each year (29 females vs. 27 males in 1978-79; 32 females vs. 14 males in 1979-80; and 31 females vs. 23 males in 1980-81). The distribution of doctoral degrees by ethnic group for this 8-year period was as follows:

white females received 168 (38.53%) and white males received 188 (43.12%) of the total doctotal degrees awarded in the 8-year period;

black females received 20 (4.59%) and black males received 13 (2.98%) of the total doctoral degrees awarded in the 8-year period;

Asian/Pacific Islander females received 16 (3.67%) and Asian/Pacific Islander males received 8 (1.83%) of the total doctoral degrees awarded in the 8-year period;

Hispanic females received 5 (1.15%) and Hispanic males received 4 (.92%) of the total doctoral degrees awarded in the 8-year period;

American Indian/Alaskan native females received 2 (.46%) and AI/AN males received 2 (.46%) of the total doctoral degrees awarded in the 8-year period. **(787)**

Ibid. . . . *showed that* during the 8 years of the study 80 (18.35%) of the doctoral degrees were awarded to minorities, compared to 9.50% of the M.L.S. degrees awarded to minorities in the same time period. **(787)**

Faculty—General Issues

■ An analysis reported in 1974 of 660 library science and library science related dissertations completed between 1925 and 1972 *showed that* 48% of the 435 doctoral recipients who received their degrees between 1953-72 worked in positions or with activities that appeared to be far removed from the scope of their dissertations. The primary exception to this general trend was library school faculty, where 63.3% taught courses that generally coincided with their dissertation topic. **(283)**

Ibid. . . . *showed that*, of the 435 doctoral recipients who received their degrees between 1953-72, there was no statistically significant relationship between type of degree earned (Ph.D., D.L.S., and Ed.D.) and the type of position held (faculty, academic libraries, public libraries, school libraries, special libraries, other) at the time of the analysis. D.L.S. recipients were as likely as Ph.D. or Ed.D. recipients to teach on library school faculties, while Ph.D. recipients were as likely as D.L.S. or Ed.D. recipients to have jobs in academic libraries, etc.   **(283)**

■   A survey reported in 1978 of traceable North American librarians who had earned library doctorates in American Library Association accredited programs between 1930 and 1975 (survey size: 568; responding: 403 or 71%) *showed that* 51.3% reported being in library education, 33.8% reported being in the field of library administration, 11.1% reported library research (as distinct from any other categories), and 3.8% reported being in library operations.   **(463)**

Ibid. . . . *showed that* respondents were generally happy with the type of work they were doing. Specifically:

of library administrators, 76.1% reported that they preferred administration to other type of work, while only 10.9% reported that they preferred education;

of individuals in library operations, 53.3% preferred this type of work, while 26.7% reported they would prefer library administration;

of library educators, 86.7% preferred this type of work, while only 7.1% reported they would prefer library administration;

of library researchers, 67.6% preferred this type of work [no information is given on those preferring alternative types of work].   **(463)**

Ibid. . . . *showed that*, based on a scoring system where "3" = essential, "2" = important, "1" = useful, and "0" = unimportant, respondents overall rated the library doctorate 2.4 in obtaining their present posts and 1.99 in performing the duties of their present posts. Specifically:

library educators rated the library doctorate 2.81 in obtaining their present posts and 2.33 in performing their duties;

library administrators ranked the library doctorate 2.06 in obtaining their present positions and 1.73 in performing their duties;

library researchers ranked the library doctorate 1.86 in obtaining their present positions and 1.51 in performing their duties;

individuals in library operations ranked the library doctorate 1.20 in obtaining their present positions and 1.07 in performing their duties. **(463)**

■ A survey reported in 1978 of full-time British and U.S. library school teaching staff (population: 16 British schools with 285 teachers, 53 accredited U.S. programs with a total of 633 teachers; responding: 134 or 47% of the British teachers and 302 or 48% of the U.S. teachers) *showed that* nonteaching professional experience of British and U.S. respondents was as follows: none (British, 4 or 3%; U.S., 30 or 9.9%), academic libraries (British, 49 or 36.6%; U.S., 215 or 71.2%), national libraries (British, 2 or 1.5%; U.S., 13 or 4.3%), public libraries (British, 96 or 71.6%; U.S., 93 or 30.8%), school libraries (British, 1 or 0.8%; U.S., 57 or 18.9%), special libraries (British, 28 or 21.0%; U.S., 93 or 30.8%). **(288)**

Ibid. . . . *showed that*, of 130 British and 297 U.S. respondents, 59 or 45.4% of the British and 180 or 60.6% of the U.S. teachers had been teaching in their present institution for less than 7 years, while 54.6% of the British and 39.4% of the U.S. teachers had been teaching in their present institution for 7 years or more. Average teaching time at their present institution was 7.5 years for the British and 6.5 years for the U.S. teachers. **(288)**

Ibid. . . . *showed that*, of 134 British and 302 U.S. respondents, 127 or 94.8% of the British and 255 or 84.4% of the U.S. teachers were members of the Library Association or American Library Association, respectively, while 11 or 8.2% of the British and 283 or 93.7% of the U.S. teachers were members of state, regional, or county library associations. **(288)**

Ibid. . . . *showed that*, for 132 British and 289 U.S. respondents, the age distribution of teachers was as follows: 21 to 30 (11 or 8.3% British; 6 or 2.1% U.S.), 31 to 40 (32 or 24.2% British; 73 or 25.3% U.S.), 41 to 50 (49 or 37.1% British; 94 or 32.5% U.S.), 51 to 60 (32 or 24.2% British; 81 or 28% U.S.), 61 to 70 (8 or 6.1% British; 35 or 12.1% U.S.). **(288)**

■ A 1978 survey of full-time faculty in 7 Canadian graduate library schools (population: 81 faculty; survey size: 71 faculty; responding: 59 or 83%) *showed that* the average age of the faculty had increased since the early 1970s. For example, 27.1% of the faculty were 55 years old or older compared to 20% of the faculty 55 years old or older in a 1971-72 survey. This compared to 9.5% overall for university teachers in Canada who were 55 years old or older in a 1975-76 study. **(551)**

Ibid. . . . *showed that* 46 (78%) respondents were Canadian citizens. This represented a 16% gain in Canadian citizens over the 1971-72 study of library schools. Overall in Canadian universities 70.6% of the university teachers were Canadian citizens [no date given]. **(551)**

Ibid. . . . *showed that* the 4 "best" library schools out of 16 as ranked by 24 respondents (voting for one's own school was allowed) and scored on a weighted scale were (in descending order of perceived quality):

1. University of Chicago
2. University of Toronto
3. University of Illinois
4. University of California, Los Angeles

Further, 23 (28.4%) of the total group of Canadian library school faculty received at least 1 degree from these 4 schools. **(551)**

Ibid. . . . *showed that* 2 (3.4%) respondents entered library education directly without having spent time in some other full-time occupation. 53 (90.0%) respondents worked in libraries before becoming library school faculty, while 4 (6.8%) had never worked in a library. **(551)**

Ibid. . . . *showed that*, of the 57 respondents who had held a full-time job before joining a library school, 27 (47.4%) received all their experience in Canada, while 18 (31.6%) had both Canadian work experience and work experience in at least 1 foreign country. Only 12 (21.1%) respondents had no Canadian work experience. **(551)**

Ibid. . . . *showed that* 44 (74.6%) respondents felt that library experience was a prerequisite for teaching library science, 14 (23.7%) felt that library experience was not a prerequisite for teaching library science, and 1 (1.7%) held no opinion. **(551)**

Ibid. . . . *showed that* 13 (22%) respondents had been in their present positions for less than 5 years, 26 (44.1%) respondents had been in their present positions between 5 and 9 years, while 20 (33.9%) respondents had been in their present positions for 10 years or longer. **(551)**

Ibid. . . . *showed that* the 5 most frequently reported professional groups to which respondents belonged were (multiple responses allowed):

      Canadian Library Association   40 (67.8%) respondents
      American Library Association   27 (45.8%) respondents

continued

Association of American Library
Schools   18 (30.5%) respondents
American Society for Information
Science   18 (30.5%) respondents
Canadian Association of Library
Schools   18 (30.5%) respondents **(551)**

■ A study reported in 1983 of 98 doctoral dissertations in library administration (taken from *Dissertations in Library Science* 1930-80 by C. H. Davis, 1980) *showed that* research continuity in the area of library administration was very limited. For example, of the 23 individuals supervising 2 or more doctoral dissertations in library administration:

4 of the supervisors had no earned Ph.D.;

of the 19 supervisors who had an earned doctorate, 4 had doctorates in fields or disciplines other than library science;

of the 15 supervisors who had doctorates in library science, only 1 supervisor had a degree in library administration.   **(560)**

Faculty—Career Issues

■ An analysis reported in 1974 of 660 library science and library science related dissertations completed between 1925 and 1972 *showed that* 48% of the 435 doctoral recipients who received their degrees between 1953-72 worked in positions or with activities that appeared to be far removed from the scope of their dissertations. The primary exception to this general trend was library school faculty, where 63.3% taught courses that generally coincided with their dissertation topic.   **(283)**

Ibid. . . . *showed that*, of the 435 doctoral recipients who received their degrees between 1953-72, there was no statistically significant relationship between type of degree earned (Ph.D., D.L.S., and Ed.D.) and the type of position held (faculty, academic libraries, public libraries, school libraries, special libraries, other) at the time of the analysis. D.L.S. recipients were as likely as Ph.D. or Ed.D. recipients to teach on library school faculties, while Ph.D. recipients were as likely as D.L.S. or Ed.D. recipients to have jobs in academic libraries, etc.   **(283)**

■ An analysis reported in 1976 of candidates for library science teaching positions at the University of Michigan School of Library Science (85 candidates for 3 positions in 1973; 40 candidates for 3 positions in 1975) *showed that*, although work on a doctorate was a desired qualification, 23% of the men and 32% of the women candidates in 1973 held only a master's degree in library science and were not pursuing further study, while in 1975 4% of the men and 20% of the women candidates held only a master's degree and were not pursuing further study. Further, while 10% of the men and 4% of the women candidates in 1973 already had doctorates, in 1975 16% of the men and 20% of the women candidates had doctorates in library science.   **(284)**

Ibid. . . . *showed that* 33% of the candidates in 1973 and 38% of the candidates in 1975 were women, 1 candidate in 1973 was black, and in 1975 1 candidate was black and 1 Mexican-American.   **(284)**

Ibid. . . . *showed that*, while the percentage of candidates 40 years old and under remained essentially the same for the 2 searches (59% in 1973; 60% in 1975), the number of men 40 and under increased (60% in 1973; 72% in 1975), while the number of women 40 and under decreased (57% in 1973; 40% in 1975).   **(284)**

Ibid. . . . *showed that* for 1975, while 67% of the women candidates had worked for 6+ years in the field, only 48% of the men candidates had done so. Overall, 18% of the candidates had worked from 0-2 years in the field, 27% had worked from 3-5 years in the field, 23% had worked from 6-8 years, 12% had worked from 9-11 years, and 20% had worked 12+ years in the field.   **(284)**

■ A survey reported in 1978 of traceable North American librarians who had earned library doctorates in American Library Association accredited programs between 1930 and 1975 (survey size: 568; responding: 403 or 71%) *showed that* 51.3% reported being in library education, 33.8% reported being in the field of library administration, 11.1% reported library research (as distinct from any other categories), and 3.8% reported being in library operations.   **(463)**

Ibid. . . . *showed that* respondents were generally happy with the type of work they were doing. Specifically:

> of library administrators, 76.1% reported that they perferred administration to other type of work, while only 10.9% reported that they preferred education;

> of individuals in library operations, 53.3% preferred this type of work, while 26.7% reported they would prefer library administration;

of library educators, 86.7% preferred this type of work, while only 7.1% reported that they would prefer library administration;

of library researchers, 67.6% preferred this type of work [no information is given on those preferring alternative types of work]. **(463)**

Ibid. . . . *showed that*, based on a scoring system where "3" = essential, "2" = important, "1" = useful and "0" = unimportant, respondents overall rated the library doctorate 2.4 in obtaining their present posts and 1.99 in performing the duties of their present posts. Specifically:

library educators rated the library doctorate 2.81 in obtaining their present posts and 2.33 in performing their duties;

library administrators ranked the library doctorate 2.06 in obtaining their present positions and 1.73 in performing their duties;

library researchers ranked the library doctorate 1.86 in obtaining their present positions and 1.51 in performing their duties;

individuals in library operations ranked the library doctorate 1.20 in obtaining their present positions and 1.07 in performing their duties. **(463)**

■ A 1978 survey of full-time faculty in 7 Canadian graduate library schools (population: 81 faculty; survey size: 71 faculty; responding: 59 or 83%) *showed that* 2 (3.4%) respondents entered library education directly without having spent time in some other full-time occupation. 53 (90.0%) respondents worked in libraries before becoming library school faculty, while 4 (6.8%) had never worked in a library. **(551)**

Ibid. . . . *showed that*, of the 57 respondents who had held a full-time job before joining a library school, 27 (47.4%) received all their experience in Canada, while 18 (31.6%) had both Canadian work experience and work experience in at least 1 foreign country. Only 12 (21.1%) respondents had no Canadian work experience. **(551)**

Ibid. . . . *showed that* 44 (74.6%) respondents felt that library experience was a prerequisite for teaching library science, 14 (23.7%) felt that library experience was not a prerequisite for teaching library science, and 1 (1.7%) held no opinion. **(551)**

Ibjd. . . . *showed that* 13 (22%) respondents had been in their present positions for less than 5 years, 26 (44.1%) respondents had been in their present positions between 5 and 9 years, while 20 (33.9%) respondents had been in their present positions for 10 years or longer.   **(551)**

Ibid. . . . *showed that*, of 6 library schools providing reliable data, 2 general patterns of teaching loads emerge. 3 schools had teaching loads "of about 6 hours per week," while 3 schools had teaching loads "hovering around the 9 to 10 hour per week mark."   **(551)**

Ibid. . . . *showed that* the average number of courses taught per year per faculty member was 4.6, with the average per school per faculty member ranging from 3.7 courses per year to 5.5 courses per year.   **(551)**

Ibid. . . . *showed that* 13 (22.0%) respondents (spread through 4 schools) were involved in extension work. Further, 45 (76%) respondents were involved in academic administration, of which 26 (57.8%) devoted at least 10% of their time to academic administration. 22 (37.3%) respondents reported an involvement in consulting activities.   **(551)**

■ A survey reported in 1978 of full-time British and U.S. library school teaching staff (population: 16 British schools with 285 teachers, 53 accredited U.S. programs with a total of 633 teachers; responding: 134 or 47% of the British teachers and 302 or 48% of the U.S. teachers) *showed that* nonteaching professional experience of British and U.S. respondents was as follows: none (British, 4 or 3%; U.S., 30 or 9.9%), academic libraries (British, 49 or 36.6%; U.S., 215 or 71.2%), national libraries (British, 2 or 1.5%; U.S., 13 or 4.3%), public libraries (British, 96 or 71.6%; U.S., 93 or 30.8%), school libraries (British, 1 or 0.8%; U.S., 57 or 18.9%), special libraries (British, 28 or 21.0%; U.S., 93 or 30.8%).
                                                                  (288)

Ibid. . . . *showed that*, of 130 British and 297 U.S. respondents, 59 or 45.4% of the British and 180 or 60.6% of the U.S. teachers had been teaching in their present institution for less than 7 years, while 54.6% of the British and 39.4% of the U.S. teachers had been teaching in their present institution for 7 years or more. Average teaching time at their present institution was 7.5 years for the British and 6.5 years for the U.S. teachers.   **(288)**

Ibid. . . . *showed that*, of 134 British and 302 U.S. respondents, 127 or 94.8% of the British and 255 or 84.4% of the U.S. teachers were members of the Library Association or American Library Association, respectively, while 11 or 8.2% of the British and 283 or 93.7% of the U.S. teachers were members of state, regional or county library associations. **(288)**

■ A survey reported in 1978 of the degree to which library doctorates were required in advertisements appearing over a 6-month period (June 1976 through December 1976) in a wide range of publications for professional positions in library schools and head administrative posts in academic libraries (46 ads for library school positions; 53 ads for head administrators in academic libraries) *showed that*, of the library school ads, 39 (84.8%) required a doctorate of some kind, with 23 (50%) requiring a library doctorate and 16 (34.8%) indicating that a subject doctorate was also acceptable. **(463)**

Ibid. . . . *showed that* 15 of the 17 positions at doctorate-granting schools required a doctorate, with 4 of those positions allowing a subject doctorate in lieu of a library doctorate;

> that 18 of the 19 positions at non-doctorate-granting schools required a doctorate, with 12 allowing a subject doctorate in lieu of a library doctorate;

> that 6 of the 10 positions in nonaccredited schools required a library doctorate, with the remaining 4 positions preferring but not insisting on a doctorate (2 preferred a library doctorate; 2 preferred a subject doctorate). **(463)**

Faculty—Continuing Education

■ A survey reported in 1983 of full-time teaching faculty in North American library schools with ALA-accredited programs concerning continuing education (survey size: 215 faculty; responding: 159 or 73.9%) *showed that* (regardless of whether respondents had used them) the 3 most highly rated continuing education activites (out of 24) in terms of perceived effectiveness were (based on a ranking system of 1-5 where 5 was the most effective):

reading the current literature in one's own teaching area (154 respondents)	4.07 average rating
research (150 respondents)	4.04 average rating
writing for publication (148 respondents)	3.84 average rating

Further, there was no statistically significant relationship between the ratings given each of the 24 activities and the subject/teaching areas of the respondents.   **(802)**

Ibid. . . . *showed that* the 6 most frequently mentioned continuing education activites (out of 24) actually used by respondents in the past 3 years or since starting teaching (whichever was shorter), were:

reading the current literature in one's own teaching area (156 respondents)	98.1% respondents
attend professional meetings (145 respondents)	91.2% respondents
informally arranged discussions with former students (138 respondents)	86.8% respondents
visits to libraries (136 respondents)	85.5% respondents
reading the current literature in nonteaching areas (133 respondents)	83.6% respondents
informal conferences with practicing librarians (131 respondents)	82.4% respondents

Further, there was no statistically significant relationship between use of a particular activity and subject/teaching area.   **(802)**

Ibid. . . . *showed that* the 4 most highly ranked continuing education activities (out of 24) in terms of perference (based on a scale of 1 to 5 where 5 is most preferred) were as follows:

reading the current literature in one's teaching area (154 respondents)	4.26 average score
research (149 respondents)	4.02 average score
attend professional meetings (152 respondents)	3.84 average score
writing for publication (149 respondents)	3.83 average score

Further, there was no statistically significant relationship between preference for an activity and subject/teaching area.   **(802)**

Ibid. . . . *showed that* in 16 (66%) out of 24 cases there was a statistically significant relationship between use of a continuing education activity and the perceived effectiveness of that activity, that in 21 (87.5%) out of 24 cases there was a statistically significant relationship between use of a continuing education activity and preference for that activity, and that in all 24 (100%) cases there was a statistically significant relationship between preference for a continuing education activity and perceived effectiveness of that activity (based on Chi square tests significant at the .05 level).

(802)

Faculty—Education

■ A 1974-75 study of university libraries including all Association of Research Libraries libraries (sample size: 92; responding: 72 or 78%) and all library schools with ALA-accredited programs (sample size: not given; responding: 44 or 80%) *showed that* responding library school deans reported that 41.8% of the library school faculty members held subject Ph.D.'s. 69.2% of the deans reported it would be necessary for a subject Ph.D. to have practical library experience to be considered for a library position, while 30.8% reported such experience would not be required.

(445)

■ An analysis reported in 1974 of 660 library science and library science related dissertations completed between 1925 and 1972 *showed that* 48% of the 435 doctoral recipients who received their degrees between 1953-72 worked in positions or with activities that appeared to be far removed from the scope of their dissertations. The primary exception to this general trend was library school faculty, where 63.3% taught courses that generally coincided with their dissertation topic. **(283)**

Ibid. . . . *showed that*, of the 435 doctoral recipients who received their degrees between 1953-72, there was no statistically significant relationship between type of degree earned (Ph.D., D.L.S., and Ed.D.) and the type of position held (faculty, academic libraries, public libraries, school libraries, special libraries, other) at the time of the analysis. D.L.S. recipients were as likely as Ph.D. or Ed.D. recipients to teach on library school faculties, while Ph.D. recipients were as likely as D.L.S. or Ed.D. recipients to have jobs in academic libraries, etc. **(283)**

■ A survey reported in 1978 of the degree to which library doctorates were required in advertisements appearing over a 6-month period (June 1976 through December 1976) in a wide range of publications for professional positions in library schools and head administrative posts in academic libraries (46 ads for library school positions; 53 ads for head administrators in academic libraries) *showed that*, of the library school ads, 39 (84.8%) required a doctorate of some kind, with 23 (50%) requiring a library doctorate and 16 (34.8%) indicating that a subject doctorate was also acceptable. **(463)**

Ibid. . . . *showed that* 15 of the 17 positions at doctorate-granting schools required a doctorate, with 4 of those positions allowing a subject doctorate in lieu of a library doctorate;

> that 18 of the 19 positions at non-doctorate-granting schools required a doctorate, with 12 allowing a subject doctorate in lieu of a library doctorate;

> that 6 of the 10 positions in nonaccredited schools required a library doctorate, with the remaining 4 positions preferring but not insisting on a doctorate (2 preferred a library doctorate; 2 preferred a subject doctorate). **(463)**

■ A 1978 survey of full-time faculty in 7 Canadian graduate library schools (population: 81 faculty; survey size: 71 faculty; responding: 59 or 83%) *showed that* 24 (40.7%) respondents reported possessing doctorates. 18 (30.5%) of the responding faculty had doctorates in library science, while 6 (10.2%) had doctorates in some other field. In Canadian universities overall, 57.8% of the faculty had doctorates in 1975-76. Further, other earned degrees held by library school faculty were as follows:

M.L.S. and M.A. or M.S.	5 (8.5%) respondents
M.L.S. and B.L.S.	11 (18.6%) respondents
M.L.S.	8 (13.6%) respondents
B.L.S. and M.A. or M.S.	3 (5.1%) respondents
B.L.S.	3 (5.1%) respondents
F.L.A. or A.L.A.	3 (5.1%) respondents
no library degree	2 (3.3%) respondents **(551)**

Ibid. . . . *showed that* the 4 "best" library schools out of 16 as ranked by 24 respondents (voting for one's own school was allowed) and scored on a weighted scale were (in descending order of perceived quality):

1. University of Chicago
2. University of Toronto
3. University of Illinois
4. University of California, Los Angeles

Further, 23 (28.4%) of the total group of Canadian library school faculty received at least 1 degree from these 4 schools. **(551)**

■ A survey reported in 1978 of full-time British and U.S. library school teaching staff (population: 16 British schools with 285 teachers, 53 accredited U.S. programs with a total of 633 teachers; responding: 134 or

47% of the British teachers and 302 or 48% of the U.S. teachers) *showed that*, in terms of nonlibrary degrees past the baccalaureate, 78 or 58.2% of the British and 134 or 44.3% of the U.S. teachers had none, 45 or 33.6% of the British and 121 or 40.1% of the U.S. teachers had a master's degree, and 11 or 8.2% of the British and 47 or 15.6% of the U.S. teachers had a Ph.D.   **(288)**

Ibid. . . . *showed that* the highest library degree or qualification of 134 British respondents was as follows: none (7 or 5.2%), associateship of the Library Association (26 or 19.4%), fellowship of the Library Association (64 or 47.7%), bachelor's in library science (2 or 1.5%), master's in library science (33 or 24.7%), certificate in typography and printing (1 or 0.7%), and Ph.D./D.L.S. (1 or 0.7%).   **(288)**

Ibid. . . . *showed that* the highest library degree or qualification of 302 U.S. respondents was as follows: none (21 or 7%), bachelor's in library science (18 or 6%), master's in library science (111 or 36.7%), advanced certificate—sixth year (10 or 3.3%), education (11 or 3.6%), Ph.D/D.L.S. (131 or 43.4%).   **(288)**

■ A study reported in 1983 of 98 doctoral dissertations in library administration (taken from *Dissertations in Library Science* 1930-80 by C. H. Davis, 1980) *showed that* research continuity in the area of library administration was very limited. For example, of the 23 individuals supervising 2 or more doctoral dissertations in library administration:

   4 of the supervisors had no earned Ph.D.;

   of the 19 supervisors who had an earned doctorate, 4 had doctorates in fields or disciplines other than library science;

   of the 15 supervisors who had doctorates in library science, only 1 supervisor had a degree in library administration.   **(560)**

Faculty—Evaluation

■ A 1978-79 survey of U.S. and Canadian library programs' deans and directors (population: 63; responding: 59 or 94%, with 23 from doctoral-level schools and 36 from master's-level-only schools) *showed that* the top 7 criteria for evaluating overall faculty performance currently in use were (in descending order of importance): (1) classroom teaching, (2) quality of publications, (3) personal qualifications such as academic degrees, professional experience, (4) research/creative activity independent of publication, (5) activity in professional societies, (6) number of publications, and

(7) campus committee work/service to college. This corresponded basically with the ranking of criteria that "should" be used except that #7 disappeared, #6 became #7 and "supervision of student research including serving on master's and doctoral committees" became #6.   **(296)**

Ibid. . . . *showed that* the top 5 kinds of information currently used to evaluate overall faculty scholarship or research performance were (in descending order of importance): (1) books as sole or senior author, (2) articles in quality journals, (3) peers at the institution, (4) dean or department chairman, (5) monographs or chapters in books. The top 5 kinds of information that "should" be used were basically the same as the ones currently used except that #4 was replaced by "peers at other institutions."   **(296)**

Ibid. . . . *showed that* there were statistically significant differences betweeen Ph.D.-granting and non-Ph.D.-granting library schools in the means used to rank 2 of the criteria each currently used for faculty evaluaiton. Ph.D schools ranked "research and/or creative activity independent of publications" as #2 compared to non-Ph.D. schools, which ranked it #5.5 (a .5 indicates a tie between 2 criteria) while "supervision of student research including serving on master's and doctoral committees" was ranked #6 by Ph.D. schools but 11 by non-Ph.D. schools. (Significant at the .05 level or better.)   **(296)**

Ibid. . . . *showed that* there were statistically significant differences between Ph.D-granting and non-Ph.D.-granting library schools in the means used to rank 3 of the criteria each thought "should" be used for faculty evaluation. Ph.D. schools ranked "classroom teaching" #2.5 (.5 indicates a tie between 2 criteria) compared to non-Ph.D. schools, who ranked it #1; Ph.D. schools ranked "research and/or creative activity independent of publications" #2.5 compared to non-Ph.D. schools, who ranked it #4; Ph.D. schools ranked "public or community service" #12 compared to non-Ph.D. schools, who ranked it #11.   **(296)**

Ibid. . . . *showed that* the top 5 sources of information currently used to rank overall faculty performance were (in descending order of importance): (1) committee evaluation, (2) chairman/director or dean evaluation, (3) systematic student ratings, (4) colleague opinions, and (5) informal student opinions. The top 5 sources that "should" be used were the same as the ones currently used except for #4, which became "content of course syllabi and examination" and #5, which became "teaching improvement activities such as participating in workshops, in-service programs." (296)

Ibid. . . . *showed that* there were no statistically significant differences between Ph.D.-granting and non-Ph.D.-granting library schools in the sources of information curently used or the sources of information that "should" be used. (296)

Ibid. . . . *showed that* there was 1 statistically significant difference between Ph.D.-granting and non-Ph.D.-granting library schools in the means used to rank the kind of information currently used to evaluate faculty scholarship or research. Ph.D. schools ranked "peers at other institutions" as #5 compared to non-Ph.D. schools, which ranked it #12. There was also 1 statistically significant difference between Ph.D.-granting and non-Ph.D.-granting schools in the means used to rank the kind of information that "should" be used to evaluate faculty scholarship or research. Ph.D. schools ranked "publications in all professional journals" as #10 compared to non-Ph.D. schools, which ranked it #3.5 (a .5 indicates a tie between 2 rankings). (Both differences were significant at the .05 level.) (296)

Faculty—Job Hunting

■ An analysis reported in 1976 of candidates for library science teaching positions at the University of Michigan School of Library Science (85 candidates for 3 positions in 1973; 40 candidates for 3 positions in 1975) *showed that*, although work on a doctorate was a desired qualification, 23% of the men and 32% of the women candidates in 1973 held only a master's degree in library science and were not pursuing further study, while in 1975 4% of the men and 20% of the women candidates held only a master's degree and were not pursuing further study. Further, while 10% of the men and 4% of the women candidates in 1973 already had doctorates, in 1975 16% of the men and 20% of the women candidates had doctorates in library science. (284)

Ibid. . . . *showed that* 33% of the candidates in 1973 and 38% of the candidates in 1975 were women, 1 candidate in 1973 was black, and in 1975 1 candidate was black and 1 Mexican-American. (284)

Ibid. . . . *showed that*, while the percentage of candidates 40 years old and under remained essentially the same for the 2 searches (59% in 1973; 60% in 1975), the number of men 40 and under increased (60% in 1973; 72% in

1975), while the number of women 40 and under decreased (57% in 1973; 40% in 1975). **(284)**

Ibid. . . . *showed that* for 1975, while 67% of the women candidates had worked for 6+ years in the field, only 48% of the men candidates had done so. Overall, 18% of the candidates had worked from 0-2 years in the field, 27% had worked from 3-5 years in the field, 23% had worked from 6-8 years, 12% had worked from 9-11 years, and 20% had worked 12+ years in the field. **(284)**

Ibid. . . . *showed that* the number of candidates with work experience in various types of libraries was as follows for 1973 and 1975, respectively: academic (68% vs. 75%), public (21% vs. 18%), school (18% vs. 25%), and special (15% vs 33%). **(284)**

Ibid. . . . *showed that* for 1975 40% of the candidates reported no publications, 28% reported 1-2 publications, 32% reported 3+ publications. **(284)**

Ibid. . . . *showed that* 1975 candidates learned about the job vacancies from the following sources: *American Libraries* (25%), library school placement service (20%), *Library Journal* (15%), professional meeting (10%), *Wilson Library Bulletin* (8%), *Special Libraries* (1%), other (20%), and Hotline (0%). **(284)**

■ A survey reported in 1978 of the degree to which library doctorates were required in advertisements appearing over a 6-month period (June 1976 through December 1976) in a wide range of publications for professional positions in library schools and head administrative posts in academic libraries (46 ads for library school positions; 53 ads for head administrators in academic libraries) *showed that*, of the library school ads, 39 (84.8%) required a doctorate of some kind, with 23 (50%) requiring a library doctorate and 16 (34.8%) indicating that a subject doctorate was also acceptable. **(463)**

Ibid. . . . *showed that* 15 of the 17 positions at doctorate-granting schools required a doctorate, with 4 of those positions allowing a subject doctorate in lieu of a library doctorate;

that 18 of the 19 positions at non-doctorate-granting schools required a doctorate, with 12 allowing a subject doctorate in lieu of a library doctorate;

that 6 of the 10 positions in nonaccredited schools required a library doctorate with the remaining 4 positions preferring but not insisting on a doctorate (2 preferred a library doctorate; 2 preferred a subject doctorate). **(463)**

Faculty—Personal Values

■ A survey reported in 1980 of the values of 44 directors of large U.S. public libraries (response: 25 or 57%), 60 full-time faculty in ALA-accredited library school programs (response: 35 or 58%), and 175 students in accredited library school programs (response: 128 or 73%) as measured by the Rokeach Value Survey *showed that* all 3 groups ranked highly: self-respect, wisdom, freedom, inner harmony, and family security. All placed a low value on salvation, national security, social recognition, pleasure, and comfortable life. **(290)**

Ibid. . . . *showed that* the top 3 values for library directors were: sense of accomplishment (lasting contribution), exciting life (a stimulating, active life), and family security (taking care of loved ones). The top 3 values for library school faculty were: sense of accomplishment (lasting contribution), self-respect (self-esteem) and wisdom (a mature understanding of life). The top 3 values for library school students were: self-respect (self-esteem), wisdom (a mature understanding of life), and freedom (independent, free choice). **(290)**

Faculty—Publications

■ A survey reported in 1978 of full-time British and U.S. library school teaching staff (population: 16 British schools with 285 teachers, 53 accredited U.S. programs with a total of 633 teachers; responding: 134 or 47% of the British teachers and 302 or 48% of the U.S. teachers) *showed that*, for 134 British and 302 U.S. respondents in the 7-year period prior to the study, 91 or 68% of the British and 181 or 60% of the U.S. teachers published no books, 43 or 32% of the British and 77 or 25.4% of the U.S. teachers published no journal articles, while 90 or 67.2% of the British and 138 or 45.7% of the U.S. teachers published no surveys and reports. **(288)**

■ A study reported in 1980 of authorship in 5 library periodicals over a 10-year period primarily in the 1970s (*College and Research Libraries, Library Journal, Library Quarterly, Library Trends,* and *RQ*) *showed that* the gender of authorship by library science faculty only was as follows:

College and Research
  Libraries (72 articles)   12.5% women; 87.5% men
Library Journal (164 articles)   32.3% women; 67.7% men
Library Quarterly (77 articles)   19.2% women; 80.8% men
Library Trends (89 articles)   29.2% women; 70.8% men
RQ (59 articles)   33.9% women; 66.1% men

Overall, 40.8% of the library science faculty were women while 59.2% were men.   **(481)**

Ibid. . . . *showed that* the occupations of authors ranged as follows for the 5 periodicals:

academic librarians	18.9% to 51.6%
public librarians	1.7% to 16.3%
other librarians	2.5% to 9.4%
library science faculty	16.6% to 30.4%
library science students	0.5% to 4.0%
other faculty	4.4% to 17.0%
other (nonlibrarian/nonfaculty)	11.3% to 28.9% **(481)**

■ A study reported in 1981 of articles submitted to and published in *Library Resources and Technical Services* during the period 1957 through 1980 concerning author characteristics *showed that* the occupations of authors for those published articles where it could be determined (1957-67: 575 articles; 1968-77: 447 articles; and 1978-80: 108 articles) were as follows:

academic librarians accounted for 46.4%, 54.8%, and 54.6% of the 1957-67, 1968-77, and 1978-80 articles, respectively;

public librarians accounted for 13.0%, 3.1%, and 3.7% of the 1957-67, 1968-77, and 1978-80 articles, respectively;

other librarians accounted for 16.9%, 16.3%, and 9.2% of the 1957-67, 1968-77, and 1978-80 articles, respectively;

library science faculty accounted for 14.1%, 16.5%, and 21.3% of the 1957-67, 1968-77, and 1978-80 articles, respectively;

library science students accounted for 1.0%, 1.3%, and 0.0% of the 1957-67, 1968-77, and 1978-80 articles, respectively;

other faculty accounted for 0.9%, 1.8%, and 0.9% of the 1957-67, 1968-77, and 1978-80 articles, respectively;

nonlibrarian/nonacademic individuals accounted for 8.5%, 6.9%, and 10.2% of the 1957-67, 1968-77, and 1978-80 articles, respectively.   **(763)**

Ibid. . . . *showed that* the papers submitted for publication during the period July 1979-June 1980 for which author occupation could be determined (32 papers accepted; 42 not accepted) were distributed as follows:

academic librarians accounted for 37.5% of the accepted papers and 73.8% of the rejected papers;

public librarians accounted for 3.1% of the accepted papers and 2.4% of the rejected papers;

other librarians accounted for 15.6% of the accepted papers and 4.8% of the rejected papers;

library science faculty accounted for 25.0% of the accepted papers and 9.5% of the rejected papers;

library science students and other faculty submitted no papers;

nonlibrarian/nonacademic individuals accounted for 18.8% of the accepted papers and 9.5% of the rejected papers. **(763)**

■ A study reported in 1981 of authorship in 5 journals in special librarianship over a 10-year period (generally the decade of the 1970s) or over the life of the journal if it had not been published for a 10-year period *showed that* the occupations of authors contributing articles broke down as follows:

academic	5.8% of total	
library science faculty	10.3% of total	
special librarians	41.6% of total	
other librarians	3.3% of total	
other faculty	5.4% of total	
information supplier	4.7% of total	
private/government	15.3% of total	**(496)**

■ A study reported in 1981 of approximately 10 years of articles published in the 1970s in 5 special library periodicals *showed that* the occupations of authors in the *Law Library Journal* were as follows:

special librarians	62.6%	
other faculty and graduate students	21.9%	
nonlibrary private/government	9.3%	
other librarians and library school students	2.5%	
academic librarians	1.6%	
information suppliers, brokers, etc.	1.1%	
library science faculty	1.1%	**(372)**

■ A study reported in 1982 of author characteristics in 5 special library journals (*Special Libraries, Journal of the American Society for Information Science, Law Library Journal, Bulletin of the Medical Library Association*, and *Online Review*) over a 10-year period (except for *Online* which began in 1977) *showed that* the 4 most frequent occupations of *Special Libraries* authors were: special librarian (43.8% authors), private/government librarians (16.4% authors), academic librarian (13.6% authors), and library science faculty (11.4% authors).   **(438)**

■ A study reported in 1982 of authorship of articles in the *Canadian Library Journal* during the period 1968 through 1980, involving 545 articles, *showed that* for the 477 articles for which author occupation could be determined, occupational distribution was as follows:

academic librarian	25.6% of total articles
public librarian	17.0% of total articles
other librarian	21.0% of total articles
library science faculty	14.5% of total articles
library science student	3.8% of total articles
other faculty	4.0% of total articles
nonlibrarian/nonacademic	14.3% of total articles

Further, for the 385 articles for which author occupation could be determined for the period 1968-77 (see citation 481), occupational distribution was as follows:

academic librarian	27.5% of total articles
public librarian	18.4% of total articles
other librarian	19.7% of total articles
library science faculty	12.7% of total articles
library science student	3.4% of total articles
other faculty	4.2% of total articles
nonlibrarian/nonacademic	14.0% of total articles **(298)**

■ A study reported in 1983 of citation and publication levels of 411 tenured-level (associate and full professors) library school faculty in the 60 U.S. library schools with ALA-accredited M.L.S. programs (citations taken from *Social Science Citation Index* for the periods 1966-70, 1971-75, and 1976-80) *showed that* there was a statistically significant difference between average publication levels for associate and full professors. Specifically, over the 15-year period the 204 associate professors published an average of 4.18 publications, while the 207 full professors published an average of 7.85 publications. (Significance level not given.)
                                                                      (784)

Ibid. . . . *showed that* there was a statistically significant difference between average citation levels for associate and full professors. Specifically, over the 15-year period the 204 associate professors were cited an average of 8.56 times, while full professors were cited an average of 36.32 times. (Significance level not given.) **(784)**

Ibid. . . . *showed that* the breakdown of publications for associate and full professors combined for the 15-year period was as follows:

0-3 publications	183 (44.5%) respondents
3-6 publications	76 (18.5%) respondents
6-12 publications	84 (20.4%) respondents
12-24 publications	47 (11.4%) respondents
24 or more publications	21 (5.1%) respondents

(784)

Ibid. . . . *showed that* the breakdown of number of citations for associate and full professors combined for the 15-year period was as follows:

0-12 citations	263 (64.0%) respondents
12-24 citations	59 (14.4%) respondents
24-48 citations	41 (10.0%) respondents
48-96 citations	24 (5.8%) respondents
96 or more citations	24 (5.8%) respondents

(784)

Ibid. . . . *showed that* the average delay between publication and citation was 6 years with an average, normalized (i.e., adjusted for associate professors who have presumably been publishing for only about 8 years compared to full professors who have been publishing for an estimated 15 years) publication rate of .5 publications per year for all associate and full professors combined and an average, normalized citation rate of 4 citations per year for all associate and full professors combined. However, many faculty members had not published at all in 15 years. Computing on the basis of faculty members who have published or been cited at least once in the 15-year period, the average, normalized publication rate for all tenured library faculty was .67 publications per year, while the average, normalized citation rate for all tenured library faculty was 5 citations per year. **(784)**

Ibid. . . . *showed that* the overall citation rate per author in *Social Science Citation Index* remained consistent from year to year and that in 1980 the average number of citations per author per year was 4.6 citations. **(784)**

Ibid. . . . *showed that* both the publication and citation rates were considerably higher for tenured faculty in Ph.D.-granting institutions than in non-Ph.D. institutions. Specifically of 207 faculty in non-Ph.D.-granting institutions and 204 faculty in Ph.D.-granting institutions:

> the average publication rate over the 15-year period was 3.76 publications per faculty member in non-Ph.D. institutions compared to 8.32 publications per faculty member in Ph.D.-granting institutions;

> the average citation rate over the 15-year period was 8.47 citations per faculty member in non-Ph.D. intsitutions compared to 36.82 citations per faculty member in Ph.D.-granting institutions.   **(784)**

Ibid. . . . *showed that*, while the 20 library schools with the highest normalized publication and citation rates included 9 of the top 10 ranked library school programs as reported by Blau and Margulies, the Spearman rank order correlation between the Blau and Margulies rankings and those 20 library schools ranked in order of average number of citations to a school's faculty was "virtually zero." In other words, within the top 20 library schools there was no relationship between the ranking of the programs and the ranking based on per capita number of citations to faculty publications.   **(784)**

Faculty—Workload and Assignments

■ A survey reported in 1978 of full-time British and U.S. library school teaching staff (population: 16 British schools with 285 teachers, 53 accredited U.S. programs with a total of 633 teachers; responding: 134 or 47% of the British teachers and 302 or 48% of the U.S. teachers) *showed that* for 124 British and 293 U.S. respondents the average number of course, seminar, and tutorial hours of instruction per week in a typical term was as follows: 31 or 25% of the British and 116 or 39.6% of the U.S. teachers reported 0 to 8 hours per week, 29 or 23.4% British and 151 or 51.5% of the U.S. teachers reported 9 to 12 hours per week, and 64 or 51.6% of the British and 26 or 8.9% of the U.S. teachers reported 13 to 16 hours per week.   **(288)**

Ibid. . . . *showed that* for 129 British and 297 U.S. respondents the number of courses taught regularly each year was as follows: 1-2 courses (40 or 31% British; 50 or 16.8% U.S.), 3-4 courses (74 or 57.4% British; 188 or 63.3% U.S.), 5-6 courses (12 or 9.3% British; 53 or 17.9% U.S.), 7-8 courses (3 or 2.3% British; 6 or 2% U.S.).   **(288)**

■ A 1978 survey of full-time faculty in 7 Canadian graduate library schools (population: 81 faculty; survey size: 71 faculty; responding: 59 or 83%) *showed that*, of 6 library schools providing reliable data, 2 general patterns of teaching loads emerge. 3 schools have teaching loads "of about 6 hours per week," while 3 schools have teaching loads "hovering around the 9 to 10 hour per week mark." **(551)**

Ibid. . . . *showed that* the average number of courses taught per year per faculty member was 4.6, with the average per school per faculty member ranging from 3.7 courses per year to 5.5 courses per year. **(551)**

Ibid. . . . *showed that* 13 (22.0%) respondents (spread through 4 schools) were involved in extension work. Further, 45 (76%) respondents were involved in academic administration, of which 26 (57.8%) devoted at least 10% of their time to academic administration. 22 (37.3%) respondents reported an involvement in consulting activities. **(551)**

■ A 1982 study of a how a single library faculty member spent his work time over a 20-week period (Spring semester) based on 4 reports an hour (4,012 reports in total) *showed that* his time was spent as follows:

teaching	2,352 reports or 58.62% time
service	481 reports or 11.99% time
research	384 reports or 9.57% time
other	795 reports or 19.82% time **(801)**

Gender and Minority Issues—Deans

■ A 1978 survey of full-time faculty in 7 Canadian graduate library schools (population: 81 faculty; survey size: 71 faculty; responding: 59 or 83%) *showed that*, of the 7 library school deans and directors, 5 were male and 2 were female. **(551)**

■ A study reported in 1983 investigating the educational and professional qualifications of the 162 individuals holding deanships (excluding acting or interim deans) of ALA-accredited library school programs in North America during the period 1960-81 *showed that* for the whole period women accounted for 39 (24.1%) of the deanships and men for 123 (75.9%) of the deanships. Further, of the 62 library school deans holding office in 1981, 13 (21%) were women and 49 (79%) were men. **(562)**

Ibid. . . . *showed that* the 29 library education programs in the U.S. that had maintained ALA accreditation throughout the period 1960-81 had 77 deans during this period, including 14 (18.2%) women and 63 (81.8%) men. The 2 Canadian library education programs that had likewise maintained ALA accreditation throughout the 1960-81 period had 9 deans, including 8 (88.9%) women and 1 (11.1%) men.   **(562)**

Ibid. . . . *showed that* the average age at which the 39 women were first appointed dean was 49.7 years, while the average age at which the 123 men were first appointed dean was 44.8 years.   **(562)**

Ibid. . . . *showed that* 144 (88.9%) of the deans had a fifth-year (master's level) library degree, including 37 (94.9%) of the women and 107 (87%) of the men. Further, 3 library schools together accounted for 40.3% of the 144 fifth-year degrees awarded deans. These were: Columbia (32 or 22.2% of the fifth-year degrees), University of Illinois (14 or 9.7% of the fifth-year degrees), and University of Michigan (12 or 8.3% or the fifth-year degrees).   **(562)**

Ibid. . . . *showed that* 67 (41.4%) of the deans held subject master's degrees, including 9 (23.1%) women and 58 (47.2%) men.   **(562)**

Ibid. . . . *showed that* 124 (76.5%) of the deans held doctorates, including 24 (61.5%) women and 100 (81.3%) men. The types of doctorates held were as follows:

Ph.D.	15 (38.4%) women;	88 (71.5%) men
D.L.S.	6 (15.4%) women;	7 (5.7%) men
Ed.D.	3 (7.7%) women;	4 (3.3%) men
Des. L.	0 (0.0%) women;	1 (0.8%) men

Further, 78 of the doctorates were in library science, while the remainder were in other subject areas.   **(562)**

Ibid. . . . *showed that*, of the 12 ALA-accredited library schools awarding a total of 77 Ph.D.'s or D.L.S.'s to the deans, the 3 schools awarding the most library science doctorates to this group of deans were: University of Chicago (15 or 19.5% of the library science doctorates), University of Michigan (14 or 18.2% of the library science doctorates), and Columbia (12 or 15.6% of the library science doctorates).   **(562)**

Ibid. . . . *showed that* the average total years of professional experience per library school dean was 17.5 years, including an average of 21.7 years of professional experience per female dean and 16.2 years of professional experience per male dean. **(562)**

Ibid. . . . *showed that* the average total years of library experience per library school dean was 10.5 years, including an average of 11.3 years per female dean and an average of 10.3 years per male dean. **(562)**

Ibid. . . . *showed that* 62 (38.3%) library school deans had previously served as faculty members of the same library school to which they were appointed dean, including 24 (61.5%) of the female deans and 38 (30.9%) of the male deans. **(562)**

Ibid. . . . *showed that* 33 (20.4%) library school deans had had previous library school administrative experience, including 7 (17.9%) women deans and 26 (21.1%) male deans. **(562)**

Ibid. . . . *showed that* 147 (90.7%) deans had had library experience. A higher proportion of women than men had received most of their library experience in school libraries (12 or 30.8% women; 10 or 8.1% men), while a larger proportion of men than women had received most of their library experience in govermental libraries (2 or 5.1% women; 14 or 11.4% men) and special libraries (no women; 7 or 5.7% men). There was little difference between the proportions of men and women who had received most of their library experience in public libraries (5 or 12.8% women; 17 or 13.8% men) or academic libraries (19 or 48.7% women; 57 or 46.3% men). **(562)**

Gender and Minority Issues—Doctoral Students

■ An analysis reported in 1974 of 660 library science and library science related dissertations completed between 1925 and 1972 *showed that*, although the absolute number of dissertations in librarianship written by women had increased steadily, the proportion of dissertations written by women had remained relatively unchanged at an average rate of 31.1% in any given year. Annual increases and decreases in the number of dissertations by women were statistically nonsignificant. **(283)**

Ibid. . . . *showed that* there was no statistically significant relationship between sex and type of degree received, between sex and research method chosen, or betweeen sex and whether the dissertation was completed. **(283)**

Ibid. . . . *showed that*, for 435 doctoral recipients who received their degrees between 1953-72, there was a statistically significant relationship between sex and current type of position held (significant at the .001 level). Specifically, a higher proportion of males (29.3%) than females (14.3%) tended to work in academic libraries, while a higher proportion of females (65.7%) than males (58.1%) tended to join library school faculties. 3.8% of the females vs. 1.4% of the males worked in public libraries, 6.7% of the females vs. 0.5% of the males worked in school libraries, and 1.9% of the females vs. 2.7% of the males worked in special libraries. 7.6% of the females and 8.0% of the males worked in "other" positions.   **(283)**

Ibid. . . . *showed that*, for 435 doctoral recipients who received their degrees between 1953-72, there was no statistically significant relationship between sex and mobility. Specifically, comparing location of job to location of school, 17.0% of the females and 9.5% of the males were in the same state, 27.4% of the females and 31.8% of the males were in contiguous states, while 55.6% of the females and 58.7% of the males were "geographically removed."   **(283)**

■   A study reported in 1983 of data gathered by the Office for Library Personnel Resources on master's- and doctoral-level degree recipients from ALA-accredited programs during the period 1973-74 through 1980-81 *showed that* during the 8-year period 436 doctoral degrees were awarded of which 213 (48.85%) went to females and 223 (51.15%) went to males. Since 1978-79 more females than males received doctoral degrees each year (29 females vs. 27 males in 1978-79; 32 females vs. 14 males in 1979-80; and 31 females vs. 23 males in 1980-81). The distribution of doctoral degrees by ethnic group for this 8-year period was as follows:

white females received 168 (38.53%) and white males received 188 (43.12%) of the total doctotal degrees awarded in the 8-year period;

black females received 20 (4.59%) and black males received 13 (2.98%) of the total doctoral degrees awarded in the 8-year period;

Asian/Pacific Islander females received 16 (3.67%) and Asian/Pacific Islander males received 8 (1.83%) of the total doctoral degrees awarded in the 8-year period;

Hispanic females received 5 (1.15%) and Hispanic males received 4 (.92%) of the total doctoral degrees awarded in the 8-year period;

American Indian/Alaskan native females received 2 (.46%) and AI/AN males received 2 (.46%) of the total doctoral degrees awarded in the 8-year period.   **(787)**

Ibid. . . . *showed that* during the 8 years of the study 80 (18.35%) of the doctoral degrees were awarded to minorities compared to 9.50% of the M.L.S. degrees awarded to minorities in the same time period. **(787)**

Gender and Minority Issues—Faculty

■ An analysis reported in 1976 of candidates for library science teaching positions at the University of Michigan School of Library Science (85 candidates for 3 positions in 1973; 40 candidates for 3 positions in 1975) *showed that*, although work on a doctorate was a desired qualification, 23% of the men and 32% of the women candidates in 1973 held only a master's degree in library science and were not pursuing further study, while in 1975 4% of the men and 20% of the women candidates held only a master's degree and were not pursuing further study. Further, while 10% of the men and 4% of the women candidates in 1973 already had doctorates, in 1975 16% of the men and 20% of the women candidates had doctorates in library science. **(284)**

Ibid. . . . *showed that* 33% of the candidates in 1973 and 38% of the candidates in 1975 were women, 1 candidate in 1973 was black, and in 1975 1 candidate was black and 1 Mexican-American. **(284)**

Ibid. . . . *showed that*, while the percentage of candidates 40 years old and under remained essentially the same for the 2 searches (59% in 1973; 60% in 1975), the number of men 40 and under increased (60% in 1973; 72% in 1975), while the number of women 40 and under decreased (57% in 1973; 40% in 1975). **(284)**

Ibid. . . . *showed that* for 1975, while 67% of the women candidates had worked for 6+ years in the field, only 48% of the men candidates had done so. Overall, 18% of the candidates had worked from 0-2 years in the field, 27% had worked from 3-5 years in the field, 23% had worked from 6-8 years, 12% had worked from 9-11 years, and 20% had worked 12+ years in the field. **(284)**

■ A 1978 survey of full-time faculty in 7 Canadian graduate library schools (population: 81 faculty; survey size: 71 faculty; responding: 59 or 83%) *showed that* the percentage of male teachers in Canadian library schools was increasing. Of the whole group of 81 library school faculty members as of 1978, 51.8% were men. In the 1971-72 study of full-time library school faculty 47.8% were men. Further, the men in the present study were not evenly distributed among the 7 library schools, and their percentage ranged from a low of 29.4% in 1 school to a high of 75.0% in another school. For Canadian university teachers generally in 1975-76, women consitiuted 14% of the total full-time faculty.   **(551)**

■ A survey reported in 1978 of full-time British and U.S. library school teaching staff (population: 16 British schools with 285 teachers, 53 accredited U.S. programs with a total of 633 teachers; responding: 134 or 47% of the British teachers and 302 or 48% of the U.S. teachers) *showed that*, for 130 British and 295 U.S. respondents, the sex of teachers was as follows: male (105 or 80.8% British; 188 or 63.7% U.S.), female (25 or 19.2% British; 107 or 36.3% U.S.).   **(288)**

Gender and Minority Issues—Library Technicians

■ A study reported in 1971 of library technician graduates during the period 1967-69 (sample size: 200; responding: 154 or 77%) *showed that* 5 (3%) of the library technician graduates were male while 149 (97%) were female.   **(398)**

Gender and Minority Issues—M.L.S. Students

■ An analysis reported in 1977 of 334 students at the University of Michigan during 1971-76 who completed a second-level library school data processing course *showed that* there was no statistically significant differ-ence between grade performance of males and females but that there was a statistically significant difference between math/science undergraduate majors and other undergraduate majors in terms of grade performance, with the math/science group averaging higher course grades (significance level .05). Undergraduate education majors averaged lower grades as a group than other undergraduate majors, but the difference was not statistically significant.   **(286)**

■ A study reported in 1983 of data gathered by the Office for Library Personnel Resources on master's- and doctoral-level degree recipients from ALA-accredited programs during the period 1973-74 through 1980-81 *showed that* for this period males in total were a declining portion of the M.L.S. graduates. While the overall annual average of male graduates for this period was 20.57%, their numbers declined from 21.76% of the total

M.L.S. graduates in 1973-74 to 17.82% of the total M.L.S. graduates in 1980-81. This decline was primarily due to the decline of white male M.L.S. graduates during this period from 19.7% of the total M.L.S. graduates in 1973-74 to 15.9% of the graduates in 1980-81. Other ethnic males fared as follows:

> black males decreased absolutely from 52 graduates in 1973-74 to 38 in 1980-81 but increased proportionately from .8% to 1.0% of the M.L.S. graduates in those years;
>
> Asian/Pacific Islanders held constant absolutely with 19 graduates in 1973-74 and 20 graduates in 1980-81 but increased proportionately from .3% to .5% of the M.L.S. graduates in those years;
>
> Hispanic males held constant absolutely with 15 graduates in 1973-74 and 15 graduates in 1980-81 but increased proportionately from .2% to .4% of the M.L.S. graduates in those years;
>
> American Indian/Alaskan native males decreased from 2 graduates in 1973-74 to 1 graduate in 1980-81. **(787)**

Ibid. . . . *showed that* black, Asian/Pacific Islander, Hispanic, American Indian/Alaskan native, and "other" males constituted only 1.97% of all M.L.S. degrees awarded during the period 1973-74 through 1980-81.

(787)

Ibid. . . . *showed that*, while their overall numbers decreased, the portion of white females receiving M.L.S. degrees annually during the 8-year period increased from 70.1% in 1973-74 to 74.6% in 1980-81. Other ethnic females fared as follows:

> black females decreased both absolutely (from 255 M.L.S.graduates in 1973-74 to 129 in 1980-81) and proportionately (from 4.0% to 3.4% of the total graduates for those years);
>
> Asian/Pacific Islander females decreased absolutely (from 131 M.L.S. graduates in 1973-74 to 98 in 1980-81) but increased proportionately (from 2.1% to 2.6% of the total graduates for those years);
>
> Hispanic females held constant absolutely (from 46 M.L.S. graduates in 1973-74 to 48 in 1980-81) but increased proportionately (from .7% to 1.3% of the total graduates for those years);
>
> American Indian/Alaskan native females increased from 4 in 1973-74 to 8 in 1980-81. **(787)**

Ibid. . . . *showed that* during the 8 years of the study 80 (18.35%) of the doctoral degrees were awarded to minorities compared to 9.50% of the M.L.S. degrees awarded to minorities in the same time period.   **(787)**

Grading

■ A study reported in 1977 of grading practices during Fall/Spring semesters for the years 1966-67, 1969-70, 1972-73, and Fall semester 1975 at the Indiana University Graduate Library School *showed that* the grade distribution for the top 3 grades was as follows: 1966-67 (58.6% A's, 37.4% B's, 2.2% C's), 1969-70 (67.4% A's, 23.3% B's, 1.8% C's), 1972-73 (63.6% A's, 28.2% B's, 1.4% C's), Fall 1975 (61.3% A's, 35.2% B's and 1.5% C's).   **(285)**

■ A survey reported in 1977 of 9 teaching faculty at the Indiana University Graduate Library School (8 responding) *showed that*, when asked to compare grading practices at IUGLS with the library school where they received their M.L.S. degree, 2 felt that IUGLS was "much more lenient," 4 felt that IUGLS was "more lenient," and 2 felt that grading practices were "about the same."   **(285)**

■ A survey reported in 1977 of a random sample of students enrolled in Indiana University's Graduate Library School Spring semester 1975-76 (population: 300; sample: 36; usable responses: 34) *showed that* 20 (59%) felt IUGLS grading practices were "much more lenient" or "more lenient" than their undergraduate institutions, 9 (26%) felt grading practices were about the same, and 5 (15%) found them to be "more" or "much more rigorous." Further, of 12 individuals in the sample who had done other graduate study, 6 "agreed" or "strongly agreed" that IUGLS grading was easier than any other graduate program with which they were familiar, 4 were "undecided," and 2 "disagreed."   **(285)**

■ An analysis reported in 1977 of 334 students at the University of Michigan during 1971-76 who completed a second-level library school data processing course *showed that* there was no statistically significant difference between grade performance of males and females but that there was a statistically significant difference between math/science undergraduate majors and other undergraduate majors in terms of grade performance, with the math/science group averaging higher course grades (significance level .05). Undergraduate education majors averaged lower grades as a group than other undergraduate majors, but the difference was not statistically significant.   **(286)**

■ A study reported in 1978 of 334 library school students [library school not specified] over a 5-year period who had taken a library school second-level computer programming course in PL/1 *showed that* undergraduate math/science majors performed statistically significantly better in the course than students with other undergraduate majors, while students with undergraduate education majors scored statistically significantly worse than students with other undergraduate majors (significance level in the first case was at the .0002 level and in the second case was at the .002 level). **(425)**

■ A study reported in 1978 of students entering the Queens College Graduate Department of Library Science in 1972 and completing the program or withdrawing by Fall 1975 (sample size: 169) *showed that* 86.4% of those students who began the program finished it. There were no statistically significant differences between finishers and nonfinishers with regard to number of years between finishing undergraduate degrees and entering library school, undergraduate GPA, verbal score on the Graduate Record Examination, or quantitative score on the Graduate Record Examination. **(291)**

Ibid. . . . *showed that* there was a statistically significant relationship between undergraduate GPA and final graduate library school GPA (significant at the .005 level). Specifically, 63% of those students with UGPAs between 3.35 and 4.0 had GGPAs over 3.76 compared to 29.3% of those with UGPAs under 3.35 who had GGPAs between 3.35 and 4.0. **(291)**

Ibid. . . . *showed that* there was a statistically significant relationship between both verbal and quantitative scores on the Graduate Record Examination and final graduate library school GPA (significance in both cases at the .001 level). Specifically, 39.1% of the students with GREV scores over 600 had GGPAs over 3.76 compared to 12% of the students with GREV scores under 400. Further, 72.2% of those with GREQ scores 600 or better had final graduate library school GPAs of 3.6 or better, while only 65.9% of those with GREQ scores between 400 and 599 had final graduate library school GPAs of 3.6 or better. **(291)**

Ibid. . . . *showed that* comparison of standardized regression coefficients (Betas) revealed that undergraduate GPA was the best predictor of final library school GPA (B = .302), verbal score on the Graduate Record Examination next best (B = .247) and number of years between finishing undergraduate work and beginning library school work (B = .187) (all significant at the .01 level). However, all 3 of the independent variables together only explained 16% of the variance in GGPA.   **(291)**

Ibid. . . . *showed that* the equation for predicting final library school GPA was: GGPA = .203 (UGPA) + .00051 (GREV) + .0088 (Interyear) + 2.76 (where Interyear is number of years between finishing undergraduate degree and beginning library school).   **(291)**

Ibid. . . . *showed that* an undergraduate GPA 4+ years old (graduating in 1968 or earlier) predicted a higher final library school GPA than the same undergraduate GPA less than 4 years old (graduating after 1968). For example, a pre-1968 3.0 UGPA was the equal of a post-1968 3.6 UGPA.
(291)

Library Technicians

■ A study reported in 1971 of library technician graduates during the period 1967-69 (sample size: 200; responding: 154 or 77%) *showed that* the average full-time salary after training was $5,357 per year compared to $4,089 (adjusted for inflation and cost of living increases) before training. This is an average difference of $1,262, a statistically significant difference at the .001 significance level.   **(398)**

Ibid. . . . *showed that* 147 (95%) respondents reported they were happy that they took the library technician program (requiring 2 years work past high school), while 7 (5%) reported they were not happy to have taken the program. Of those unhappy, 4 reported they were not displeased with the courses but because they could not find a job after graduation.   **(398)**

Ibid. . . . *showed that,* of 91 respondents, 70 (77%) felt their course work had done a "good" or "excellent" job of preparing them for their present position, 16 (18%) felt that it had done a "fair" job, and 5 (5%) felt that it had done a "poor" or "unsatisfactory" job of preparation.
(398)

Ibid. . . . *showed that,* of 91 respondents, 64 (70.3%) felt they were accepted as part of the library staff, 13 (14.3%) felt they were moderately accepted by the library staff, 12 (13.2%) felt they were considered another clerical assistant, and 2 (2.2%) felt they were not accepted by the professional librarian.   **(398)**

Ibid. . . . *showed that* before entering the library technician program 61 (40%) respondents had worked in a high school library, 7 (4%) in a college or university library, 7 (4%) in a public library, and 8 (5%) worked as volunteers in an elementary school library. **(398)**

Ibid. . . . *showed that* 5 (3%) of the library technician graduates were male while 149 (97%) were female. **(398)**

■ A 1977 study of library technician positions (a library technician was defined as a graduate of a 2-year undergraduate program with specialization in library techniques and procedures) in Ontario academic libraries (survey size: 15 libraries; responding: 12 or 80% libraries) *showed that* the number of library technicians employed at the time of the survey in the 12 libraries totaled 27 individuals. Overall for all 12 libraries, library technicians constituted 5.2% of the total staff and 6.5% of the nonprofessional staff. **(549)**

Ibid. . . . *showed that* 10 (83.3%) of the responding libraries reported that they did not have a position classification designated specifically for library technicians. **(549)**

Ibid. . . . *showed that*, of 5 respondents ranking the importance of courses taken by library technicians, the courses were (in descending order of importance):

1. library techniques
2. library-related courses
3. communications
4. business
5. human relations and social sciences
6. humanities
7. sciences **(549)**

M.L.S. Graduates—General Issues

■ A survey of 1976 graduates of the Indiana University Graduate Library School with 73.2% (131) responding, *showed that*:

11.5%	unemployed
2.3%	further education (including library doctorate)
7.6%	jobs outside library field
75.6%	professional jobs
3.1%	clerical positions in libraries **(007)**

■ A study reported in 1978 of students entering the Queens College Graduate Department of Library Science (master's level) in 1972 and completing the program or withdrawing by Fall 1975 (sample size: 169) *showed that* 86.4% of those students who began the program finished it. There were no statistically significant differences between finishers and nonfinishers with regard to number of years between finishing undergraduate degrees and entering library school, undergraduate GPA, verbal score on the Graduate Record Examination, or quantitative score on the Graduate Record Examination.   **(291)**

■ A 1980 survey of randomly selected American Library Association personal members (sample size: 3,000 members; responding: 1,987 or 67.1%, including 1,583 full-time members employed at the time of the survey, which provided the subsample analyzed here) *showed that* men appeared to be more heavily represented in ALA membership than their overall numbers in librarianship would suggest, although the female/male ratio for graduates of ALA-approved programs was fairly close to the female/male ratio in ALA membership. Specifically, women made up 75.8% of the ALA membership that was currently [at the time of the survey] employed full-time, while men made up 24.1% of such membership. This compared to the full population of U.S. librarians as reported in the 1970 census, in which the ratio was 84% female to 16% male, while the average ratio of females to males obtaining degrees from ALA-accredited programs during the period 1972-80 was 79% females to 21% males.

(668)

■ A study reported in 1983 of data gathered by the Office for Library Personnel Resources on master's- and doctoral-level degree recipients from ALA-accredited programs during the period 1973-74 through 1980-81 *showed that* the number of master's-level graduates dropped from 6,323 in 1973-74 to 3,776 in 1980-81, a decline of 40%. The number of earned doctoral degrees awarded remained fairly constant during that period, ranging (with the exception of 1974-75 when 78 doctoral degrees were awarded) from 46 awarded in 1979-80 to 56 awarded in 1978-79.   **(787)**

M.L.S. Graduates—Gender and Minority Issues

■ A study reported in 1983 of data gathered by the Office for Library Personnel Resources on master's- and doctoral-level degree recipients from ALA-accredited programs during the period 1973-74 through 1980-81 *showed that* for this period males in total were a declining portion of the M.L.S. graduates. While the overall annual average of male graduates for this period was 20.57%, their numbers declined from 21.76% of the total

M.L.S. graduates in 1973-74 to 17.82% of the total M.L.S. graduates in 1980-81. This decline was primarily due to the decline of white male M.L.S. graduates during this period from 19.7% of the total M.L.S. graduates in 1973-74 to 15.9% of the graduates in 1980-81. Other ethnic males fared as follows:

> black males decreased absolutely from 52 graduates in 1973-74 to 38 in 1980-81 but increased proportionately from .8% to 1.0% of the M.L.S. graduates in those years;

> Asian/Pacific Islanders held constant absolutely with 19 graduates in 1973-74 and 20 graduates in 1980-81 but increased proportionately from .3% to .5% of the M.L.S. graduates in those years;

> Hispanic males held constant absolutely with 15 graduates in 1973-74 and 15 graduates in 1980-81 but increased proportionately from .2% to .4% of the M.L.S. graduates in those years;

> American Indian/Alaskan native males decreased from 2 graduates in 1973-74 to 1 graduate in 1980-81.   **(787)**

Ibid. . . . *showed that*, while their overall numbers decreased, the portion of white females receiving M.L.S. degrees annually during the 8-year period increased from 70.1% in 1973-74 to 74.6% in 1980-81. Other ethnic females fared as follows:

> black females decreased both absolutely (from 255 M.L.S. graduates in 1973-74 to 129 in 1980-81) and proportionately (from 4.0% to 3.4% of the total graduates for those years);

> Asian/Pacific Islander females decreased absolutely (from 131 M.L.S. graduates in 1973-74 to 98 in 1980-81) but increased proportionately (from 2.1% to 2.6% of the total graduates for those years);

> Hispanic females held constant absolutely (from 46 M.L.S. graduates in 1973-74 to 48 in 1980-81) but increased proportionately (from .7% to 1.3% of the total graduates for those years);

> American Indian/Alaskan native females increased from 4 in 1973-74 to 8 in 1980-81.   **(787)**

Ibid. . . . *showed that* a comparison of the total number of M.L.S. graduates during the 8-year period by percentage of ethnic breakdown with the percent of the ethnic population in the U.S. was as follows:

white	90.50% grads; 76.70% pop.
black	4.61% grads; 11.69% pop.

continued

Asian/Pacific Islander	2.47% grads;	1.55% pop.	
Hispanic	1.43% grads;	6.45% pop.	
American Indian/			
Alaskan native	0.16% grads;	0.63% pop.	
other	.83% grads;	2.98% pop.	**(787)**

Ibid. . . . *showed that* during the 8 years of the study 80 (18.35%) of the doctoral degrees were awarded to minorities, compared to 9.50% of the M.L.S. degrees awarded to minorities in the same time period.   **(787)**

M.L.S. Graduates—Medical Library Education Program

■   A survey reported in 1973 of 16 past and present medical library education programs (8 degree programs; 8 internship programs) *showed that*, as of the date of the survey, 113 students had completed the degree programs while 125 students had completed the internship programs. **(694)**

M.L.S. Graduates—Projections

■   A study reported in 1982 comparing U.S. government projections (taken from *Projections of Educational Statistics*) for the number of graduates from library science degree programs with actual numbers of graduates from such programs *showed that* for all 3 kinds of library degrees the long-term projections were extremely inaccurate and even the shortest-term projections were quite inaccurate except for doctoral candidates. For example:

in 1979-80, 73 doctoral degrees in library science were actually granted, while the projected number of doctoral degrees for 1979-80 in 1971 was 40, in 1973 was 60, in 1976 was 90, and in 178 was 80;

in 1979-80, 5,374 master's degrees in library science were actually granted, while the projected number of master's degrees for 1979-80 in 1971 was 19,280, in 1973 was 10,940, in 1976 was 10,250, and in 1978 was 8,920;

in 1979-80, 398 bachelor's degrees in library science were actually granted, while the projected number of bachelor's degrees for 1979-80 in 1971 was 1,580, in 1973 was 1,520, in 1976 was 1,410, and in 1978 was 940.   **(665)**

Ibid. . . . *showed that* the number of doctoral degrees granted in library science rose from 14 in 1960-61 to a high of 102 in 1972-73 and declined to 73 in 1979-80. **(665)**

Reference Education

■ A report on a statewide Teletype reference service provided by library school students at the University of Iowa in an advanced reference course, involving 460 questions received in the first 6 months of 1974 from college libraries or public library regional centers, *showed that* 61% of the questions were answered completely successfully, 13% received nearly complete answers, 10% of the answers may have been minimally useful to the patron, and for 16% there were no available answers. **(146)**

Ibid. . . . *showed that* the average time spent searching for answers to the 460 questions was 1.9 hours, with 145 (31%) of the questions requiring a half hour or less to answer, 222 (48%) requiring an hour or less to answer, and only 43 (9%) requiring more than 5 hours of searching. **(146)**

■ A survey reported in 1983 of 249 special library respondents in 28 major firms (126 of the respondents had a master's degree in library science or the equivalent) *showed that* the 3 library school courses out of 9 ranked by the most respondents as "important" or "very important" were:
online searching (43% respondents took the course in library school; 83% rated it as "important" or "very important");

specialized reference (93% respondents took the course in library school; 76% rated it as "important" or "very important");

general reference (97% respondents took the course in library school; 69% rated it as "important" or "very important"). **(443)**

Relations with the Field

■ A 1979 survey of Canadian librarians in 3 groups (librarians who were or had been executives of a library or library-related associations in Canada; library administrators and department heads in public or academic libraries located within 20 miles of a library school; and library school full-time faculty) concerning the interaction [no time period given] between the library field and library schools (survey size: 120 association librarians, 120 library administrators, and [65] library school faculty; responding: 78 or 65% association librarians, 90 or 75% library administrators, and 43 or 66% library school faculty) *showed that* the number of direct contact activities between library school students and both groups of library practitioners (interviews, observation visits, tours, guest lecturers in classes, field work supervisor, etc.) averaged 3.3 activities per practitioner with the following breakdown:

0 activities per practitioner	10% practitioners	
1-2 activities per practitioner	27% practitioners	
3-4 activities per practitioner	31% practitioners	
5-8 activities per practitioner	32% practitioners	**(554)**

Ibid. . . . *showed that* interaction related to course preparation (e.g., what elements should be included in a course, course assignments, examples from experience, etc.) averaged .8 activities per both groups of practitioners with the following breakdown:

0 activities per practitioner	54% practitioners	
1 activity per practitioner	23% practitioners	
2 activities per practitioner	15% practitioners	
3 activities per practitioner	8% practitioners	**(554)**

Ibid. . . . *showed that* interaction related to degree programs (e.g., serving on an accreditation team, curriculum committee, etc.) was as follows:

54% of the practitioners had volunteered suggestions or recommended topics for the curriculum;

11% had been asked to review a program;

10% had sat on a curriculum or other library school committee;

and 3 respondents had served as members of an accreditation team.   **(554)**

Ibid. . . . *showed that* interaction related to research, publication, and association work was as follows:

20% of the practitioners reported interaction with library school faculty on research;

14% of the practitioners reported interaction with the library school faculty in publications;

56% of the practitioners reported interaction with the library school faculty in association work.   **(554)**

Ibid. . . . *showed that* interaction involving reciprocal activities (e.g., practitioners seeking information or assistance from library school faculty on an informal or formal basis, enrollment in continuing education courses, etc.) averaged 3.1 activities per practitioner with a breakdown as follows:

0 activities per practitioner	7% practitioners
1-2 activities per practitioner	36% practitioners
3-4 activities per practitioner	33% practitioners
5-7 activities per practitioner	24% practitioners **(554)**

Ibid. . . . *showed that* interaction with practitioners reported by library school faculty in terms of course planning and presentation was as follows:

63% of the instructors consulted with practitioners concerning 3 elements: course elements, course assignments, and illustrations of theory;

80% of the instructors consulted with practitioners concerning 2 of the 3 elements listed above. **(554)**

Ibid. . . . *showed that* interaction with practitioners reported by library school faculty in terms of association work was as follows: 93% of the faculty reported they were active on association committees, while 86% of the faculty reported they were active in working on association conferences and programs. **(554)**

Ibid. . . . *showed that* 44% of the faculty members reported that practitioners had called upon them for information or advice 10 or more times in the past 3 years. **(554)**

School Librarianship

■ A 1964 survey by the Committee on Professional Status and Growth of AASL (American Association of School Librarians) of institutions listed in the USDE Directory as offering a program of teacher education (population: 1,209; sample size: 683 or 56.5%; responding: 398 or 32%) *showed that* while responding institutions tended to rate themselves average on other measures of educational effectiveness, 57% (214) of the institutions answering this particular question rated themselves as having minimal or no success in providing experiences for students to work with boys and girls in school library situations. **(069)**

Ibid. . . . *showed that* of responding institutions 18% (68) reported they did not provide specific opportunity for use of materials in school library situations; 51% (196) reported that they do not use the adequacy of the collection as 1 criterion in the selection of schools as teaching centers; and 64% (249) do not use the presence of a school library and librarian as a requirement for selecting a school as a teaching center.   **(069)**

Ibid. . . . *showed that*, of the 268 responding institutions reporting one or more courses, 82 have a laboratory school library and 124 report an organized collection of materials either in addition to or in place of a laboratory school library.   **(069)**

Ibid. . . . *showed that* 268 of responding institutions offered 1 or more courses for future teachers dealing entirely with printed or AV materials, with the effective use of such materials, or with the nature and function of the school library.   **(069)**

School Rankings—Perceptual Basis

■   A 1978 survey of full-time faculty in 7 Canadian graduate library schools (population: 81 faculty; survey size: 71 faculty; responding: 59 or 83%) *showed that* the 4 "best" library schools out of 16 as ranked by 24 respondents (voting for one's own school was allowed) and scored on a weighted scale were (in descending order of perceived quality):

1. University of Chicago
2. University of Toronto
3. University of Illinois
4. University of California, Los Angeles

Further, 23 (28.4%) of the total group of Canadian library school faculty received at least 1 degree from these 4 schools.   **(551)**

■   A study reported in 1978 comparing peer ratings of graduate programs (Roose-Andersen ratings of graduate faculty in 10 scientific fields) with bibliometric ratings of those programs (number of papers published and "quality" of papers based on the papers' citation ratings), involving analysis of 127,000 papers from 450 journals in 10 fields published during the period 1965-73 and programs in 115 universities, *showed that* the correlations between peer and bibliometric ratings were as follows (fields included—biochemistry, chemistry, developmental biology, mathematics, microbiology, pharmacology, physics, physiology, psychology, and zoology):

between peer ratings and total number of papers published in the programs, the rank correlations ranged from .635 to .898;

between peer ratings and "quality" of papers published in the programs, the rank correlations ranged from .275 to .834;

between peer ratings and total influence (product of total number of papers published and "quality" of papers), the rank correlations ranged from .647 to .910.

(All correlations Spearman rank correlations.)   **(622)**

■ A survey reported in 1981 of the perceived ranking of the quality of North American library school programs as ranked by Association for Research Libraries [top] administrators and library school faculties (responses received from 59 or 56.2% of 105 ARL administrators and from faculties of 56 or 81.2% of the 69 library schools) *showed that* the 5 programs at the master's level most frequently mentioned as among the top 10 programs in North America by 248 library faculty and 55 ARL administrators were as follows:

LIBRARY FACULTY	ARL ADMINISTRATORS
Illinois (150 responses)	Illinois (44 responses)
Michigan (133 responses)	Michigan (41 responses)
North Carolina (127 responses)	California, Berkeley (38 responses)
UCLA (112 responses)	Chicago (38 responses)
Chicago (112 responses)	UCLA (37 responses) **(491)**

Ibid. . . . *showed that* the 4 programs at the doctoral level providing preparation for library education and research most frequently mentioned as among the top 5 programs in North America by 248 library faculty and 52 ARL administrators were as follows:

LIBRARY FACULTY	ARL ADMINISTRATORS
Chicago (145 responses)	Chicago (43 responses)
Illinois (116 responses)	Columbia (31 responses)
Michigan (91 responses)	Illinois (29 responses)
Columbia (90 responses)	Michigan (26 responses) **(491)**

Ibid. . . . *showed that* the 4 or 5 programs at the doctoral level providing preparation for library administration most frequently mentioned as among the top 5 programs in North America by 201 library faculty and 46 ARL administrators were as follows:

LIBRARY FACULTY	ARL ADMINISTRATORS
Columbia (84 responses)	California, Berkeley (22 responses)
Illinois (81 responses)	Columbia (22 responses)
Michigan (78 responses)	Michigan (20 responses)
Rutgers (72 responses)	Chicago (19 responses)
	Illinois (19 responses) **(491)**

Ibid. . . . *showed that* the 5 faculties most frequently mentioned as among the top 10 in North America in contributing to advancement of the library profession by 248 library faculty and 49 ARL administrators were as follows:

LIBRARY FACULTY	ARL ADMINISTRATORS
Illinois (151 responses)	Illinois (33 responses)
Chicago (140 responses)	Chicago (31 responses)
Pittsburgh (129 responses)	Michigan (28 responses)
Columbia (103 responses)	Columbia (27 responses)
Michigan (97 responses)	California, Berkeley (25 responses) **(491)**

School Rankings—Productivity Basis

■ An analysis reported in 1974 of 660 library science and library science related dissertations completed between 1925 and 1972 *showed that*, while the 660 dissertations came from a total of 68 private and public academic institutions, "three-fifths" of them were written at 6 schools: University of Chicago, University of Michigan, Columbia University, University of Illinois, Case Western Reserve University, and Rutgers University. Between 1925-50 the University of Chicago produced 2/3 of the 100 dissertations written; since the early 1960s Columbia and University of Michigan each produced twice as many dissertations as the University of Chicago. **(283)**

■ A study reported in 1978 comparing peer ratings of graduate programs (Roose-Andersen ratings of graduate faculty in 10 scientific fields) with bibliometric ratings of those programs (number of papers published and "quality" of papers based on the papers' citation ratings), involving analysis of 127,000 papers from 450 journals in 10 fields published during the period 1965-73 and programs in 115 universities, *showed that* the correlations between peer and bibliometric ratings were as follows (fields included—biochemistry, chemistry, developmental biology, mathematics, microbiology, pharmacology, physics, physiology, psychology, and zoology):

between peer ratings and total number of papers published in the programs, the rank correlations ranged from .635 to .898;

between peer ratings and "quality" of papers published in the programs, the rank correlations ranged from .275 to .834;

between peer ratings and total influence (product of total number of papers published and "quality" of papers), the rank correlations ranged from .647 to .910.

(All correlations Spearman rank correlations.) **(622)**

■ A 1980 survey of first-time-appointed academic library directors during the period 1970-80 (survey size: 230 directors; responding: 141 or 61.3%, including 98 males and 43 females) *showed that* the 132 respondents with a U.S. master's degree in library science received their degrees from a total of 44 schools. The 3 schools with the most master's degree graduates among the respondents were: Michigan (12 or 9.0% respondents), Columbia (10 or 7.6% respondents), and Simmons (10 or 7.6% respondents). Further, of the 14 black respondents, 6 (42.9%) received their M.L.S. from Atlanta. **(785)**

■ A study reported in 1983 of 98 doctoral dissertations in library administration (taken from *Dissertations in Library Science* 1930-80 by C. H. Davis, 1980) *showed that* the 3 most productive library schools (out of 18) in this area were:

Florida State	13 (13.3%) dissertations
Indiana	13 (13.3%) dissertations
University of Pittsburgh	11 (11.2%) dissertations

Further, the 3 library schools with the oldest doctoral programs (University of Chicago; University of Illinois, Urbana; and Columbia University) had each only produced 6 doctoral dissertations in the area of library administration, while Indiana's first dissertation in library administration appeared in 1970 and Florida State's first such dissertation appeared in 1972. **(560)**

■ A study reported in 1983 investigating the educational and professional qualifications of the 162 individuals holding deanships (excluding acting or interim deans) of ALA-accredited library school programs in North America during the period 1960-81 *showed that* 144 (88.9%) of the deans had a fifth-year (master's level) library degree, including 37 (94.9%) of the women and 107 (87%) of the men. Further, 3 library schools together accounted for 40.3% of the 144 fifth-year degrees awarded deans. These were: Columbia (32 or 22.2% of the fifth-year degrees), University of Illinois (14 or 9.7% of the fifth-year degrees), and University of Michigan (12 or 8.3% or the fifth-year degrees). **(562)**

Ibid. . . . *showed that*, of the 12 ALA accredited library schools awarding a total of 77 Ph.D.'s or D.L.S.'s to the deans, the 3 schools awarding the most library science doctorates to this group of deans were: University of Chicago (15 or 19.5% of the library science doctorates), University of Michigan (14 or 18.2% of the library science doctorates), and Columbia (12 or 15.6% of the library science doctorates). **(562)**

■ A study reported in 1983 of data compiled on 153 Association of Research Libraries and major public library directors *showed that* all but 1 of the 153 directors graduated from a library school, with the top 7 schools (in terms of graduating major library directors) graduating 50.7% of the directors. Columbia graduated 19 (12.5%), Illinois 13 (8.6%), Michigan 13 (8.6%), Simmons 11 (7.2%), Chicago 7 (4.6%), Louisiana State 7 (4.6%), and Wisconsin (Madison) 7 (4.6%). **(275)**

■ A study reported in 1983 of citation and publication levels of 411 tenured-level (associate and full professors) library school faculty in the 60 U.S. library schools with ALA-accredited M.L.S. programs (citations taken from *Social Science Citation Index* for the periods 1966-70, 1971-75, and 1976-80) *showed that*, while the 20 library schools with the highest normalized publication and citation rates included 9 of the top 10 ranked library school programs as reported by Blau and Margulies, the Spearman rank order correlation between the Blau and Margulies rankings and those 20 library schools ranked in order of average number of citations to a school's faculty was "virtually zero." In other words, within the top 20 library schools there was no relationship between the ranking of the programs and the ranking based on per capita number of citations to faculty publications. **(784)**

Students—Attitudes

■ A 1976 survey of students enrolled in the Graduate Library School at Indiana University (population: 194; responding: 147 or 76%) [whether in master's or doctoral program not stated] *showed that* 17% agreed, 38% disagreed, and 45% were uncertain as to whether librarianship lacked theory to give it direction and purpose. Of those already holding an advanced degree, 33% felt that librarianship lacked theory, while only 12% of those without an advanced degree felt that librarianship lacked theory. This was a statistically significant difference (significant at the .05 level). **(293)**

Ibid. . . . *showed that* 35% agreed that librarianship should be more concerned with "why" than "how," 20% disagreed, and 45% were unsure. 42% of the women vs. 16% of the men agreed that librarianship should be more concerned with "why" than "how." This was a statistically significant difference (significant at the .05 level). **(293)**

Ibid. . . . *showed that* 50% of the students agreed that library school courses should stress "how-to-do-it," while 11% disagreed, and 39% were uncertain. However, when asked if library schools should prepare students for the immediate tasks of their first job rather than teach principles useful for the future, only 3% agreed, 67% disagreed, and 30% were unsure. **(293)**

■ A study during the 1977-78 academic year of students and faculty at 2 Canadian library schools (School of Library and Information Science at the University of Western Ontario and the Faculty of Library Science at the University of Toronto) concerning philosophical orientation (study size: 161 beginning students, 120 graduates, and 50 faculty) *showed that*, given the 2 poles of custodial versus assistance orientation in librarianship, scores revealed a progression from a custodial orientation toward an assistance orientation as one moved from beginning students to graduates to faculty. **(552)**

Ibid. . . . *showed that*, on the issue of censorship, scores revealed a progression moving away from censorship tendencies as one moved from beginning students to graduates to faculty. **(552)**

Ibid. . . . *showed that* on the issue of promotion of libraries and library services there was almost no difference at all among beginning students, graduates and faculty. **(552)**

Students—Personality Traits and Values

■ A 1967 study of 35 male summer school library students at the University of Oklahoma who were given the California Psychological Inventory Questionnaire *showed that* as a group they scored statistically significantly higher on the femininity scale (18.17 mean with a standard deviation of 2.95) than American males as a group (16.26 mean with a standard deviation of 3.63) at the .01 significance level. The male librarians studied tended toward gentleness and appreciativeness rather than amibition, activity, or innovation. **(201)**

■ A 1977 study in a library school at a major university in the western United States involving 16 males and 26 females taking the Bem Sex-Role Inventory *showed that* there were no statistically significant differences between library school males and the normative male group on masculinity, femininity, or androgyny scores. **(485)**

Ibid. . . . *showed that* there were no statistically significant differences between library school females and the normative female group on masculinity or androgyny scores. There were statistically significant differences between the 2 groups on femininity scores, with the library school females scoring higher (significanct at the .05 level). **(485)**

Ibid. . . . *showed that* a comparison of scores for library school males and library school females showed a statistically significant difference on masculinity, femininity, and androgyny scores, with males scoring higher on the masculinity scales and females scoring higher on the female and androgynous scales (significant at the .01 level). **(485)**

■ A 1979-80 study of 61 students enrolled in an LST 600 Foundations of Librarianship course in the Library Science/Educational Technology program at the University of North Carolina, Greensboro using the Cognitive Style Inventory (developed by J. E. Hill), *showed that* as a group the students revealed the following major strengths (indicated by a score of 32 to 40): TVL, 33.2 (prefer to learn through reading than hearing); QT, 32.1 (prefer to learn through the sense of touch); QCEM, 32.1 (empathy); QCES, 35.0 (esthetics), QCET, 33.8 (ethics), QCP, 32.1 (sense of other's personal space needs), QCTM, 33.8 (willing to function within established time frames). **(295)**

■ A survey reported in 1980 of the values of 44 directors of large U.S. public libraries (response: 25 or 57%), 60 full-time faculty in ALA-accredited library school programs (response: 35 or 58%),and 175 students in accredited library school programs (response: 128 or 73%) as measured by the Rokeach Value Survey *showed that* all 3 groups ranked highly: self-respect, wisdom, freedom, inner harmony, and family security. All placed a low value on salvation, national security, social recognition, pleasure, and comfortable life. **(290)**

Ibid. . . . *showed that* the top 3 values for library directors were: sense of accomplishment (lasting contribution), exciting life (a stimulating, active life), and family security (taking care of loved ones).

The top 3 values for library school faculty were: sense of accomplishment (lasting contribution), self-respect (self-esteem), and wisdom (a mature understanding of life).

The top 3 values for library school students were: self-respect (self-esteem), wisdom (a mature understanding of life), and freedom (independent, free choice). **(290)**

■ A survey reported in 1981 that requested a systematic sample of special librarians to take the Rokeach Value Survey (sample size: 200; responding: 101), which was then compared to Value Survey results from librarians in public libraries, library school faculty, and library school students, *showed that* special librarians differed most from these other groups in the importance they assigned to sense of accomplishment. Public librarians and library school faculty ranked it higher (both ranked it first of 18), while library school students ranked it lower (ninth of 18). Special librarians ranked it sixth of 18. These differences were statistically significant at the .05 level. **(434)**

■ A 1983 study of 70 graduate library school students at North Texas State University (replicating an earlier study on library students' cognitive styles) based on the Hill Cognitive Style Inventory *showed that* the replication validated the results of the earlier study. Specifically, when average scores on the 28 test items were compared between the original study and the replicated study, there were statistically significant differences on only 3 of the items. Further, even though the 3 items had statistically significant different scores, the different scores were not large enough to change the interpretation of the test results. Consequently the implications for the education of library science students remained unchanged, i.e., library science students preferred to learn though the written word and sensory input rather than through auditory signals. This suggested use of reading assignments, independent study, use of visuals, hands-on experience, etc. **(804)**

Students—Practices

■ A 1976 survey of students enrolled in the Graduate Library School at Indiana University (population: 194; responding: 147 or 76%) [whether in master's or doctoral program not stated] *showed that* the number of hours per week students reported reading nonrequired library-related literature was as follows: none (20%), 1 hour (26%), 2 hours (23%), 3 hours (12%), 4 hours (10%), and 5+ hours (9%). **(293)**

Ibid. . . . *showed that* 36% of the students did not browse library periodicals, but of those who did the 4 most commonly browsed library periodicals were as follows: *Library Journal* (59 or 40% of the total respondents), *Booklist* (22 or 15%), *Publishers Weekly* (16 or 11%), *Choice* (14 or 15%).
(293)

Teaching Techniques

■   A report on a statewide Teletype reference service provided in 1974 by library school students at the University of Iowa in an advanced reference course, involving 460 questions received from college libraries or public library regional centers, *showed that* 61% of the questions were answered completely successfully, 13% received nearly complete answers, 10% of the answers may have been minimally useful to the patron, and for 16% there were no available answers.   **(146)**

■   A 1975-76 study at the Graduate Library School of the University of Arizona involving 63 students completing the basic reference course (30 students in the control group using a traditional lecture method of presentation; 33 in the experimental group using self-paced audio tapes in place of the lecture) *showed that* there was no statistically significant difference between the 2 groups in their ability to understand the theoretical concerns of the reference process, no statistically significant difference between the 2 groups in their knowledge of reference tools, and no statistically significant difference in their satisfaction with the methodology of the course.   **(287)**

Ibid. . . . *showed that* students in the audio-tutorial course did express to a statistically significant degree more satisfaction with their own performance and knowledge than students in the lecture course (significance level .05).   **(287)**

■   A study reported in 1976 in the library school at UCLA involving 24 students in 2 classes studying flowcharting *showed that*, while the class given programmed learning required only 3 hours compared to 6 hours for the traditional classroom approach to cover the material, there was no statistically significant difference between the pre- and post-test scores of the 2 groups (significance level at .05).   **(327)**

■   A 1979-80 study of 61 students enrolled in an LST 600 Foundations of Librarianship course in the Library Science/Educational Technology program at the University of North Carolina, Greensboro, using the Cognitive

Style Inventory (developed by J. E. Hill), *showed that* as a group the students revealed the following major strengths (indicated by a score of 32 to 40): TVL, 33.2 (prefer to learn through reading than hearing); QT, 32.1 (prefer to learn through the sense of touch); QCEM, 32.1 (empathy); QCES, 35.0 (esthetics), QCET, 33.8 (ethics), QCP, 32.1 (sense of other's personal space needs), QCTM, 33.8 (willing to function within established time frames). **(295)**

■ A 1983 study of 70 graduate library school students at North Texas State University (replicating an earlier study on library students' cognitive styles) based on the Hill Cognitive Style Inventory *showed that* the replication validated the results of the earlier study. Specifically, when average scores on the 28 test items were compared between the original study and the replicated study, there were statistically significant differences on only 3 of the items. Further, even though the 3 items had statistically significant different scores, the different scores were not large enough to change the interpretation of the test results. Consequently the implications for the education of library science students remained unchanged, i.e., library science students preferred to learn though the written word and sensory input rather than through auditory signals. This suggested use of reading assignments, independent study, use of visuals, hands-on experience, etc. **(804)**

Undergraduate Programs

■ A study reported in 1982 comparing U.S. government projections (taken from *Projections of Educational Statistics*) for the number of graduates from library science degree programs with actual numbers of graduates from such programs *showed that* for all 3 kinds of library degrees the long-term projections were extremely inaccurate and even the shortest-term projections were quite inaccurate except for doctoral candidates. For example:

in 1979-80, 73 doctoral degrees in library science were actually granted, while the projected number of doctoral degrees for 1979-80 in 1971 was 40, in 1973 was 60, in 1976 was 90, and in 178 was 80;

in 1979-80, 5,374 master's degrees in library science were actually granted, while the projected number of master's degrees for 1979-80 in 1971 was 19,280, in 1973 was 10,940, in 1976 was 10,250, and in 1978 was 8,920;

in 1979-80, 398 bachelor's degrees in library science were actually granted, while the projected number of bachelor's

degrees for 1979-80 in 1971 was 1,580, in 1973 was 1,520, in
1976 was 1,410, and in 1978 was 940.   **(665)**

Ibid. . . . *showed that* the number of bachelor's degrees awarded in library
science rose from 439 in 1960-61 to a high of 1,164 in 1973-74 and declined
to 398 in 1979-80.   **(665)**

2.

Professional Issues

Bibliometrics

General

■ A study reported in 1983 comparing peer rating of medical articles with citation counts (taken from *Science Citation Index* for the 5 years following the articles' date of publication), involving 279 "first order papers" (all 1974 research papers abstracted in the 1975 or 1976 volumes of the *Yearbook of Cancer*, highest peer rating), 276 "second order papers" (random sample of the 1974 research papers that were only listed in the 1975 or 1976 volumes of the *Yearbook of Cancer*, next highest peer rating), and 315 "average" papers (no special peer rating) published in 1974 on the subject of cancer research randomly selected from *Biological Abstracts*, *showed that* the more highly regarded articles tended to be cited more than other articles to a statistically significant degree (significant at the .005 level). Specifically, the average percentage of papers cited per year was as follows:

first-order group	73.7% of papers
second-order group	72.7% of papers
average group	55.7% of papers

while the average number of citations per paper for the 5-year period was as follows:

first-order group	30.59 citations	
second-order group	24.60 citations	
average group	11.17 citations	**(657)**

Ibid. . . . *showed that* comparison of citation ratings for the 3 groups using only 1974 and 1975 citations (citations made during these 2 years took place before the *Yearbook of Cancer* could have been a factor in calling attention to the articles) indicated as well that the more highly regarded articles were cited more than other articles to a statistically significant degree (significance level at the .001 level). This suggests that the quality of the article itself was the factor leading to the generally higher number of citations. **(657)**

Academic

■ A study reported in 1978 comparing peer ratings of graduate programs (Roose-Andersen ratings of graduate faculty in 10 scientific fields) with bibliometric ratings of those programs (number of papers published and "quality" of papers based on the papers' citation ratings), involving analysis of 127,000 papers from 450 journals in 10 fields published during the period 1965-73 and programs in 115 universities, *showed that* the correlations between peer and bibliometric ratings were as follows (fields included—biochemistry, chemistry, developmental biology, mathematics, microbiology, pharmacology, physics, physiology, psychology, and zoology):

> between peer ratings and total number of papers published in the programs, the rank correlations ranged from .635 to .898;
>
> between peer ratings and "quality" of papers published in the programs, the rank correlations ranged from .275 to .834;
>
> between peer ratings and total influence (product of total number of papers published and "quality" of papers), the rank correlations ranged from .647 to .910.

(All correlations Spearman rank correlations.) **(622)**

■ A study reported in 1980 comparing the subjective rating by science faculty of the importance of the average article in a group of scientific journals compared to the rating of importance of the average article in those journals based on a citation count (faculty survey size: not given; responding: 298 or 25%, involving 56 journals in 10 scientific fields) *showed that* the agreement between subjective and citation-based rating of journals was quite good in most fields. Specifically, the average overall correlation between the subjective and citation rating was r = .78, with the correlations in the 7 most strongly correlated fields ranging from r = .76 (psychology) to r = .96 (geoscience). In the 3 least correlated fields the correlations ranged from r = .37 (electrical engineering) to r = .69 (physics). **(625)**

■ A study reported in 1983 investigating the relationship between the scholarliness of academic papers and their impact by comparing the number of references in each of 110 papers (taken from the *American Sociological Review* and the *American Journal of Sociology* during the years 1972-73) to the number of citations listed for each of the papers in *Social Science Citation Index*, 1972-81, *showed that* there was a very modest but statistically significant relationship between scholarliness and impact. Specifically, the correlation coefficient (partial gamma coefficient) was .26 and significant at the .03 level. **(659)**

Career Issues—General Issues

General

■ A 1968 survey of library staff members belonging to the Staff Organization Round Table (SORT) of ALA who did not have collective bargaining contracts (2,185 individuals responding, including 1,047 from large public libraries, 614 from small public libraries, and 524 from academic libraries; 39% professionals, 14% subprofessionals, and 46% nonprofessionals) *showed that* the following ratios obtained between librarians and populations/enrollments:

public elementary & secondary schools—.57 librarians/1,000 enrollees
college & university libraries—2.7 librarians/1,000 enrollees
public libraries—.11 librarians/1,000 population
special libraries—.054 librarians/1,000 population   **(074)**

■ A study reported in 1981 of academic job openings listed in *Library Journal* during the period 1970-79 (2,531 openings) *showed that* 1,237 (49%) were public service positions, 897 (35%) were technical service openings, and 397 (16%) were administrative openings.   **(495)**

Ibid. . . . *showed that* a cyclical pattern of job availability took place during the decade, beginning with a decline in 1970-72 (from 263 positions in 1970 to 167 in 1972) followed by an upswing in 1973-76 (from 229 positions in 1973 to 354 positions in 1976), which was followed by another decline in 1977-79 (from 317 positions in 1977 to 200 positions in 1979).   **(495)**

Ibid. . . . *showed that* the regional distribution of job openings listed generally corresponded to the distribution of academic librarians employed in that region (based on 1970 statistics) in the Southeast, Southwest, and West, while the Northeast had fewer openings compared to the number of academic librarians employed in that area and the Midwest had more. Specifically:

Northeast	26% openings	32% present positions
Southwest	15% openings	16% present positions
Midwest	33% openings	26% present positions
Southwest	10% openings	10% present positions
West	16% openings	16% present positions **(495)**

Academic

■ A 1969 survey of the 71 ARL libraries (57 responding; 55 or 77.5% usable) concerning librarians as teachers *showed that*, of the library staff members who also have teaching assignments in academic departments, 56.4% hold joint appointments; 20.0% do not hold joint appointments; and 23.6% of the responding libraries reported that the issue was "not applicable."   **(196)**

■ A survey reported in 1978 of 407 academic and public libraries who had filled professional positions (61% [no number given] responding with 233 or 57% usable responses) *showed that* there was an average of 73 applicants for each academic library position and 47 for each public library position. Broken down by level: entry level averaged 92 applicants per position for academic libraries and 65 for public libraries; departmental level averaged 58 applicants per academic library position and 36 per public library position; administrative level averaged 73 applicants per academic position and 50 per public position.   **(227)**

Ibid. . . . *showed that* in academic libraries there was an average of 110 applicants per reference position, 109 per audiovisual position, 69 per acquisitions position, and 55 per cataloging position [conflicting data given concerning circulation], while in public libraries there was an average of 31 applicants per cataloging position and 26 per reference position, with no data available for other positions.   **(227)**

■ A study reported in 1978 of 23 middle managers and 11 administrators in 5 Association of Research Libraries libraries as well as a review of ads for 82 middle managerial positions in academic libraries posted in 1975 *showed that*, of the 82 middle management positions, 13.4% were staff specialists (e.g., systems analysts, personnel directors, etc.), 26.8% were in technical services, and 59.8% were in public services.   **(423)**

■ A 1979 survey of members of the ACRL Discussion Group of Personnel Officers (sample size: 45; responding: 30) concerning entry-level requirements for professionals *showed that* 24 out of 27 agreed that previous nonprofessional experience was an important requirement for an entry-level position. The "majority" also indicated that the experience should be in an academic library.   **(240)**

Ibid. . . . *showed that* for long-term growth the skills respondents mentioned were in the following areas: management skills (10 respondents), computer background (6 respondents), advanced degrees (5 respondents), and depth of subject expertise (5 respondents).   **(240)**

Public

■ A survey reported in 1967 of midwestern librarians (37 men, 408 women, total 445) in small public libraries (i.e., serving populations of 10,000 to 35,000) *showed that* 54.3% of the librarians with professional degrees worked in communities with median incomes of less than $7,000, while 72.2% of the librarians with less training worked in such communities; 19.4% of the librarians with professional degrees worked in communities with median incomes $10,000+, while only 6.5% of the librarians with less training worked in such communities. A positive correlation (correlation coefficient = .20) between professional training and community income was determined (no significance level given).   **(282)**

■ A survey reported in 1978 of 407 academic and public libraries who had filled professional positions (61% [no number given] responding with 233 or 57% usable responses) *showed that* there was an average of 73 applicants for each academic library position and 47 for each public library position. Broken down by level: entry level averaged 92 applicants per position for academic libraries and 65 for public libraries; departmental level averaged 58 applicants per academic library position and 36 per public library position; administrative level averaged 73 applicants per academic position and 50 per public position.   **(227)**

Ibid. . . . *showed that* in academic libraries there was an average of 110 applicants per reference position, 109 per audiovisual position, 69 per acquisitions position, and 55 per cataloging position [conflicting data given concerning circulation], while in public libraries there was an average of 31 applicants per cataloging position and 26 per reference position, with no data available for other positions.   **(227)**

School

■ A 1983 survey of a systematic sample of school library media centers concerning data for fiscal year 1982-83 (survey size: 2,000 centers; responding: 1,297; usable: 1,251 or 62%) *showed that* a comparison of schools with (666 schools) and without (597 schools) district-level library media coordinators revealed that schools without district coordinators spent more money per student on resources and had more books per student than schools with district coordinators. However, schools with district coordinators paid media specialists higher salaries, had more AV items per student, had more clerical assistance, and used more adult volunteers than schools without district coordinators. Specifically:

> total materials expenditure per student in schools with coordinators averaged $8.80 and in schools without coordinators averaged $10.92;

> average books per student in schools with coordinators averaged 18 and in schools without coordinators averaged 20;

> number of AV items per student in schools with coordinators averaged 3.45 and in schools without coordinators averaged 3.03;

media specialist salary in schools with coordinators averaged $20,699 and in schools without coordinators averaged $19,354;

the number of clerical assistants and adult volunteers in schools with coordinators averaged .83 and 2.46, respectively, and in schools without coordinators averaged .77 and 1.85, respectively.   **(056)**

Special

■   A 1972 survey of prison law libraries (sample size: 90; responding: 68% [no number given, 62 assumed]) *showed that* the type of prison law library staff was as follows (multiple responses allowed when more than 1 staff member):

noninmate with library degree	7 (11.3%)	
noninmate without library degree	36 (58.1%)	
inmate with library degree	1 (1.6%)	
inmate without library degree	33 (53.2%)	**(389)**

■   A 1974 survey of a random sample of U.S. museum libraries (including history, art, and science museums) listed in the 1973 *Official Museum Directory* (population: 2,556; sample size: 856; responding: 374 or 43.7%) *showed that* only 50% of the libraries had a librarian and only 47% of them possessed a degree in library science. The largest number of librarians were in libraries with 1,000-5,000 book titles, but full-time librarians were not reported until library size began to reach 10,000 titles.   **(412)**

■   A preliminary analysis reported in 1976 of a survey of American Association of Law Libraries members (survey size: "approximately 2,000" individuals; responding: "approximately 1,400" or 70%, of which responses from 888 respondents were analyzed at the time of the report) *showed that* the library size (in volumes) in which respondents worked was as follows:

small (50,000 vols. or less)	41% respondents	
medium (50-100,000 vols.)	22% respondents	
large (100-200,000 vols.)	22% respondents	
very large (200,000 vols. or more)	15% respondents	**(793)**

Ibid. . . . *showed that* the type of library in which respondents worked was as follows:

law school libraries	45% respondents
bar or lawyer association	
libraries	5% respondents

continued

law firm libraries	21% respondents
non-law firm libraries	6% respondents
government libraries	23% respondents

This represented a 10% drop in members employed in law school libraries and a 13% increase in members employed in law firms [from the earlier 1970 survey of AALL members]. **(793)**

■ A survey reported in 1980 of 23 special librarians who became officers in their organizations *showed that* "almost half" of the 23 belonged to 5 organizations (3 banks and 2 advertising companies). **(431)**

Ibid. . . . *showed that* "two-thirds" had been with their present employers 5 years or more, while "one-half" had been with their present employers for 10 years or more. Further, "almost all" had been special librarians for at least "three-fourths" of their professional careers and "one-half" had worked only as special librarians. "Two-thirds" of them supervised 7 or more employees. **(431)**

Ibid. . . . *showed that* "almost one-half" considered their appointment to officership a promotion; the rest did not. Further, "an overwhelming number" reported that the appointment had had little effect on their job functions or position on the organizational chart. **(431)**

Ibid. . . . *showed that*, of external factors (those over which the respondent had little control) influencing the appointment to officer rank, the 1 "most frequently mentioned" was a supportive management. The "next most frequently cited external factor" was the women's movement and affirmative action. **(431)**

Ibid. . . . *showed that*, of personal factors influencing the appointment to officer rank, the 2 "most frequently" mentioned were hard work and the development of a service-oriented staff. **(431)**

Career Issues—Accredited Library Degree Programs

General

■ A study reported in 1982 of academic job advertisements at 5-year intervals (1959, 1964, 1969, 1974, and 1979) over a 20-year period taken from 3 library journals (*Library Journal, ALA Bulletin/American Librar-*

ies, and *College and Research Libraries/College and Research Libraries News*), excluding jobs that were primarily administrative or technical in nature for a total of 1,254 jobs, *showed that* in 1959, 48 (26.0%) of the jobs advertised required an M.L.S., of which only 9 (4.9%) of the jobs required an ALA-accredited M.L.S., while by 1979, 244 (97.6%) of the jobs required an M.L.S., of which 193 (77.2%) required an ALA-accredited M.L.S.   **(515)**

Academic

■ A study reported in 1978 of 23 middle managers and 11 administrators in 5 Association of Research Libraries libraries as well as a review of ads for 82 middle managerial positions in academic libraries posted in 1975 *showed that* 43 (52.4%) of the ads listed an ALA-accredited library master's degree as a qualification, 37 (45.1%) listed library master's degree without specifying ALA-accredited, 30 (36.6%) listed second master's degree, 4 (4.9%) listed Ph.D., 1 (1.2%) listed an other professional degree, and 1 stated that a master's degree was not required.   **(423)**

Ibid. . . . *showed that* of 23 middle managers, 21 (91.3%) had ALA-accredited master's degrees, none had unaccredited library master's degrees, 13 (56.5%) had second master's degrees, 1 (4.3%) had a Ph.D. and 2 (8.7%) had an other professional degree.   **(423)**

■ A study reported in 1982 of academic job advertisements at 5-year intervals (1959, 1964, 1969, 1974, and 1979) over a 20-year period taken from 3 library journals (*Library Journal, ALA Bulletin/American Libraries*, and *College and Research Libraries/College and Research Libraries News*), excluding jobs that were primarily administrative or technical in nature for a total of 1,254 jobs, *showed that* in 1959, 48 (26.0%) of the jobs advertised required an M.L.S., of which only 9 (4.9%) of the jobs required an ALA-accredited M.L.S., while by 1979, 244 (97.6%) of the jobs required an M.L.S., of which 193 (77.2%) required an ALA-accredited M.L.S.   **(515)**

Career Issues—Career Patterns

Academic

■ A 1975 survey of 530 (87% responding) academic librarians in 9 southern states out of a total academic librarian population of 1,964, investigating the relationship between job mobility and career advancement, *showed that*, of the respondents who had changed jobs, 91% had subsequently received a salary increase. The size of the increase, however, was related to the reasons for the move. Of those librarians who had moved for career reasons, 24% made salary gains of $8,000 or more; of those who moved for noncareer reasons, only 16% received salary increases of $8,000 or more.   **(165)**

Career Issues—Community Size

Public

■   A survey reported in 1967 of midwestern librarians (37 men, 408 women, total 445) in small public libraries (i.e., serving populations of 10,000 to 35,000) *showed that* 54.3% of the librarians with professional degrees worked in communities with median incomes of less than $7,000, while 72.2% of the librarians with less training worked in such communities; 19.4% of the librarians with professional degrees worked in communities with median incomes $10,000+, while only 6.5% of the librarians with less training worked in such communities. A positive correlation (correlation coefficient = .20) between professional training and community income was determined (no significance level given).   **(282)**

Ibid. . . . *showed that* there was a slight statistical relationship (correlation coefficient = .14) between size of community and professional education of the librarian. 29.4% of the libraians with professional degrees and 40.3% of the librarians with less education worked in libraries serving communities of 10,000 to 14,999, while 16.5% of the librarians with professional degrees and 10.9% of the librarians with less education worked in libraries serving communities of 30,000 to 34,999 (no significance level given). **(282)**

Career Issues—Doctorates

General

■   A survey reported in 1978 of traceable North American librarians who had earned library doctorates in American Library Association accredited programs between 1930 and 1975 (survey size: 568; responding: 403 or 71%) *showed that*, based on a scoring system where "3" = essential, "2" = important, "1" = useful and "0" = unimportant, respondents overall rated the library doctorate 2.4 in obtaining their present posts and 1.99 in performing the duties of their present posts. Specifically:

> library educators rated the library doctorate 2.81 in obtaining
> their present posts and 2.33 in performing their duties;

library administrators ranked the library doctorate 2.06 in obtaining their present positions and 1.73 in performing their duties;

library researchers ranked the library doctorate 1.86 in obtaining their present positions and 1.51 in performing their duties;

individuals in library operations ranked the library doctorate 1.20 in obtaining their present positions and 1.07 in performing their duties.   **(463)**

Ibid. . . . *showed that* 51.3% reported being in library education, 33.8% reported being in the field of library administration, 11.1% reported library research (as distinct from any other categories), and 3.8% reported being in library operations.   **(463)**

■ An analysis reported in 1974 of 660 library science and library science related dissertations completed between 1925 and 1972 *showed that* 48% of the 435 doctoral recipients who received their degrees between 1953-72 worked in positions or with activities that appeared to be far removed from the scope of their dissertations. The primary exception to this general trend was library school faculty, where 63.3% taught courses that generally coincided with their dissertation topic.   **(283)**

Ibid. . . . *showed that*, of the 435 doctoral recipients who received their degrees between 1953-72, there was no statistically significant relationship between type of degree earned (Ph.D., D.L.S., and Ed.D.) and the type of position held (faculty, academic libraries, public libraries, school libraries, special libraries, other) at the time of the analysis. D.L.S. recipients were as likely as Ph.D. or Ed.D. recipients to teach on library school faculties, while Ph.D. recipients were as likely as D.L.S. or Ed.D. recipients to have jobs in academic libraries, etc.   **(283)**

Ibid. . . . *showed that*, for 435 doctoral recipients who received their degrees between 1953-72, there was a statistically significant relationship between sex and current type of position held (significant at the .001 level). Specifically, a higher proportion of males (29.3%) than females (14.3%) tended to work in academic libraries, while a higher proportion of females (65.7%) than males (58.1%) tended to join library school faculties. 3.8% of the females vs. 1.4% of the males worked in public libraries, 6.7% of the females vs. 0.5% of the males worked in school libraries, and 1.9% of the females vs. 2.7% of the males worked in special libraries. 7.6% of the females and 8.0% of the males worked in "other" positions.   **(283)**

Ibid. . . . *showed that*, for 435 doctoral recipients who received their degrees between 1953-72, there was no statistically significant relationship between sex and mobility. Specifically, comparing location of job to location of school, 17.0% of the females and 9.5% of the males were in the same state, 27.4% of the females and 31.8% of the males were in contiguous states, while 55.6% of the females and 58.7% of the males were "geographically removed." **(283)**

Academic

■ A 1974-75 study of university libraries including all Association of Research Libraries libraries (sample size: 92; responding: 72 or 78%) and all library schools with ALA-accredited programs (sample size: not given; responding: 44 or 80%) *showed that* responding libraries reported [some individuals apparently worked in more than 1 area] that 52 (30.1%) subject Ph.D.'s were employed in archives/special collections, 44 (25.4%) in subject bibliography, 39 (22.5%) in administration, 34 (19.7%) in reference or technical services, and 6 (3.5%) as branch librarians. **(445)**

Ibid. . . . *showed that*, of 72 responding library directors and 44 responding library school deans, the number who felt it was desirable to hire subject Ph.D.'s in the following positions was as follows: administration (50% library directors; 74.2% deans), reference (70.8% library directors; 83.9% deans), bibliography (87.5% library directors; 93.6% deans), archives (86.1% library directors; 87.1% deans), and technical services (34.7% library directors; 3.2% deans). **(445)**

Ibid. . . . *showed that*, of 39 responding library school deans, 71% reported that the subject Ph.D.'s they had placed had not had library experience. Nevertheless, 60.7% of these 71% had received positions with advanced salaries according to the library school deans. 42.7% of the library directors reported they would hire a subject Ph.D. without library experience (but with an M.L.S.) at an advanced salary while 45.6% said they would not. The remainder indicated that it depended on the position, the individual, or both. However, when referring to specific salary levels, 64.7% of the library directors indicated they would hire a subject Ph.D. (with M.L.S.) at a higher level than they would an M.L.S. only. **(445)**

Ibid. . . . *showed that* 22.4% of the responding library directors would allow graduate study for the Ph.D. to be considered library experience, while 68.6% would not, and 9% indicated that it depended upon the position. Further, 16.4% of the responding library directors would allow previous teaching experience to influence salary levels, while 76.1%

indicated they would not, and 7.5% said it would depend upon the position. **(445)**

■ A study reported in 1978 of 23 middle managers and 11 administrators in 5 Association of Research Libraries libraries as well as a review of ads for 82 middle managerial positions in academic libraries posted in 1975 *showed that* 43 (52.4%) of the ads listed an ALA-accredited library master's degree as a qualification, 37 (45.1%) listed library master's degree without specifying ALA-accredited, 30 (36.6%) listed second master's degree, 4 (4.9%) listed Ph.D., 1 (1.2%) listed an other professional degree, and 1 stated that a master's degree was not required. **(423)**

Ibid. . . . *showed that*, of 23 middle managers, 21 (91.3%) had ALA-accredited master's degrees, none had unaccredited library master's degrees, 13 (56.5%) had second master's degrees, 1 (4.3%) had a Ph.D., and 2 (8.7%) had an other professional degree. **(423)**

■ A study reported in 1981 of job listings for college and university libraries reported in *Library Journal* and *College and Research Libraries News* during 1970-79 (5,269 job listings) *showed that* overall for the survey period for nondirector university positions 1.9% required a Ph.D., 27.0% required a second master's, while 71% required no additional educational certification. Overall for nondirector college positions, 2.8% required a Ph.D., 21.4% required a second master's, while 75.8% required no additional educational certification. **(494)**

Career Issues—Education, General

Academic

■ A study reported in 1978 of 23 middle managers and 11 administrators in 5 Association of Research Libraries libraries as well as a review of ads for 82 middle managerial positions in academic libraries posted in 1975 *showed that* 43 (52.4%) of the ads listed an ALA-accredited library master's degree as a qualification, 37 (45.1%) listed library master's degree without specifying ALA-accredited, 30 (36.6%) listed second master's degree, 4 (4.9%) listed Ph.D., 1 (1.2%) listed an other professional degree, and 1 stated that a master's degree was not required. **(423)**

Ibid. . . . *showed that*, of 23 middle managers, 21 (91.3%) had ALA-accredited master's degrees, none had unaccredited library master's degrees, 13 (56.5%) had second master's degrees, 1 (4.3%) had a Ph.D., and 2 (8.7%) had an other professional degree.   **(423)**

■ A study reported in 1981 of job listings for college and university libraries reported in *Library Journal* and *College and Research Libraries News* during 1970-79 (5,269 job listings) *showed that* educational requirements for nondirector positions generally increased from 1970 through 1976, with a peak in the 1974-76 period and decline in educational requirements subsequently. The only exception to this pattern was college director positions, whose educational requirements increased throughout the survey period.   **(494)**

Ibid. . . . *showed that* overall for the survey period for nondirector university positions 1.9% required a Ph.D., 27.0% required a second master's, while 71% required no additional educational certification. Overall for nondirector college positions, 2.8% required a Ph.D., 21.4% required a second master's, while 75.8% required no additional educational certification.   **(494)**

Ibid. . . . *showed that* both director and nondirector positions in the university environment listed statistically significantly higher educational requirements than director and nondirector positions in the college environment (significant at the .05 level or less).   **(494)**

Public

■ A survey reported in 1967 of midwestern librarians (37 men, 408 women, total 445) in small public libraries (i.e., serving populations of 10,000 to 35,000) *showed that*:

of those librarians under 30 years of age, 91.6% had completed 4 years of college;

of librarians in their 30s, 85.0% had completed college;

of librarians in their 40s, 65.3% had completed college;

of librarians in their 50s, 52.0% had completed college;

of librarians in their 60s, 53.1% had completed college;

and of those librarians 70+, 50.0% had completed college.   **(282)**

Ibid. . . . *showed that*, of the respondents as a group, 36.0% had no college degree, 26.4% had no more than a college degree, 13.3% had no

more than a fifth-year bachelor's degree, and 24.1% had no more than a
master's degree.   **(282)**

Ibid. . . . *showed that* 54.3% of the librarians with professional degrees
worked in communities with median incomes of less than $7,000, while
72.2% of the librarians with less training worked in such communities;
19.4% of the librarians with professional degrees worked in communities
with median incomes $10,000+, while only 6.5% of the librarians with less
training worked in such communities. A positive correlation (correlation
coefficient = .20) between professional training and community income
was determined (no significance level given).   **(282)**

Ibid. . . . *showed that* there was a slight statistical relationship (correlation
coefficient = .14) between size of community and professional education of
the librarian. 29.4% of the librarians with professional degrees and 40.3%
of the librarians with less education worked in libraries serving communities of 10,000 to 14,999, while 16.5% of the librarians with professional
degrees and 10.9% of the librarians with less education worked in libraries
serving communities of 30,000 to 34,999 (no significance level given). **(282)**

Special

■ A 1974 survey of a random sample of U.S. museum libraries (including
history, art, and science museums) listed in the 1973 *Official Museum
Directory* (population: 2,556; sample size: 856; responding: 374 or 43.7%)
showed that only 50% of the libraries had a librarian and only 47% of them
possessed a degree in library science. The largest number of librarians
were in libraries with 1,000-5,000 book titles, but full-time librarians were
not reported until library size began to reach 10,000 titles.   **(412)**

■ A preliminary analysis reported in 1976 of a survey of American
Association of Law Libraries members (survey size: "approximately
2,000" individuals; responding: "approximately 1,400" or 70%, of which
responses from 888 respondents were analyzed at the time of the report)
showed that education of respondents was as follows:

graduate degrees in library science	50%	respondents
degree in law	26%	respondents
both of the above	17%	respondents
working on 1 of the above	9%	respondents

Since an earlier survey of AALL members in 1970, the number of
members with law degrees had increased from 40% to 43%, the mem-

bers holding both degrees decreased from 23% to 17% and the members holding neither degree decreased from 25% to 16%. Further, AALL members who had completed a formal course in law librarianship or legal bibliography had increased to 54% compared to the 1970 survey.   (793)

Career Issues—Extended Degree Programs

General

■ A 1978 survey of a randomly selected sample of 32 public, 29 academic, 32 special, and 25 school library directors (responding: public, 19 or 59.4%; academic, 24 or 82.8%; special, 18 or 56.3%; and school, 12 or 48.0%) *showed that* 45.07% of the respondents indicated "agree" or "strongly agree" to the statement that an entry-level applicant with an extended library master's degree (1 and 1/2 to 2-year program rather than a 1-year program) would be given hiring preference over an applicant with a degree from a 1-year program.   (292)

Career Issues—Foreign Languages

Academic

■ A study reported in 1982 of academic job advertisements at 5-year intervals (1959, 1964, 1969, 1974, and 1979) over a 20-year period taken from 3 library journals (*Library Journal, ALA Bulletin/American Libraries*, and *College and Research Libraries/College and Research Libraries News*), excluding jobs that were primarily administrative or technical in nature for a total of 1,254 jobs, *showed that* generally the number of qualifications for professional jobs had increased during the 20-year period. Specifically, the number of jobs requiring:

a foreign language increased from 38 (20.5%) of the jobs in 1959 to 88 (35.2%) of the jobs in 1979;

computer expertise increased from 0 in 1959 to 103 (41.2%) of the jobs in 1979;

subject background increased from 20 (10.8%) of the jobs in 1959 to 81 (32.4%) of the jobs in 1979;

AV knowledge increased from 1 (.5%) of the jobs in 1959 to 18 (7.2%) of the jobs in 1979;

teaching experience increased from 2 (1.1%) of the jobs in
1959 to 11 (4.4%) of the jobs in 1979;

specific library expertise increased from 10 (5.4%) of the jobs
in 1959 to 52 (20.8%) of the jobs in 1979;

communicative ability increased from 2 (1.1%) of the jobs in
1959 to 34 (13.6%) of the jobs in 1979;

administrative ability increased from 1 (.5%) job in 1959 to 28
(11.2%) of the jobs in 1979.   **(515)**

■ A 1979 survey of members of the ACRL Discussion Group of
Personnel Officers (sample size: 45; responding: 30) concerning entry-level
requirements for professionals *showed that* 4 respondents reported that a
foreign language was required for entry-level positions in their libraries, 16
reported that it was "very important" or "helpful," while only 1 respondents reported it was unimportant. The languages most often required
were Romance languages (26 respondents) or German (22 respondents).
                                                                (240)

Ibid. . . . *showed that* 20 respondents reported cataloging as requiring a
foreign language, 11 reported "some reference positions" requiring foreign languages, and 7 reported subject specialist positions requiring a
foreign language.   **(240)**

Career Issues—Job Satisfaction

General

■ A survey reported in 1978 of traceable North American librarians who
had earned library doctorates in American Library Association accredited
programs between 1930 and 1975 (survey size: 568; responding: 403 or
71%) *showed that* respondents were generally happy with the type of work
they were doing. Specifically:

of library administrators 76.1% reported that they preferred
administration to other types of work, while only 10.9%
reported that they preferred education;

of individuals in library operations, 53.3% preferred this type
of work, while 26.7% reported they would prefer library
administration;

of library educators 86.7% preferred this type of work, while
only 7.1% reported they would prefer library administration;

of library researchers 67.6% preferred this type of work [no information is given on those preferring alternative types of work]. **(463)**

Academic

■ A survey reported in 1975 to determine levels of job satisfaction, using a Maslow needs hierarchy, of 202 men and women library professionals from 23 college and university libraries in the greater New York metropolitan area *showed that* in terms of needs fulfillment (degree to which job met needs) men and women showed similar levels of fulfillment in lower-order needs, i.e., social and security needs, but that women expressed statistically significant lower levels of fulfillment than men in meeting esteem and autonomy needs. **(103)**

Ibid. . . . *showed that* in terms of needs deficiency (size of gap between actual and desired degree to which job fills needs) women had statistically significantly higher deficiencies than men in security, autonomy, esteem, and self-actualization. There was no statistically significant difference between men and women in the area of social needs. **(103)**

Ibid. . . . showed in terms of importance of needs (degree to which respondents considered the need important) both men and women ranked autonomy and self-actualization needs as most important. The judged importance of security, social, and esteem needs was similar for both men and women, while women considered autonomy and self-actualization as having less importance than men. **(103)**

Career Issues—Joint Degree Programs

Academic

■ A survey reported in 1983 of directors of Association for Research Libraries concerning their attitudes toward joint degree programs (resulting in both a library degree and a degree in some other field) (population surveyed: 111 directors; responding: 93 or 84%) *showed that* only 9 (9.7%) respondents opposed joint degree programs, while 38 (40.9%) felt that "most academic disciplines" were suitable for joint programs. The 2 disciplines most frequently mentioned as desirable for joint programs were computer science (47 or 50.3% respondents) and management or business (47 or 50.3% respondents). **(803)**

Ibid. . . . *showed that* in considering applicants for jobs, directors reported they would consider the joint degree as follows:

asset	70 (75.3%)	respondents
irrelevant	12 (12.9%)	respondents
liability	2 (2.2%)	respondents
no response	9 (9.7%)	respondents **(803)**

Ibid. . . . *showed that* 54 (58.1%) respondents felt that joint graduate degrees were equal to the same degrees earned independently, 27 (29.0%) felt they were not equal, and 12 (12.9%) did not respond.   **(803)**

Ibid. . . . *showed that* directors' responses to hiring job applicants with joint graduate degrees compared to hiring applicants with just the M.L.S. degree were as follows:

6 (6.5%) respondents reported that there would be no preference between the candidates;

65 (69.9%) reported they would be more likely to hire the candidate with the joint degrees, while 2 (2.2%) reported they would be more likely to hire the candidate with the M.L.S. only;

47 (50.5%) reported they would pay more to a candidate with the joint degrees, while 20 (21.5%) reported they would not pay more;

43 (46.2%) reported they felt 2 graduate degrees were desirable for nearly all professional positions, 3 (3.2%) reported that they felt 2 graduate degrees were undesirable for most positions, 54 (58.1%) reported they felt 2 graduate degrees were desirable for specialist positions, and 30 (32.3%) reported they felt 2 graduate degrees were desirable for administrative positions.   **(803)**

Career Issues—Library School Grades

General

■ A survey reported in 1977 of the larger employers of librarians in the state of Indiana, including academic, public, special, and school libraries (31 institutions or systems queried; 30 responding), *showed that* the top-ranked criteria for hiring (ranked #1 by 20 respondents) was how the candidate handled the personal interview. Further, 18 ranked work experience second or third, and 20 ranked recommendations from former employers second or third. 27 ranked library school grades as fourth, fifth, or sixth in importance.   **(285)**

Career Issues—Library Work Experience

General

■ A study reported in 1982 of academic job advertisements at 5-year intervals (1959, 1964, 1969, 1974, and 1979) over a 20-year period taken from 3 library journals (*Library Journal, ALA Bulletin/American Librar-ies,* and *College and Research Libraries/College and Research Libraries News*), excluding jobs that were primarily administrative or technical in nature for a total of 1,254 jobs, *showed that* in 1959, 70 (37.8%) of the jobs advertised required library experience, of which 20 (10.8%) required specialized experience, while by 1979, 171 (68.4%) of the jobs required library experience, of which 138 (55.2%) required specialized experience.
(515)

Ibid. . . . *showed that* generally prior experience was associated with higher salaries, while subject master's degrees were associated with higher salaries only recently. Specifically, advertised salaries of positions requir-ing experience were statistically significantly higher than salaries of posi-tions not requiring experience in 4 of the 5 years studied (significance level at .001 or better), while advertised salaries of positions requiring subject master's degrees were statistically significantly higher only in the 1974 and 1979 periods studied (significance level at .05 or better).   **(515)**

Academic

■ A study of academic job advertisements at 5-year intervals (1959, 1964, 1969, 1974, and 1979) over a 20-year period taken from 3 library journals (*Library Journal, ALA Bulletin/American Libraries* and *College and Research Libraries/College and Research Libraries News*), excluding jobs that were primarily administrative or technical in nature for a total of 1,254 jobs, *showed that* in 1959, 70 (37.8%) of the jobs advertised required library experience, of which 20 (10.8%) required specialized experience, while by 1979, 171 (68.4%) of the jobs required library experience, of which 138 (55.2%) required specialized experience.   **(515)**

■ A 1979 survey of members of the ACRL Discussion Group of Personnel Officers (sample size: 45; responding: 30) concerning entry-level requirements for professionals *showed that* 24 out of 27 agreed that previous nonprofessional experience was an important requirement for an entry-level position. The "majority" also indicated that the experience should be in an academic library.   **(240)**

School

■ A 1983 survey of a systematic sample of school library media centers concerning data for fiscal year 1982-83 (survey size: 2,000 centers; responding: 1,297; usable: 1,251 or 62%) *showed that* a comparison of schools with (666 schools) and without (597 schools) district-level library media coordinators revealed that schools without district coordinators spent more money per student on resources and had more books per student than schools with district coordinators. However, schools with district coordinators paid media specialists higher salaries, had more AV items per student, had more clerical assistance, and used more adult volunteers than schools without district coordinators. Specifically:

total materials expenditure per student in schools with coordinators averaged $8.80 and in schools without coordinators averaged $10.92;

average books per student in schools with coordinators averaged 18 and in schools without coordinators averaged 20;

number of AV items per student in schools with coordinators averaged 3.45 and in schools without coordinators averaged 3.03;

media specialist salary in schools with coordinators averaged $20,699 and in schools without coordinators averaged $19,354;

the number of clerical assistants and adult volunteers in schools with coordinators averaged .83 and 2.46, respectively, and in schools without coordinators averaged .77 and 1.85, respectively.   **(798)**

Special

■ A preliminary analysis reported in 1976 of a survey of American Association of Law Libraries members (survey size: "approximately 2,000" individuals; responding: "approximately 1,400" or 70%, of which responses from 888 respondents were analyzed at the time of the report) *showed that* the experience of the respondents (as law librarians) was as follows:

3 years or less	36% respondents
4-7 years experience	26% respondents
8-10 years experience	13% respondents
over 10 years experience	26% respondents

This is a younger group than indicated by an earlier survey of AALL members in 1970, which *showed that* 46% respondents had over 10 years of experience while 22% had 3 years or less of law library experience. **(793)**

Career Issues—Mobility

Academic

■ A 1975 survey of 530 academic librarians (87% responding) in 9 southern states out of a total academic librarian population of 1,964, investigating the relationship between job mobility and career advancement, *showed that*, of the respondents who had changed jobs, 91% had subsequently received a salary increase. The size of the increase, however, was related to the reasons for the move. Of those librarians who had moved for career reasons, 24% made salary gains of $8,000 or more; of those who moved for noncareer reasons, only 16% received salary increases of $8,000 or more. **(165)**

Career Issues—Salaries

General

■ A 1980 survey of randomly selected American Library Association personal members (sample size: 3,000 members; responding: 1,987 or 67.1%, including 1,583 full-time members employed at the time of the survey, which provided the subsample analyzed here) *showed that* the average annual librarian's salary by type of library was as follows:

academic librarian	$16,710 average salary
public librarian	$15,300 average salary
special librarian	$15,120 average salary
school librarian	$14,700 average salary

These salary rankings have remained fairly constant since at least 1970, when the ALA salary survey showed the following average annual librarian's salary by type of library:

academic librarian	$12,523 average salary	
special librarian	$12,084 average salary	
public librarian	$11,135 average salary	
school librarian	$10,623 average salary	**(668)**

■ A study reported in 1982 of academic job advertisements at 5-year intervals (1959, 1964, 1969, 1974, and 1979) over a 20-year period taken from 3 library journals (*Library Journal, ALA Bulletin/American Librar-*

ies, and *College and Research Libraries/College and Research Libraries News*), excluding jobs that were primarily administrative or technical in nature for a total of 1,254 jobs, *showed that*, although advertised salaries in real dollars rose sharply between 1959 and 1969, they dropped sharply between 1969 and 1979, so that although a small absolute increase remained, there was no statistically significant difference between the salaries advertised in 1959 and 1979 when adjusted in terms of real dollars. The average salary in 1959 was $5,614, in 1969 was (after adjustment) $7,592, and in 1979 (after adjustment) was $5,926.   **(515)**

Ibid. . . . *showed that* generally prior experience was associated with higher salaries, while subject master's degrees were associated with higher salaries only recently. Specifically, advertised salaries of positions requiring experience were statistically significantly higher than salaries of positions not requiring experience in 4 of the 5 years studied (significance level at .001 or better), while advertised salaries of positions requiring subject master's degrees were statistically significantly higher only in the 1974 and 1979 periods studied (significance level at .05 or better).   **(515)**

Academic

■ A 1966 survey of Catholic college and university libraries in institutions with at least 1,000 full-time students (sample size: 70; responding: 56 or 80%) *showed that* 12 respondents (22%) reported that librarian salaries are less than that of the teaching faculty, 32 (60%) reported that salaries of librarians and teaching faculty were approximately the same, 8 (15%) reported the salaries were the same, and 1 (1.8%) reported that librarian salaries were possibly higher.   **(187)**

■ A 1967 survey of 4-year state colleges and universities (sample size: 321; responding: 200 or 62.3%; usable: 183 or 57%) *showed that* faculty and librarians were most likely to be treated alike with regard to fringe benefits (89.6% institutions), tenure criteria (77.6% institutions), sabbatical leave (74.3% institutions), participation in faculty government (71.0% institutions), and use of academic titles (65.0% institutions). They were least likely to be treated alike in rate of pay (29.0% institutions), academic vacations (33.9% institutions), and promotion policies (49.7% institutions).   **(186)**

■ A 1968 survey of academic library salaries in a 7-state area (North and South Dakota, Minnesota, Iowa, Nebraska, Wyoming, and Montana) (sample size: 96; responding: 68 or 70.8%) *showed that* 34 (51.5%) of responding libraries reported that salaries for librarians were equal to those of faculty members with equivalent background and experience.

However, a comparison of salary information provided through the survey from some of these responding institutions with published AAUP salary information shows a number of cases where the equality of salaries for librarians and teaching faculty is in fact not supported. **(198)**

■ A survey of academic libraries reported in 1970 (sample size: 120; responding: 65) concerning fringe benefits in academic libraries *showed that* librarians had faculty rank in 73% of responding institutions; had salaries equal with faculty in 80% of responding institutions; had sabbaticals equal with faculty in 54% of cases; had yearly increments in 98% of cases; and raises on merit in 79% of cases. **(200)**

■ A 1970 survey of Canadian community college libraries concerning academic status, salaries, and fringe benefits (sample size: 108; responding: 49; usable: 43 or 39.8%) *showed that*, for librarians with equivalent background and experience with the teaching faculty, 57% of the libraries reported that librarian and teaching faculty salaries were equal, 23% of the institutions reported that librarians' salaries were greater, and 20% of the institutions reported that librarians's salaries were lower than that of the teaching faculty. **(537)**

■ A 1972 survey of law school libraries listed in the 1977 *AALS Directory of Law Teachers* (population: 167: responding: 158 or 95%) *showed that* 77 (49%) respondents reported that they felt that the law school's autonomy from or integration with the university library did affect salary levels for law librarians, particularly in so far as the other campus librarians were concerned. 60 (38%) felt that this was not the case, 5 (3%) did not know, and 16 (10%) did not answer the question. Of those that felt the autonomy/integration issue did make a difference, the "overwhelming majority" felt that the difference resulted in higher salaries. **(362)**

■ A 1974-75 study of university libraries including all Association of Research Libraries libraries (sample size: 92; responding: 72 or 78%) and all library schools with ALA-accredited programs (sample size: not given; responding: 44 or 80%) *showed that*, of 39 responding library school deans, 71% reported that the subject Ph.D.'s they had placed had not had library experience. Nevertheless, 60.7% of these 71% had received positions with advanced salaries according to the library school deans. 42.7% of the library directors reported they would hire a subject Ph.D. without library experience (but with an M.L.S.) at an advanced salary while 45.6% said they would not. The remainder indicated that it depended on the position, the individual, or both. However, when referring to specific salary levels, 64.7% of the library directors indicated they would hire a subject Ph.D. (with M.L.S.) at a higher level than they would an M.L.S. only. **(445)**

Ibid. . . . *showed that* 22.4% of the responding library directors would allow graduate study for the Ph.D. to be considered library experience, while 68.6% would not and 9% indicated that it depended upon the position. Further, 16.4% of the responding library directors would allow previous teaching experience to influence salary levels, while 76.1% indicated they would not, and 7.5% said it would depend upon the position.   **(445)**

■ A 1975 survey of 530 academic librarians (87% responding) in 9 southern states out of a total academic librarian population of 1,964, investigating the relationship between job mobility and career advancement, *showed that* of the respondents who had changed jobs, 91% had subsequently received a salary increase. The size of the increase, however, was related to the reasons for the move. Of those librarians who had moved for career reasons, 24% made salary gains of $8,000 or more; of those who moved for noncareer reasons, only 16% received salary increases of $8,000 or more.   **(165)**

Ibid. . . . *showed that* on the average women librarians who had left their last positions for career-related reasons increased their salaries by $1,861 less than men who had also moved for career reasons. Women who left their positions for noncareer reasons increased their salaries (average increase $3,586) by $2,742 less than men (average increase $6,328) who left their positions for noncareer reasons. These are both statistically significant differences.   **(165)**

■ A study reported in 1982 of academic job advertisements at 5-year intervals (1959, 1964, 1969, 1974, and 1979) over a 20-year period taken from 3 library journals (*Library Journal, ALA Bulletin/American Libraries*, and *College and Research Libraries/College and Research Libraries News*), excluding jobs that were primarily administrative or technical in nature for a total of 1,254 jobs, *showed that*, although advertised salaries in real dollars rose sharply between 1959 and 1969, they dropped sharply between 1969 and 1979, so that although a small absolute increase remained, there was no statistically significant difference between the salaries advertised in 1959 and 1979 when adjusted in terms of real dollars. The average salary in 1959 was $5,614, in 1969 was (after adjustment) $7,592, and in 1979 (after adjustment) was $5,926.   **(515)**

Ibid. . . . *showed that* generally prior experience was associated with higher salaries, while subject master's degrees were associated with higher salaries only recently. Specifically, advertised salaries of positions requiring experience were statistically significantly higher than salaries of positions not requiring experience in 4 of the 5 years studied (significance level at .001 or better), while advertised salaries of positions requiring subject master's degrees were statistically significantly higher only in the 1974 and 1979 periods studied (significance level at .05 or better). **(515)**

■ A 1980 survey of academic librarians in Alabama, Georgia, and Mississippi concerning faculty status (sample size: 416; responding: 271; usable: 267 or 64.2%) *showed that*, of 220 respondents who reported having faculty status, 64.1% reported that their salaries were "at least less by $1,000" than the salaries of other faculty members, 23.6% reported that their salaries were "comparable," 6.8% reported that their salaries were "at least more by $1,000" than the salaries of other faculty members, and 5.5% did not respond. **(502)**

■ The annual survey of law school libraries and librarians conducted in 1980 by the American Bar Association, American Association of Law Libraries, and Association of American Law Schools (population: not given; response: 168 libraries) *showed that* the median salary of full-time professional law school librarians in the U.S. (excluding head law school librarians) was overall $16,950, while by size of library it was as follows:

small (under 70,000 vols.)	$15,680
medium (70,000-99,999 vols.)	$15,550
medium-large (100,000-199,999 vols.)	$16,100
large (200,000+)	$18,350 **(382)**

Public

■ A survey reported in 1967 of midwestern librarians (37 men, 408 women, total 445) in small public libraries (i.e., serving populations of 10,000 to 35,000) *showed that* 54.3% of the librarians with professional degrees worked in communities with median incomes of less than $7,000, while 72.2% of the librarians with less training worked in such communities; 19.4% of the librarians with professional degrees worked in communities with median incomes $10,000+, while only 6.5% of the librarians with less training worked in such communities. A positive correlation (correlation coefficient = .20) between professional training and community income was determined (no significance level given). **(282)**

School

■ A 1983 survey of a systematic sample of school library media centers concerning data for fiscal year 1982-83 (survey size: 2,000 centers; responding: 1,297; usable: 1,251 or 62%) *showed that* the average years of experience and salary for library media specialists by type of library were as follows:

elementary school (587 schools): 10.04 years of experience with a salary of $19,596;

junior high/middle school (308 schools): 11.79 years of experience with a salary of $21,613;

senior high school (304 schools): 12.02 years of experience with a salary of $20,069;

other (49 schools): 9.84 years of experience with a salary of $15,954. **(056)**

Ibid. . . . *showed that* a comparison of privately supported (72) and publicly supported (1,179) school library media centers revealed that media specialists in private schools served fewer students, had more money to spend on resources, administered smaller collections, and earned more modest salaries. Specifically:

enrollment averaged 460 students for private schools and 669 for public schools;

total materials expenditure per student averaged $12.55 for private schools and $9.62 public schools;

the number of books per student averaged 27.08 for private schools and 18.44 for public schools;

the number of AV items per student averaged 3.2 for private schools and 3.26 for public schools;

in private schools the media specialist averaged 8.92 years of experience with a salary of $13,880, while in public schools the media specialist averaged 11.08 years of experience with a salary of $20,389. **(056)**

Special

■ A 1978 survey of law school libraries listed in the 1977 *AALS Directory of Law Teachers* (population: 167: responding: 158 or 95%) *showed that* 77 (49%) respondents reported that they felt that the law school's autonomy from or integration with the university library did affect salary levels for law librarians, particularly in so far as the other campus librarians were concerned. 60 (38%) felt that this was not the case, 5 (3%) did not know, and 16 (10%) did not answer the question. Of those that felt the autonomy/integration issue did make a difference, the "overwhelming majority" felt that the difference resulted in higher salaries. **(362)**

■ A 1974 survey of a random sample of U.S. museum libraries (including history, art, and science museums) listed in the 1973 *Official Museum Directory* (population: 2,556; sample size: 856; responding: 374 or 43.7%)

showed that 74% of the museum librarians reported receiving salaries with the salary ranging from $2,000 to $24,000 per year. Publicly funded salaries averaged $10,069, while privately funded salaries averaged $9,439. The median length of service in the library and museum field reported by museum librarians was 10 years. **(412)**

Ibid. . . . *showed that* annual salaries for librarians in art museum libraries averaged $10,969, in science museum libraries $10,995, in history museum libraries around $9,000, in general libraries just over $8,000, and in other types of museum libraries between $7-8,000. **(412)**

■ A survey of 1976 data on U.S. law libraries serving a local bar (survey size: not given; responding: 74 libraries) *showed that* the average salary for professional librarians (excluding head librarians) was $15,396, with a median of $15,156 and a range from $5,595 to $41,112. Further, the starting salaries for professional librarians averaged $9,757, with a median of $9,000 and a range from $5,564 to $14,292. **(648)**

■ A preliminary analysis reported in 1976 of a survey of American Association of Law Libraries members (survey size: "approximately 2,000" individuals; responding: "approximately 1,400" or 70%, of which responses from 888 respondents were analyzed at the time of the report) *showed that*, of the 45% who worked in law schools, 46% had faculty status and 36% had faculty rank. Of those with faculty rank:

23% were professors (including 68% males; 32% females);

33% were associate professors (including 65% males; 35% females);

and 26% were assistant professors (including 53% males; 47% females). **(793)**

■ A 1979 survey of libraries in accredited North American veterinary schools (population: 25 libraries; responding: 23 or 92%) *showed that*, of the 18 veterinary libraries housed separately, the salaries of the head librarian ranged from $14,125 to $21,853, with an average salary of $17,275 and a median salary of $17,300. Of all 23 respondents, the average salary of the head veterinary librarian was $18,192. **(740)**

■ A 1980 survey of the private law library and corporate law library membership of the American Association of Law Libraries, excluding part-time librarians (population: 585; responding: 382; usable: 360 or 61%) *showed that* the average salary for private law librarians (81% of 360 usable responses) was $19,563, while the average salary for corporate law librarians (17% of 360 usable responses) was $22,154. **(377)**

Ibid. . . . *showed that* of 316 responses average salaries were:

$17,955 for 19 private/governmental and $25,487 for 12 corporate respondents whose highest subject degree was an associate degree, no degree, or no college degree;

$18,986 for 183 private/governmental and $18,341 for 30 corporate respondents whose highest subject degree was at the bachelor's level;

$20,444 for 41 private/governmental and $28,416 for 6 corporate respondents whose highest subject degree was at the master's level;

$26,027 for 18 private/governmental and $28,087 for 7 corporate respondents whose highest subject degree was either a J.D. or LL.B. **(377)**

■ The annual survey of law school libraries and librarians conducted in 1980 by the American Bar Association, American Association of Law Libraries, and Association of American Law Schools (population: not given; response: 168 libraries) *showed that* the median salary of full-time professional law school librarians in the U.S. (excluding head law school librarians) was overall $16,950, while by size of library it was as follows:

small (under 70,000 vols.)	$15,680
medium (70,000-99,999 vols.)	$15,550
medium-large (100,000-199,999 vols.)	$16,100
large (200,000+)	$18,350 **(382)**

Ibid. . . . *showed that* the median dollar amount of fringe benefits received by full-time professional law school librarians in the U.S. (excluding head law school librarians) was overall $2,850,while by size of library it was as follows:

small (under 70,000 vols.)	$1,880
medium (70,000-99,999 vols.)	$2,447
medium-large (100,000-199,999 vols.)	$2,805
large (200,000+ vols.)	$3,263 **(382)**

■ A survey reported in 1980 of law librarians on the AALSL (American Association of Legal Services Librarians) *Newsletter* mailing list (population: 128; responding: 53 or 41.4%) *showed that*, of the 12 professional librarians reporting salaries, the average salary for 8 librarians with 0-5 years experience was $14,951; for 3 librarians with 6-10 years experience the average salary was $16,988 with a median of $14,981. 1 respondent reported 16-20 years of experience and a salary of $19,700. **(370)**

■ A 1980 survey of the private law library and corporate law library membership of the American Association of Law Libraries, excluding part-time librarians (population: 585; responding: 382; usable: 360 or 61%) *showed that*, of 342 respondents, the average salary of 59 respondents with American Association of Law Libraries certification was $23,503, while the average salary for 283 respondents without such certification was $19,660. **(377)**

■ An annual survey reported in 1981 of North American county law libraries (population: not given; respondents: not given) *showed that* the overall average salary of professional librarians (excluding head librarians) in county law libraries for FY 1980-81 was $19,428 with a range of $6,000 to $31,644. **(379)**

Ibid. . . . *showed that* the overall average starting salary for professional librarians in county law libraries for FTY 1980-81 was $13,494 with a range of $7,746 to $18,800. **(379)**

■ An annual survey reported in 1981 of state law libraries in North America (no population given; no response given) *showed that* the average salary for professional librarians in state law libraries (excluding head librarians) was $17,577 with a range of $6,000 to $31,122. **(380)**

Ibid. . . . *showed that* the average starting salary for professional librarians in state law libraries was $14,169 with a range of $5,000 to $22,056. **(380)**

■ An annual survey reported in 1981 of U.S. and Puerto Rican court law libraries (no population given; no response given) *showed that* the average salary for FY 1980-81 for professional librarians (excluding head librarians) in court law libraries was $38,546 and ranged from $10,860 to $42,302. **(381)**

Ibid. . . . *showed that* the average salary in FY 1980-81 for starting professional librarians in court law libraries was $17,351 and ranged from $13,300 to $23,808. **(381)**

■ A study reported in 1983 of 3 surveys made by the American Medical Association's Division of Library and Archival Services in 1969, 1973, and 1979 concerning the status of health sciences libraries in the U.S. (survey size for each survey ran between 12,000-14,000 health-related organizations with a response rate for each survey around 95%) *showed that* in 1979 "some 51%" of hospital library personnel were professional library staff, 39% were library technicians/library assistants, and 10% were other library staff. Further, 7% of the professional staff earned $7,000-9,999 per year, 49.5% of the professional staff earned $10,000-14,999 per year, and 43.4% of the professional staff earned $15,000-19,999 per year.   **(747)**

Career Issues—Second Master's Degree

General

■ A 1978 survey of a randomly selected sample of 32 public, 29 academic, 32 special, and 25 school library directors (responding: public, 19 or 59.4%; academic, 24 or 82.8%; special, 18 or 56.3%; and school, 12 or 48.0%) *showed that* 39.4% of the respondents indicated "agree" or "strongly agree" with the statement that an entry-level applicant with a second master's degree in the humanities or social sciences would be given hiring preference over an applicant without a second degree, while 52.3% of the respondents indicated "agree" or "strongly agree" if the applicant's second degree was in science or technology. The second degree in science or technology was especially important for special library directors, whose response rate for "agree" or "strongly agree" was 76.46%.   **(292)**

Ibid. . . . *showed that* 15.78% of the public, 39.99% of the special, 47.82% of the academic, and 83.32% of the school library directors indicated "agree" or "strongly agree" with the statement that beginning librarians with 2 master's degrees are paid more than beginning librarians with 1 master's degree while 11.1% of the public, 15.78% of the academic, 43.75% of the special, and 66.66% of the school library directors indicated "agree" or "strongly agree" with the statement that beginning librarians with an extended library master's degree (1 and 1/2 to 2 years) were paid more than librarians with a 1-year degree.   **(292)**

Ibid. . . . *showed that* 21.04% of the public, 38.88% of the special, 54.54% of the academic, and 81.81% of the school library directors indicated "agree" or "strongly agree" with the statement that after 6-8 years of experience librarians with 2 master's degrees would be paid more than librarians with 1 degree, while 36.24% of the respondents indicated "agree" or "strongly agree" with the statement that librarians with an extended library master's degree (1 and 1/2 to 2 years) would be earning more than librarians with a 1-year library master's degree. **(292)**

Ibid. . . . *showed that* 21.04% of the public, 28.57% of the academic, 44.44% of the special, and 66.66% of the school library directors indicated "agree" or "strongly agree" with the statement that in terms of advancement librarians with 2 master's degrees would be more likely to hold administrative positions than librarians with 1 master's degree, while 45.72% of the respondents indicated "agree" or "strongly agree" with the statement that in terms of advancement librarians with an extended master's degree (1 and 1/2 to 2 years) would be more likely to hold administrative positions than librarians with 1-year master's degrees.
(292)

■ A study reported in 1982 of academic job advertisements at 5-year intervals (1959, 1964, 1969, 1974, and 1979) over a 20-year period taken from 3 library journals (*Library Journal, ALA Bulletin/American Libraries*, and *College and Research Libraries/College and Research Libraries News*), excluding jobs that were primarily administrative or technical in nature for a total of 1,254 jobs, *showed that*, in 1959, 1 (.5%) job required a subject master's degree and no particular subject was specified, while by 1979, 69 (27.6%) of the jobs required a subject master's degree, of which 40 (16.0%) required a specific subject area. **(515)**

Ibid. . . . *showed that* generally prior experience was associated with higher salaries, while subject master's degrees were associated with higher salaries only recently. Specifically, advertised salaries of positions requiring experience were statistically significantly higher than salaries of positions not requiring experience in 4 of the 5 years studied (significance level at .001 or better), while advertised salaries of positions requiring subject master's degrees were statistically significantly higher only in the 1974 and 1979 periods studied (significance level at .05 or better). **(515)**

Academic

■ A 1968 survey of academic library salaries in a 7-state area (North and South Dakota, Minnesota, Iowa, Nebraska, Wyoming, and Montana) (sample size: 96; responding: 68 or 70.8%) *showed that* nearly 15% of librarians in responding institutions had at least 2 master's degrees. Such individuals are employed in 31 of the 66 responding libraries. However, only 16 institutions (24.2%) automatically paid extra for such additional academic preparation. **(198)**

■ A study reported in 1978 of 23 middle managers and 11 administrators in 5 Association of Research Libraries libraries as well as a review of ads for 82 middle managerial positions in academic libraries posted in 1975 *showed that* 43 (52.4%) of the ads listed an ALA-accredited library master's degree as a qualification, 37 (45.1%) listed library master's degree without specifying ALA-accredited, 30 (36.6%) listed second master's degree, 4 (4.9%) listed Ph.D., 1 (1.2%) listed an other professional degree, and 1 stated that a master's degree was not required.   **(423)**

Ibid. . . . *showed that*, of 23 middle managers, 21 (91.3%) had ALA-accredited master's degrees, none had unaccredited library master's degrees, 13 (56.5%) had second master's degrees, 1 (4.3%) had a Ph.D., and 2 (8.7%) had an other professional degree.   **(423)**

■ A 1979 survey of members of the ACRL Discussion Group of Personnel Officers (sample size: 45; responding: 30) concerning entry-level requirements for professionals *showed that* 1 respondent reported a second master's degree as required, 8 reported it necessary for specific positions, and 15 reported it as preferred.   **(240)**

■ A study reported in 1982 of academic job advertisements at 5-year intervals (1959, 1964, 1969, 1974, and 1979) over a 20-year period taken from 3 library journals (*Library Journal, ALA Bulletin/American Libraries*, and *College and Research Libraries/College and Research Libraries News*), excluding jobs that were primarily administrative or technical in nature for a total of 1,254 jobs, *showed that*, in 1959, 1 (.5%) job required a subject master's degree and no particular subject was specified, while by 1979 69 (27.6%) of the jobs required a subject master's degree, of which 40 (16.0%) required a specific subject area.   **(515)**

Ibid. . . . *showed that* generally prior experience was associated with higher salaries, while subject master's degrees were associated with higher salaries only recently. Specifically, advertised salaries of positions requiring experience were statistically significantly higher than salaries of positions not requiring experience in 4 of the 5 years studied (significance level at .001 or better), while advertised salaries of positions requiring subject master's degrees were statistically significantly higher only in the 1974 and 1979 periods studied (significance level at .05 or better).   **(515)**

■ A study reported in 1981 of job listings for college and university libraries reported in *Library Journal* and *College and Research Libraries News* during 1970-79 (5,269 job listings) *showed that* overall for the survey period for nondirector university positions 1.9% required a Ph.D., 27.0% required a second master's, while 71% required no additional educational certification. Overall for nondirector college positions, 2.8% required a Ph.D., 21.4% required a second master's while 75.8% required no additional educational certification. **(494)**

Career Issues—Specific Course Work

General

■ A 1978 survey of a randomly selected sample of 32 public, 29 academic, 32 special, and 25 school library directors (responding: public, 19 or 59.4%; academic, 24 or 82.8%; special, 18 or 56.3%; and school, 12 or 48.0%) *showed that* 73.14% of the respondents indicated "agree" or "strongly agree" with the statement that an entry-level applicant with 2 or 3 computer-related library science courses would be given hiring preference for a technical service position, while 46.03% agreed that an applicant would be given hiring preference for a public service position. **(292)**

Ibid. . . . *showed that* 22.54% of the respondents indicated "agree" or "strongly agree" with the statement that an entry-level applicant with a graduate or undergraduate statistics course would be given hiring preference. **(292)**

Ibid. . . . *showed that* 48.57% of the respondents indicated "agree" or "strongly agree" with the statement that an entry-level applicant with a library course in administration would be given hiring preference. **(292)**

Ibid. . . . *showed that* 52.86% of the respondents indicated "agree" or "strongly agree" with the statement that an entry-level applicant with a library audiovisual course would be given hiring preference. However, only 11.1% of the special library directors reported agreeing or strongly agreeing, while 91.66% of the school library directors so reported. **(292)**

Academic

■ A 1979 survey of members of the ACRL Discussion Group of Personnel Officers (sample size: 45; responding: 30) concerning entry-level requirements for professionals *showed that* 4 respondents reported that a foreign language was required for entry-level positions in their libraries, 16 reported that it was "very important" or "helpful," while only 1 respondent reported it was unimportant. The languages most often required were Romance languages (26 respondents) or German (22 respondents).

(240)

Ibid. . . . *showed that*, assuming the basic courses have been taken, 6 respondents mentioned courses involving business skills, 5 mentioned courses involving automation/computer networking, 4 mentioned courses involving online reference and/or cataloging, and 2 mentioned courses involving research skills as best preparation for beginning librarians in academic libraries.   **(240)**

Ibid. . . . *showed that* for long-term growth the skills respondents mentioned were in the following areas: management skills (10 respondents), computer background (6 respondents), advanced degrees (5 respondents), and depth of subject expertise (5 respondents).   **(240)**

Special

■ A survey reported in 1983 of 249 special library respondents in 28 major firms (126 of the respondents had a master's degree in library science or the equivalent) *showed that* those library courses that special librarians ranked most highly are not those that academic librarians (according to other reported research) ranked highly. A comparison of course rankings by special librarians and by ARL library directors in terms of importance for subsequent job performance indicated that the 5 courses that special librarians ranked most highly received only an average rank of 10.2 out of 19 by the ARL librarians. For special librarians these top 5 courses were (in descending order of importance):

1. online searching
2. specialized reference
3. programming
4. management/administration
5. general reference

The top 5 library school courses ranked by ARL directors were not given.

(443)

Ibid. . . . *showed that* the 3 library school courses out of 9 ranked by the most respondents as "important" or "very important" were:

online searching (43% respondents took the course in library school; 83% rated it as "important" or "very important");

specialized reference (93% respondents took the course in library school; 76% rated it as "important" or "very important");

general reference (97% respondents took the course in library school; 69% rated it as "important" or "very important"). **(443)**

Ibid. . . . *showed that* the 4 courses that the most respondents with library school degrees wished they had taken were (multiple responses allowed): programming (45 or 35.7% respondents), online searching (37 or 29.4% respondents), computer science (30 or 23.8% respondents), and management and business administration (22 or 17.5% respondents). **(443)**

Community Service

Academic

■ A survey reported in 1968 of all ARL directors plus all other state university library directors concerning the degree to which librarians participate in traditional faculty activities (72 responding) *showed that* for participation in nonprofessional local activities 39% of respondents reported that they neither gave time nor expenses. However, 59% of respondents gave time alone, while 39% did not. **(182)**

Faculty Status—General Issues

Academic

■ A 1964 survey of 60 private liberal arts colleges (49 responding) *showed that* 25 institutions gave faculty rank or status to all librarians, 12 gave faculty rank or status to the head librarian only, 9 gave it to specific staff members (usually department heads and higher), and 3 do not give it to any library staff. **(170)**

■ A 1966 survey of Catholic college and university libraries in institutions with at least 1,000 full-time students (sample size: 70; responding: 56 or 80%) *showed that*, of the library directors, 5 (9%) hold rank of dean or equivalent, 44 (78%) hold faculty rank, 2 (3%) hold faculty status, and 5 (9%) hold no rank. In 39 libraries (70%) librarians hold faculty rank, in 7 (12%) they hold faculty status, and in 9 (16%) they hold no rank. **(187)**

■ A 1967 survey of 4-year state colleges and universities (sample size: 321; responding: 200 or 62.3%; usable: 183 or 57%) *showed that* 26 (14.2%) of reporting libraries grant full faculty status to librarians. An additional 21 libraries were very close to full status (e.g., not allowed complete academic vacations or to participate fully in faculty government) and if added to the 26 original libraries bring the total to 25.7%. **(186)**

Ibid. . . . *showed that* faculty and librarians were most likely to be treated alike with regard to fringe benefits (89.6% institutions), tenure criteria (77.6% institutions), sabbatical leave (74.3% institutions), participation in faculty government (71.0% institutions), and use of academic titles (65.0% institutions). They were least likely to be treated alike in rate of pay (29.0% institutions), academic vacations (33.9% institutions), and promotion policies (49.7% institutions). **(186)**

■ A survey reported in 1968 of 71 ARL libraries plus a group of 29 institutions (mostly state universities) (87 responses; 70 usable responses, i.e., institutions where the librarians had faculty status), *showed that* 26 respondents reported that librarians had full faculty rank and title; 13 repondents reported patterns of equivalent rank corresponding to the customary academic titles of rank such as instructor to professor; 7 respondents reported a pattern of assimilated rank, i.e., library title "with the rank of" academic rank; and 24 respondents reported a miscellaneous set of patterns under the general rubric of academic status. **(184)**

■ A 1969 survey of the 71 ARL libraries (57 responding; 55 or 77.5% usable) concerning librarians as teachers *showed that*, of responding libraries, 45.5% had librarian title with librarian rank; 30.9% had librarian title with professorial rank; 9.0% reported that title and rank depended upon appointment; 5.5% reported librarians had professorial title with professorial rank; 1.8% reported that librarians had librarian title with no specified rank; and 7.3% did not respond to the question. **(196)**

Ibid. . . . *showed that*, of the library staff members who also have teaching assignments in academic departments, 56.4% hold joint appointments; 20.0% do not hold joint appointments; and 23.6% of the responding libraries reported that the issue was "not applicable." **(196)**

■ A 1970 survey of Canadian community college libraries concerning academic status, salaries, and fringe benefits (sample size: 108; responding: 49; usable: 43 or 39.8%) *showed that* 35% reported holding faculty status, 60% reported holding librarian's titles and professorial or administrator's rank, and 5% reported they were uncertain of their status. **(537)**

■ A survey of academic libraries reported in 1970 (sample size: 120; responding: 65) concerning fringe benefits in academic libraries *showed that* librarians had faculty rank in 73% of responding institutions; had salaries equal with faculty in 80% of responding institutions; had sabbaticals equal with faculty in 54% of cases; had yearly increments in 98% of cases; and raises on merit in 79% of cases. **(200)**

■ A survey in 1972 of a stratified random sample of full-time professional librarians in private and public junior colleges, colleges, and universities in the 10 counties of southern California (sample size: 216; responding: 174 [81%]) was analyzed by stepwise regression and *showed that* the following relationship was statistically significant at the .05 level or better: Members of ALA/ACRL were more likely than nonmembers to agree that librarians should have the same rank and titles as faculty. **(092)**

■ A study reported in 1975 of the degree to which 2-year college libraries (sample size: 26; responding: 23) in the state of Ohio conformed to the "Guidelines for Two-Year College Learning Resources Programs" established by the ACRL Board of Directors in 1972 *showed that* in the majority of cases the professional staff had faculty rank, status, benefits, and responsibilities, although in very few cases was advanced study, research, or publication required. **(127)**

■ A preliminary analysis reported in 1976 of a survey of American Association of Law Libraries members (survey size: "approximately 2,000" individuals; responding: "approximately 1,400" or 70%, of which responses from 888 respondents were analyzed at the time of the report) *showed that*, of the 45% who worked in law schools, 46% had faculty status and 36% have faculty rank. Of those with faculty rank:

23% were professors (including 68% males; 32% females);

33% were associate professors (including 65% males; 35% females);

and 26% were assistant professors (including 53% males; 47% females). **(793)**

■ A 1978 survey of law school libraries listed in the 1977 *AALS Directory of Law Teachers* (population: 167; responding: 158 or 95%) *showed that* 67 (42%) respondents reported that professional law school librarians other than the head law school librarian held full faculty status/rank, while 91 (58%) reported that they did not. 59 (37%) respondents reported that professional law school librarians other than the head law school librarian either had or were working toward tenure, while 98 (62%) reported this was not the case, and 1 (0.6%) reported some either held or were working toward tenure. **(362)**

■ A 1979 survey of libraries in accredited North American veterinary schools (population: 25 libraries; responding: 23 or 92%) *showed that*, of 23 respondents, 15 (65.2%) reported faculty status. **(740)**

■ A survey reported in 1980 of Association of Research Libraries directors in academic libraries (population: 94; responding: 68 or 72%) concerning publication requirements for professional library staff *showed that* 28 (41%) respondents reported librarians held academic status, 24 (35%) reported librarians held faculty status, and 16 (24%) reported a status of "other." **(480)**

■ A survey reported in 1980 of nondirector, professional law librarians (1 in each school) in U.S. accredited law schools, with the names of individuals being selected randomly from the *Directory of Law Librarians* (1978 edition) (sample size: 145; responding: 103 or 71%) *showed that*, of 99 respondents:

35 (35.3%) reported that professional law librarians other than the director or head librarian had faculty status or rank in their institutions;

56 (56.5%) reported that professional law librarians other than the director or head librarian did not have faculty status or rank;

5 (5.1%) reported that some of the professional law librarians other than the director or head librarian had faculty status or rank;

and 3 (3.0%) reported that the professional law librarians other than the director or head librarian had faculty status but not faculty rank. **(371)**

Ibid. . . . *showed that* the "overwhelming number of law librarians" who reported having faculty status or rank were employed in public rather than private law schools. **(371)**

Ibid. . . . *showed that*, of 78 respondents, the source that granted faculty status and/or tenure was:

law school faculty	28 (35.9%) respondents
general university faculty	19 (24.4%) respondents

continued

university library	7 (9.0%) respondents
law library faculty	3 (3.8%) respondents
other	21 (26.9%) respondents **(371)**

■ A 1980 survey of academic librarians in Alabama, Georgia, and Mississippi concerning faculty status (sample size: 416; responding: 271; usable: 267 or 64.2%) *showed that* 82.4% of the respondents reported having faculty status at their institution. However, of the 47 respondents who did not have faculty status, 29.8% reported that their institution offered the possibility of tenure for librarians. **(502)**

Ibid. . . . *showed that* 49.4% of the respondents agreed with the statement "faculty status/rank with its requirement for research and publication for promotion places unrealistic demands on librarians for their advancement." 24.0% disagreed, 21.0% were undecided, and 5.6% gave no response. **(502)**

■ A survey reported in 1981 of library directors in 4-year colleges and universities in 7 Rocky Mountain states (survey size: 76; responding: 64 or 84%) concerning faculty status of librarians *showed that* faculty status for all librarians was most likely to be granted in a university library, while faculty status for library directors only was most likely to be granted in a private rather than public institution. Specifically, 22 (92%) of the university libraries, 11 (50%) of the liberal arts colleges, and 6 (43%) of the professional schools granted faculty status to all librarians. These differences were statistically significant at the .005 level. Further, 6 (15%) of the publicly supported schools gave faculty status to directors only, while 9 (40.9%) of the private schools gave faculty status to directors only. This difference was statistically significant at the .05 level. **(492)**

Ibid. . . . *showed that* 30 (75%) respondents reported that librarians' rank was identical with teaching faculty, 32 (80%) reported that tenure for librarians was identical with teaching faculty, and 33 (83%) reported that promotion eligibility was the same for librarians as for teaching faculty. **(492)**

Ibid. . . . *showed that* 62 (96%) respondents reported that at least some of the librarians had faculty status. Specifically, of the 62 respondents, 15 (24.2%) reported that only the director had faculty status, 40 (64.5%) reported that all the librarians had faculty status, while 7 (11.3%) reported some combination in between. **(492)**

■ A study reported in 1981 at Southern Illinois University, Carbondale, investigating teaching faculty perception of librarians (survey size: 507; responding: 386; usable: 384 or 75.7%) *showed that* 201 (57%) of the teaching faculty felt that librarians should have faculty rank and status, whereas 148 (43%) felt librarians should not. Of these 148 (multiple responses allowed), 58% gave as their reason for denying librarians faculty rank and status "insufficient teaching," 40% gave "insufficient research and publication," 13% gave "insufficient service," and 27% gave "insufficient education." 37% gave a variety of other reasons.   **(493)**

■ A survey reported in 1981 of Association of Research Libraries directors concerning the acceptability of nonlibrary/information science publications in the promotion and tenure of academic librarians (population: 108; responding: 82 or 75.9%) *showed that* 46 (56.1%) respondents reported their librarians had faculty status, 35 (42.7%) reported their librarians did not have faculty status, and 1 (1.2%) did not reply.   **(503)**

■ A study reported in 1982 of academic job advertisements at 5-year intervals (1959, 1964, 1969, 1974, and 1979) over a 20-year period taken from 3 library journals (*Library Journal, ALA Bulletin/American Libraries*, and *College and Research Libraries/College and Research Libraries News*), excluding jobs that were primarily administrative or technical in nature for a total of 1,254 jobs, *showed that* the percentage of advertised positions offering faculty status, while fluctuating, did not substantially change over the 20-year period. Specifically, in 1959, 85 (45.9%) of the positions indicated faculty status, while in 1979, 112 (44.8%) of the positions indicated faculty status.   **(515)**

■ A survey reported in 1983 of head librarians of accredited institutions of higher education in New York state including 2-year colleges, 4-year colleges, universities, and graduate/professional schools (survey size: 264; responding: 188 or 71%) concerning faculty status for librarians on their staff *showed that* the following applied:

none have faculty status	18.0% of total
very few have faculty status	8.0% of total
about half have faculty status	.5% of total
most have faculty status	7.0% of total
all have faculty status	65.0% of total **(516)**

Ibid. . . . *showed that*, as the academic level of the institutions rises, the percentage of librarians with faculty status falls. Specifically, 79% of the 2-year colleges, 64% of the 4-year colleges, 54% of the universities, and 50% of the graduate/professional schools have faculty status for their librarians.   **(516)**

Ibid. . . . *showed that* faculty status for all librarians was reported in 88% of 76 publicly supported institutions, in 64% of 47 private, church-related institutions, and in 40% of 65 private, independent institutions.   **(516)**

Ibid. . . . *showed that* librarians were more likely to have the responsibilities of faculty than the rights of faculty. For example, of the 137 libraries that reported that their librarians had faculty status, only 22% of the respondents had academic-year appointments, while 66% reported the importance of a second graduate degree, and 56% the importance of publishing activity in achieving tenure and promotion.   **(516)**

Ibid. . . . *showed that*, of the total respondents, librarians had the following academic rights (multiple responses allowed):

eligible to serve on the campus governing board	76% of total
eligible for release time for professional activities	68% of total
eligible for sabbatical and other professional leaves	64% of total
eligible for tenure	58% of total
eligible for research funds	55% of total
given professorial titles	30% of total
given release time for research	20% of total
academic-year appointment	16% of total **(516)**

■ A survey reported in 1983 of the U.S. academic members of the Association of Research Libraries concerning faculty status for professionals (population: 89 libraries; responding: 89 or 100%, including 57 state and 32 private institutions) *showed that* 35 (61.4%) of the libraries in state institutions and 6 (18.7%) of the libraries in private institutions granted librarians faculty status.   **(788)**

Ibid. . . . *showed that* the types of rank assigned the majority of librarians were as follows:

faculty rank was assigned by 20 (35.1%) of the state and 1 (3.1%) of the private institutions;

equivalent rank was assigned by 21 (36.8%) of the state and 7 (21.9%) of the private institutions;

numerical rank was assigned by 13 (22.8%) of the state and 20 (62.5%) of the private institutions;

"other" was used in 3 (5.3%) of the state and 4 (12.5%) of the private institutions.   **(788)**

Ibid. . . . *showed that* the benefits and privileges given librarians in state institutions versus private institutions were as follows:

faculty rank	20 (35.1%) state;	1 (3.1%) private
indefinite tenure	34 (59.6%) state;	4 (12.5%) private
research funds	51 (89.5%) state;	13 (40.6%) private
travel funds	all libraries	
research leave	47 (82.5%) state;	25 (78.1%) private
sabbatical leave	35 (61.4%) state;	10 (31.3%) private
tuition break	41 (71.9%) state;	28 (87.5%) private
option of 9-month appointment	15 (26.3%) state;	7 (21.9%) private

(788)

Ibid. . . . *showed that*, while no respondents reported the possibility of moving librarians from nonfaculty status to faculty status, 4 (7.0%) of the state institutions reported the possibility of shifting librarians from faculty to nonfaculty status. Most of the libraries (53 or 93.0% of the state institutions and 32 or all of the private institutions), however, reported no plans for change in either direction.   **(788)**

Special

■ A preliminary analysis reported in 1976 of a survey of American Association of Law Libraries members (survey size: "approximately 2,000" individuals; responding: "approximately 1,400" or 70%, of which responses from 888 respondents were analyzed at the time of the report) *showed that*, of the 45% who work in law schools, 46% have faculty status and 36% have faculty rank. Of those with faculty rank:

23% were professors (including 68% males; 32% females);

33% were associate professors (including 65% males; 35% females);

and 26% were assistant professors (including 53% males; 47% females).   **(793)**

■ A 1978 survey of law school libraries listed in the 1977 *AALS Directory of Law Teachers* (population: 167; responding: 158 or 95%) *showed that* 67 (42%) respondents reported that professional law school librarians other than the head law school librarian held full faculty status/rank, while 91 (58%) reported that they did not. 59 (37%) respondents reported that professional law school librarians other than the head law school librarian either had or were working toward tenure, while 98 (62%) reported this was not the case, and 1 (0.6%) reported some either held or were working toward tenure.   **(362)**

■ A 1979 survey of libraries in accredited North American veterinary schools (population: 25 libraries; responding: 23 or 92%) *showed that*, of 23 respondents, 15 (65.2%) reported faculty status. **(740)**

■ A survey reported in 1980 of nondirector, professional law librarians (1 in each school) in U.S. accredited law schools, with the names of individuals being selected randomly from the *Directory of Law Librarians* (1978 edition) (sample size: 145; responding: 103 or 71%), *showed that*, of 99 respondents:

> 35 (35.3%) reported that professional law librarians other than the director or head librarian had faculty status or rank in their institutions;
>
> 56 (56.5%) reported that professional law librarians other than the director or head librarian did not have faculty status or rank;
>
> 5 (5.1%) reported that some of the professional law librarians other than the director or head librarian had faculty status or rank;
>
> and 3 (3.0%) reported that the professional law librarians other than the director or head librarian had faculty status but not faculty rank. **(371)**

Ibid. . . . *showed that* the "overwhelming number of law librarians" who reported having faculty status or rank were employed in public rather than private law schools. **(371)**

Ibid. . . . *showed that*, of 78 respondents, the source that granted faculty status and/or tenure was:

law school faculty	28 (35.9%)	respondents
general university faculty	19 (24.4%)	respondents
university library	7 (9.0%)	respondents
law library faculty	3 (3.8%)	respondents
other	21 (26.9%)	respondents **(371)**

Faculty Status—Directors

Academic

■ A 1964 survey of 60 private liberal arts colleges (49 responding) *showed that* 25 institutions gave faculty rank or status to all librarians, 12 gave faculty rank or status to the head librarian only, 9 gave it to specific

staff members (usually department heads and higher), and 3 do not give it
to any library staff. **(170)**

Ibid. . . . *showed that* 13 institutions gave sabbatical leave to all librarians; 8 gave it to the head librarian only; 2 gave it to the head librarian, assistant librarian, and department head; and 26 have no definite
policy or did not answer the question. Where sabbaticals are granted, the most
usual pattern was full pay for 1 semester or half pay for 2 semesters.

(170)

■ A 1966 survey of Catholic college and university libraries in institutions
with at least 1,000 full-time students (sample size: 70; responding: 56 or
80%) *showed that*, of the library directors, 5 (9%) hold rank of dean or
equivalent, 44 (78%) hold faculty rank, 2 (3%) hold faculty status, and
5 (9%) hold no rank. In 39 libraries (70%) librarians hold faculty rank,
in 7 (12%) they hold faculty status, and in 9 (16%) they hold no rank.

(187)

■ A 1976 survey of head law librarians in North American schools
(sample size: 178; responding: 154 or 86.7%) *showed that* 62 (41%) of the
law school library directors held full professor status, 38 (26%) held
associate professor status, 30 (20%) held assistant professor status, 3 (2%)
held instructor status, 17 (11%) held no faculty status, and 4 did not reply.

(357)

■ A 1978 survey of law school libraries listed in the 1977 *AALS Directory
of Law Teachers* (population: 167; responding: 158 or 95%) *showed that*
150 head law school librarians reported they held full faculty rank or status
while 8 reported they did not, and that 130 heads reported that they had or
were working toward tenure while 25 reported that this was not the case
and 3 did not reply. **(362)**

Ibid. . . . *showed that*, for head law school librarians, their faculty status/
rank and/or tenure was or would be held in the following bodies:

law school	130 respondents
law library faculty (3 joint with law school)	8 respondents
both law school and university library	8 respondents
university library	4 respondents
university general faculty	1 respondent
none	3 respondents
no reply	4 respondents **(362)**

Ibid. . . . *showed that* 151 respondents reported that the head law school librarian attended faculty meetings in the law school, while 32 attended faculty meetings in the library system; 141 voted in law school faculty meetings, while 28 voted in library faculty meetings; and 143 were voting members of faculty committees in the law school, while 29 were voting members of faculty committees in the library. **(362)**

Ibid. . . . *showed that* 82 (52%) respondents felt it desirable that head law school librarians carry teaching responsibilities, 15 (10%) felt that head law school librarians should teach but only legal bibliography, 21 (13%) reported mixed feelings, and 40 (25%) felt that head law school librarians should not teach. **(362)**

■ A survey reported in 1981 of library directors in 4-year colleges and universities in 7 Rocky Mountain states (survey size: 76; responding: 64 or 84%) concerning faculty status of librarians *showed that* 62 (96%) respondents reported that at least some of the librarians had faculty status. Specifically, of the 62 respondents, 15 (24.2%) reported that only the director had faculty status, 40 (64.5%) reported that all the librarians had faculty status, while 7 (11.3%) reported some combination in between. **(492)**

Ibid. . . . *showed that* faculty status for all librarians was most likely to be granted in a university library, while faculty status for library directors only was most likely to be granted in a private rather than public institution. Specifically, 22 (92%) of the university libraries, 11 (50%) of the liberal arts colleges, and 6 (43%) of the professional schools granted faculty status to all librarians. These differences were statistically significant at the .005 level. Further, 6 (15%) of the publicly supported schools gave faculty status to directors only, while 9 (40.9%) of the private schools gave faculty status to directors only. This difference was statistically significant at the .05 level. **(492)**

Special

■ A 1976 survey of head law librarians in North American schools (sample size: 178; responding: 154 or 86.7%) *showed that* 62 (41%) of the law school library directors held full professor status, 38 (26%) held associate professor status, 30 (20%) held assistant professor status, 3 (2%) held instructor status, 17 (11%) held no faculty status, and 4 did not reply. **(357)**

■   A 1978 survey of law school libraries listed in the 1977 *AALS Directory of Law Teachers* (population: 167; responding: 158 or 95%) *showed that* 150 head law school librarians reported they held full faculty rank or status while 8 reported they did not, and that 130 heads reported that they had or were working toward tenure while 25 reported that this was not the case and 3 did not reply.   **(362)**

Ibid. . . . *showed that*, for head law school librarians, their faculty status/ rank and/or tenure was or would be held in the following bodies:

law school	130 respondents
law library faculty (3 joint with law school)	8 respondents
both law school and university library	8 respondents
university library	4 respondents
university general faculty	1 respondent
none	3 respondents
no reply	4 respondents **(362)**

Ibid. . . . *showed that* 151 respondents reported that the head law school librarian attended faculty meetings in the law school, while 32 attended faculty meetings in the library system; 141 voted in law school faculty meetings, while 28 voted in library faculty meetings; and 143 were voting members of faculty committees in the law school, while 29 were voting members of faculty committees in the library.   **(362)**

Ibid. . . . *showed that* 82 (52%) respondents felt it desirable that head law school librarians carry teaching responsibilities, 15 (10%) felt that head law school librarians should teach but only legal bibliography, 21 (13%) reported mixed feelings, and 40 (25%) felt that head law school librarians should not teach.   **(362)**

Faculty Status—Sabbaticals

Academic

■   A 1964 survey of 60 private liberal arts colleges (49 responding) *showed that* 13 institutions gave sabbatical leave to all librarians; 8 gave it to the head librarian only; 2 gave it to the head librarian, assistant librarian, and department head; and 26 have no definite policy or did not answer the question. Where sabbaticals are granted, the most usual pattern is full pay for 1 semester or half pay for 2 semesters.   **(170)**

■ A 1967 survey of 4-year state colleges and universities (sample size: 321; responding: 200 or 62.3%; usable: 183 or 57%) *showed that* faculty and librarians were most likely to be treated alike with regard to fringe benefits (89.6% institutions), tenure criteria (77.6% institutions), sabbatical leave (74.3% institutions), participation in faculty government (71.0% institutions), and use of academic titles (65.0% institutions). They were least likely to be treated alike in rate of pay (29.0% institutions), academic vacations (33.9% institutions), and promotion policies (49.7% institutions). **(186)**

■ A 1970 survey of Canadian community college libraries concerning academic status, salaries, and fringe benefits (sample size: 108; responding: 49; usable: 43 or 39.8%) *showed that* 23% of the libraries offer sabbatical leave for librarians, 40% do not, and 37% either do not offer sabbatical leave or do not know if sabbatical leave is offered to librarians. **(537)**

■ A survey of academic libraries reported in 1970 (sample size: 120; responding: 65) concerning fringe benefits in academic libraries *showed that* librarians had faculty rank in 73% of responding institutions; had salaries equal with faculty in 80% of responding institutions; had sabbaticals equal with faculty in 54% of cases; had yearly increments in 98% of cases; and raises on merit in 79% of cases. **(200)**

■ A survey reported in 1981 of library directors in 4-year colleges and universities in 7 Rocky Mountain states (survey size: 76; responding: 64 or 84%) concerning faculty status of librarians *showed that*, although sabbatical leaves were reported possible for librarians in 33 (83%) institutions, research leaves were only available in 32 (80%) institutions and research funds were only available in 28 (70%) institutions. **(492)**

■ A survey reported in 1983 of head librarians of accredited institutions of higher education in New York state, including 2-year colleges, 4-year colleges, universities, and graduate/professional schools (survey size: 264; responding: 188 or 71%) concerning faculty status for librarians *showed that*, of the total respondents, librarians had the following academic rights (multiple responses allowed):

eligible to serve on the campus governing board	76% of total
eligible for release time for professional activities	68% of total
eligible for sabbatical and other professional leaves	64% of total
eligible for tenure	58% of total

continued

eligible for research funds   55% of total
given professorial titles   30% of total
given release time for research   20% of total
academic-year appointment   16% of total   (516)

■ A survey reported in 1983 of the U.S. academic members of the
Association of Research Libraries concerning faculty status for professionals (population: 89 libraries; responding: 89 or 100%, including 57 state
and 32 private institutions) *showed that* the benefits and privileges given
librarians in state institutions versus private institutions were as follows:

faculty rank   20 (35.1%) state; 1 (3.1%) private
indefinite tenure   34 (59.6%) state; 4 (12.5%) private
research funds   51 (89.5%) state; 13 (40.6%) private
travel funds   all libraries
research leave   47 (82.5%) state; 25 (78.1%) private
sabbatical leave   35 (61.4%) state; 10 (31.3%) private
tuition break   41 (71.9%) state; 28 (87.5%) private
option of 9-month
  appointment   15 (26.3%) state; 7 (21.9%) private (788)

Faculty Status—Tenure and Promotion

Academic

■ A survey reported in 1968 of 71 ARL libraries plus a group of 29
institutions (mostly state universities) (87 responses; 70 usable responses,
i.e., institutions where the librarians had faculty status) *showed that* the 6
most important criteria for promotion and tenure according to all respondents were: success in teaching, research and publication, professional
competence and activity, service to the university, creative work (artistic,
dramatic, etc.) and public service.   (184)

■ A 1969 survey of the 71 ARL libraries (57 responding; 55 or 77.5%
usable) concerning librarians as teachers *showed that* in 47.3% of responding libraries the criteria for appointment, promotion, and tenure of
librarians were different from those of the teaching faculty; in 27.3% of the
libraries the criteria were the same; and in 14.5% of the libraries the
criteria were similar.   (196)

■ A 1978 survey of law school libraries listed in the 1977 *AALS Directory
of Law Teachers* (population: 167; responding: 158 or 95%) *showed that* 67
(42%) respondents reported that professional law school librarians other

than the head law school librarian held full faculty status/rank, while 91 (58%) reported that they did not. 59 (37%) respondents reported that professional law school librarians other than the head law school librarian either had or were working toward tenure, while 98 (62%) reported this was not the case, and 1 (0.6%) reported some either held or were working toward tenure. **(362)**

■ A survey reported in 1980 of nondirector, professional law librarians (1 in each school) in U.S. accredited law schools, with the names of individuals being selected randomly from the *Directory of Law Librarians* (1978 edition) (sample size: 145; responding: 103 or 71%) *showed that*, of 78 respondents, the source that granted faculty status and/or tenure was:

law school faculty	28 (35.9%) respondents
general university faculty	19 (24.4%) respondents
university library	7 (9.0%) respondents
law library faculty	3 (3.8%) respondents
other	21 (26.9%) respondents **(371)**

Ibid. . . . *showed that*, of 101 respondents:

32 (31.6%) reported that professional law librarians other than the director or head of libraries were granted or permitted to work toward tenure;

58 (57.4%) reported that professional law librarians other than the director or head of libraries were not granted or permitted to work toward tenure;

4 (4.0%) reported that some of the professional law librarians other than the director or head of libraries were granted or permitted to work toward tenure;

4 (4.0%) reported that professional law librarians other than the director or head of libraries were granted or permitted to work toward tenure under another name, e.g., "continuing appointment," "trustees appointment," "career appointment," or "permanent status";

3 (3.0%) gave miscellaneous other answers. **(371)**

■ A survey reported in 1980 of Association of Research Libraries directors in academic libraries (population: 94; responding: 68 or 72%) concerning publication requirements for professional library staff *showed that* librarians at 39 (57%) institutions were eligible for tenure, while librarians at 29 (43%) institutions were not eligible for tenure. All librarians at institutions with faculty status were elibible for tenure (24 institutions), librarians at 14 institutions where they held academic status were elibible for tenure, and librarians at 1 institution where their status was indicated "other" were eligible for tenure.   **(480)**

■ A 1980 survey of academic librarians in Alabama, Georgia, and Mississippi concerning faculty status (sample size: 416; responding: 271; usable: 267 or 64.2%) *showed that* 82.4% of the respondents reported having faculty status at their institution. However, of the 47 respondents who did not have faculty status, 29.8% reported that their institution offered the possibility of tenure for librarians.   **(502)**

Ibid. . . . *showed that*, of 220 respondents who reported having faculty status, 36.4% reported that promotion criteria for librarians were the same as for other faculty, while 36.3% reported that they were not, and 27.3% reported that they did not know the promotion criteria.   **(502)**

■ A survey reported in 1981 of library directors in 4-year colleges and universities in 7 Rocky Mountain states (survey size: 76; responding: 64 or 84%) concerning faculty status of librarians *showed that* 30 (75%) respondents reported that librarians' rank was identical with teaching faculty, 32 (80%) reported that tenure for librarians was identical with teaching faculty, and 33 (83%) reported that promotion eligibility was the same for librarians as for teaching faculty.   **(492)**

■ A survey reported in 1981 of Association of Research Libraries directors concerning the acceptability of nonlibrary/information science publications in the promotion and tenure of academic librarians (population: 108; responding: 82 or 75.9%) *showed that* 13 (15.9%) respondents reported that publication was essential for promotion and tenure at their institution, 67 (81.7%) reported that publication was not essential for promotion and tenure, and 2 (2.4%) did not reply.   **(503)**

Ibid. . . . *showed that* the importance of publications in subject fields compared to publications in library/information science for the promotion and tenure of librarians was reported as follows:

more importance	2 (2.4%)	respondents
same importance	54 (65.9%)	respondents
less importance	4 (4.9%)	respondents
no importance	5 (6.1%)	respondents
no answer	17 (20.7%)	respondents **(503)**

■ A survey reported in 1983 of head librarians of accredited institutions of higher education in New York state, including 2-year colleges, 4-year colleges, universities, and graduate/professional schools (survey size: 264; responding: 188 or 71%) concerning faculty status for librarians *showed that*, of the total respondents, librarians had the following academic rights (multiple responses allowed):

eligible to serve on the campus governing board	76% of total
eligible for release time for professional activities	68% of total
eligible for sabbatical and other professional leaves	64% of total
eligible for tenure	58% of total
eligible for research funds	55% of total
given professorial titles	30% of total
given release time for research	20% of total
academic-year appointment	16% of total **(516)**

■ A survey reported in 1983 of the U.S. academic members of the Association of Research Libraries concerning faculty status for professionals (population: 89 libraries; responding: 89 or 100%, including 57 state and 32 private institutions) *showed that* the types of final appointments that could be achieved by a majority of the professional staff were as follows:

indefinite tenure was the practice in 34 (59.7%) of the state and 4 (12.5%) of the private institutions;

continuing appointments were the practice in 19 (33.3%) of the state and 22 (68.8%) of the private institutions;

and term appointments were the practice in 4 (7.0%) of the state and 6 (18.7%) of the private institutions.

Further, indefinite tenure and continuing appointments were "perceived by respondents as nearly identical." **(788)**

Special

■ A 1978 survey of law school libraries listed in the 1977 *AALS Directory of Law Teachers* (population: 167; responding: 158 or 95%) *showed that* 67 (42%) respondents reported that professional law school librarians other than the head law school librarian held full faculty status/rank, while 91 (58%) reported that they did not. 59 (37%) respondents reported that professional law school librarians other than the head law school librarian either had or were working toward tenure, while 98 (62%) reported this was not the case, and 1 (0.6%) reported some either held or were working toward tenure. **(362)**

■ A survey reported in 1980 of nondirector, professional law librarians (1 in each school) in U.S. accredited law schools with the names of individuals being selected randomly from the *Directory of Law Librarians* (1978 edition) (sample size: 145; responding: 103 or 71%) *showed that*, of 78 respondents, the source that granted faculty status and/or tenure was:

law school faculty	28 (35.9%)	respondents
general university faculty	19 (24.4%)	respondents
university library	7 (9.0%)	respondents
law library faculty	3 (3.8%)	respondents
other	21 (26.9%)	respondents **(371)**

Ibid. . . . *showed that*, of 101 respondents:

32 (31.6%) reported that professional law librarians other than the director or head of libraries were granted or permitted to work toward tenure;

58 (57.4%) reported that professional law librarians other than the director or head of libraries were not granted or permitted to work toward tenure;

4 (4.0%) reported that some of the professional law librarians other than the director or head of libraries were granted or permitted to work toward tenure;

4 (4.0%) reported that professional law librarians other than the director or head of libraries were granted or permitted to work toward tenure under another name, e.g., "continuing appointment," "trustees appointment," "career appointment," or"permanent status";

3 (3.0%) gave miscellaneous other answers.   **(371)**

Gender Issues—General Issues

General

■ An analysis reported in 1974 of 660 library science and library science related dissertations completed between 1925 and 1972 *showed that*, for 435 doctoral recipients who received their degrees between 1953-72, there was a statistically significant relationship between gender and current type of position held (significant at the .001 level). Specifically, a higher proportion of males (29.3%) than females (14.3%) tended to work in academic libraries, while a higher proportion of females (65.7%) than males (58.1%) tended to join library school faculties. 3.8% of the females vs. 1.4% of the males worked in public libraries, 6.7% of the females vs. 0.5% of the males worked in school libraries, and 1.9% of the females vs. 2.7% of the males worked in special libraries. 7.6% of the females and 8.0% of the males worked in "other" positions. **(283)**

Academic

■ A survey reported in 1978 of 407 academic and public libraries who had filled professional positions (responding: 61% [no number given]; usable responses: 233 or 57%) *showed that* in academic libraries females were hired in 47% of the cases with the pool estimated at 48%, while in public libraries 37% of positions were filled by females out of an estimated pool of 30%. **(227)**

Public

■ A survey reported in 1978 of 407 academic and public libraries who had filled professional positions (responding: 61% [no number given]; usable responses: 233 or 57%) *showed that* in academic libraries females were hired in 47% of the cases with the pool estimated at 48%, while in public libraries 37% of positions were filled by females out of an estimated pool of 30%. **(227)**

Special

■ A survey reported in 1971 of the professional law librarians listed as members of the American Association of Law Libraries (population: not given; response: "approximately 50%," no number given) *showed that*, of 426 female respondents, 286 (67.1%) were head law libarians, 76 (17.8%) were assistant head law librarians, 29 (6.8%) were catalogers, and 35 (8.2%) were "other." **(383)**

■ A survey reported in 1972 of black employment in law school libraries (sample size: 136; responding: 95 or 70%) *showed that* responding libraries reported a total of 12 black law librarians out of 346 professional law librarians (3.4% of the professional law librarians). This included 7 black women out of 204 women professionals (2%) and 5 black men out of 123 male professionals (1.4%). **(386)**

■ A preliminary analysis reported in 1976 of a survey of American Association of Law Libraries members (survey size: "approximately 2,000" individuals; responding: "approximately 1,400" or 70%, of which responses from 888 respondents were analyzed at the time of the report) *showed that*, of the 45% who work in law schools, 46% have faculty status and 36% have faculty rank. Of those with faculty rank:

23% were professors (including 68% males; 32% females);

33% were associate professors (including 65% males; 35% females);

and 26% were assistant professors (including 53% males; 47% females). **(793)**

■ A survey reported in 1980 of 23 special librarians who became officers in their organizations *showed that*, of external factors (those over which the respondent had little control) influencing the appointment to officer rank, the one "most frequently mentioned" was a supportive management. The "next most frequently cited external factor" was the women's movement and affirmative action. **(431)**

Gender Issues—Age

General

■ A survey reported in 1967 of selected head college librarians (sample size: 660; responding: 414 or 62.7%) *showed that* men tended to become head librarians at an earlier age than women librarians. Of the 85 librarians who were under 40 years of age, 65 (76.46%) were men. Only in the 50+ years old category do women have a higher percentage of head positions, 130 (68.42%) compared to 60 (31.58%) for men. **(177)**

■ A study reported in 1981 of information on chief librarians generated in a 1975-76 survey of Canadian librarians in public, special, and academic libraries (study size: 96 chief librarians including 49 females and 47 males) *showed that* women chief librarians tend to be younger than males. For example, the average age of female chief librarians was 44.5 years compared to 46.4 years for males. Further, 17 (34.7%) of the women were in their 30s compared to 12 (25.5%) of the males, while 13 (27.7%) of the males and 9 (18.4%) of the females were in their 40s. **(557)**

Gender Issues—Career Patterns

General

■ An analysis reported in 1974 of 660 library science and library science related dissertations completed between 1925 and 1972 *showed that*, for 435 doctoral recipients who received their degrees between 1953-72, there was a statistically significant relationship between sex and current type of position held (significant at the .001 level). Specifically, a higher proportion of males (29.3%) than females (14.3%) tended to work in academic libraries, while a higher proportion of females (65.7%) than males (58.1%) tended to join library school faculties. 3.8% of the females vs. 1.4% of the males worked in public libraries, 6.7% of the females vs. 0.5% of the males worked in school libraries, and 1.9% of the females vs. 2.7% of the males worked in special libraries. 7.6% of the females and 8.0% of the males worked in "other" positions.   **(283)**

■ A study reported in 1979 of M.L.S. graduates from the University of Toronto between 1972 and 1977 and the University of Western Ontario between 1968-76 living in Canada (sample size: 300 males and 498 females; responding: 172 or 57.3% males and 204 or 40.9% females) *showed that*, by the second job, 27% of the males compared to 0% of the females were in administrative and related positions; by the third job, 41% of the males and 17% of the females were in administrative and related positions.

(553)

■ A 1980 survey of randomly selected American Library Association personal members (sample size: 3,000 members; responding: 1,987 or 67.1%, including 1,583 full-time members employed at the time of the survey, which provided the subsample analyzed here) *showed that*, of ALA members, men tended to be concentrated in academic libraries while women tended to be concentrated in public libraries. Specifically, the proportion of male and female ALA members in different types of libraries was as follows:

in school libraries: 3.5% of the male ALA members and 17.0% of the female ALA members;

in public libraries: 22.8% of the male ALA members and 30.7% of the female ALA members;

in academic libraries: 44.6% of the male ALA members and 27.7% of the female ALA members;

in special and other libraries: 25.7% of the male ALA members and 22.4% of the female ALA members;

in nonlibrary/other: 3.4% of the male ALA members and 2.2% of the female ALA members.   **(668)**

Ibid. . . . *showed that*, while women outnumbered men in all categories of library positions on an absolute basis, a higher proportion of men were found in director or associate/assistant director positions than their overall numbers would suggest, while a higher proportion of women than their numbers would suggest were found in public services, children's services, as school librarians or media specialists. Gender representation was fairly proportionate for department heads and in technical services. Specifically:

directors: 99 females compared to 77 males, representing 11.2% of the female respondents and 28.9% of the male respondents;

associate/assitant directors: 157 females compared to 27 males, representing 3.7% of the female respondents and 10.2% of the male respondents;

department heads: 157 females compared to 50 males, representing 17.8% of the female respondents and 18.7% of the male respondents;

public services (other): 120 females compared to 24 males, representing 13.5% of the female respondents and 9.0% of the male respondents;

technical services (other): 53 females compared to 23 males, representing 6.0% of the female respondents and 8.6% of the male respondents;

school librarians: 17 females compared to 1 male, representing 1.9% of the female respondents and 0.4% of the male respondents;

media specialists: 57 females compared to 6 males, representing 6.4% of the female respondents and 2.3% of the male respondents;

children's services: 37 females compared to 1 male, representing 4.2% of the female respondents and 0.4% of the male respondents. **(668)**

■ A study of a portion of the COSWL data reported in 1981 involving the responses of 739 personal members (195 men; 544 women) of the American Library Association who were at the time of the study employed in libraries and who had received their professional library degrees prior to 1971 *showed that* 64.7% of the male library directors, 45.6% of male middle managers, and 32.6% of male librarians/other reported a career pattern involving different positions in different libraries, compared to 45.8% of female library directors, 44.9% of female middle managers, and 35.3% of female librarians/other so reporting. This was the most common career pattern for both groups. **(241)**

■ A study reported in 1981 of information on chief librarians generated in a 1975-76 survey of Canadian librarians in public, special, and academic libraries (study size: 96 chief librarians including 49 females and 47 males) *showed that* career pattern for chief librarians was as follows:

started in their 20s and took no breaks (24 or 53.3% women; 22 or 56.4% men)

started in their 20s and took a break of less than 5 years (7 or 15.6% women; 0 men);

started in their 20s and took a break of more than 5 years (2 or 4.4% women; 1 or 2.6% men);

started in their 30s (12 or 26.7% women; 16 or 41% men). **(557)**

Ibid. . . . *showed that* length of career of chief librarians was as follows:

less than 10 years	15 (31.3%) women;	11 (23.4%) men
10-19 years	14 (29.2%) women;	21 (44.7%) men
20-29 years	10 (20.8%) women;	11 (23.4%) men
30 or more years	9 (18.7%) women;	4 (8.5%) men **(557)**

Academic

■ A survey reported in 1967 of selected head college librarians (sample size: 660; responding: 414 or 62.7%) *showed that* men were more likely than women to be heads of tax-supported college libraries, while women tended to be heads of privately supported college libraries. Out of 143 head librarians in tax-supported colleges, 82 (57.34%) were men, while out of 271 head librarians in privately supported schools 152 (56.09%) were women. **(177)**

Ibid. . . . *showed that* men were more likely than women to be head librarians of larger colleges. Out of 114 head librarians of colleges with enrollments ranging from 1,500 to 5,000 (the largest category in the study), 72 (63.15%) were men. The percentage of male head librarians decreased as college size decreased to the smallest category of colleges (less than 500 students), where 46 (63.89%) of the head librarians were women and 26 (36.11%) were men. **(177)**

Ibid. . . . *showed that* women head librarians tended to change positions less often than men. Of 173 head librarians who had been in their present positions for over 10 years, 112 (64.80%) were women. Of 82 head librarians who had been in their present positions for over 16 years, 60 (73.17%) were women. **(177)**

Ibid. . . . *showed that* men tended to become head librarians at an earlier age than women librarians. Of the 85 librarians who were under 40 years of age, 65 (76.46%) were men. Only in the 50+ years old category did women have a higher percentage of head positions, 130 (68.42%) compared to 60 (31.58%) for men. **(177)**

■ A 1972 study of U.S. medical school libraries and other large biomedical libraries (collection of 35,000+ volumes and staff of 3 or more) concerning the status of women professionals (survey size: 160 libraries; responding: 143; usable: 140 or 87.5%) *showed that* males tended to work in the larger medical libraries while females tended to work in the smaller medical libraries. Specifically, out of 893 females and 261 males, 306 (34%) of the females and 101 (39%) of the males worked in the largest 25 libraries, while 82 (9%) of the females and 16 (6%) of the males worked in the smallest 25 libraries. **(709)**

Ibid. . . . *showed that*, during the time span 1968-69 through 1973-74, women held 47.7% of all Medical Library Association positions, constituted 60% of the officers, 43.3% of the board members, 52.5% of the committee chairs or cochairs, and 35.6% of the delegates. Further, during the period 1950 to 1972, 14 women (and 9 men) served as MLA presidents. **(709)**

■ A 1975 survey of 530 (87% responding) academic librarians in 9 southern states out of a total academic librarian population of 1,964, investigating the relationship between job mobility and career advancement, *showed that*, although job mobility was similar for men and women librarians, the reasons for job changes were not. 94% of the men left a prior position for career-related reasons, while only 75% of the women did. The remaining men and women left their prior positions for either personal or family reasons. **(165)**

Ibid. . . . *showed that*, of the respondents who had changed jobs, 91% had subsequently received a salary increase. The size of the increase, however, was related to the reasons for the move. Of those librarians who had moved for career reasons, 24% made salary gains of $8,000 or more; of those who moved for noncareer reasons, only 16% received salary increases of $8,000 or more. **(165)**

Ibid. . . . *showed that* on the average women librarians who had left their last positions for career-related reasons increased their salaries by $1,861 less than men who had also moved for career reasons. Women who left their positions for noncareer reasons increased their salaries (average increase $3,586) by $2,742 less than men (average increase $6,328) who left their positions for noncareer reasons. These are both statistically significant differences.   **(165)**

Ibid. . . . *showed that* on the average women changed jobs every 5.2 years while men changed jobs every 4.8 years. This was not a statistically significant difference.   **(165)**

■ A random sample of directors of academic libraries in the U.S. undertaken in 1976 (sample size: 266; response: 215 or 80.8%) *showed that* there was a statistically significant tendency for women library directors to have been hired internally in both public and private institutions regardless of organizational size. In private institutions 55.6% of the women had been internal candidates compared to 21.8% men; in public institutions 44.4% of the women candidates had been internal compared to 11.7% of the men.
                                                                         (121)

Special

■ A 1972 study of U.S. medical school libraries and other large biomedical libraries (collection of 35,000+ volumes and staff of 3 or more) concerning the status of women professionals (survey size: 160 libraries; responding: 143; usable: 140 or 87.5%) *showed that* males tended to work in the larger medical libraries while females tended to work in the smaller medical libraries. Specifically, out of 893 females and 261 males, 306 (34%) of the females and 101 (39%) of the males worked in the largest 25 libraries, while 82 (9%) of the females and 16 (6%) of the males worked in the smallest 25 libraries.   **(709)**

Ibid. . . . *showed that*, during the time span 1968-69 through 1973-74, women held 47.7% of all Medical Library Association positions, constituted 60% of the officers, 43.3% of the board members, 52.5% of the committee chairs or cochairs, and 35.6% of the delegates. Further, during the period 1950 to 1972, 14 women (and 9 men) served as MLA presidents.
                                                                         (709)

■ A preliminary analysis reported in 1976 of a survey of American Association of Law Libraries members (survey size: "approximately 2,000" individuals; responding: "approximately 1,400" or 70%, of which responses from 888 respondents were analyzed at the time of the report) *showed that* the library size (in volumes) in which respondents worked was as follows:

small (50,000 vols. or less)   41% respondents
medium (50-100,000 vols.)   22% respondents
large (100-200,000 vols.)   22% respondents
very large (200,000 vols. or more) 15% respondents   **(793)**

Ibid. . . . *showed that* the type of library in which respondents worked was
as follows:

law school libraries   45% respondents
bar or lawyer association
   libraries   5% respondents
law firm libraries   21% respondents
non-law firm libraries   6% respondents
government libraries   23% respondents

This represented a 10% drop in members employed in law school libraries
and a 13% increase in members employed in law firms [from the earlier
1970 survey of AALL members].   **(793)**

Gender Issues—Demographics

Special

■ A preliminary analysis reported in 1976 of a survey of American
Association of Law Libraries members (survey size: "approximately
2,000" individuals; responding: "approximately 1,400" or 70%, of which
responses from 888 respondents were analyzed at the time of the report)
showed that the membership appeared to consist of 68% women and 32%
men. An earlier survey of AALL members in 1970 suggested that the
membership consisted of 53% women and 36% men.   **(793)**

Gender Issues—Directors

General

■ A 1980 survey of randomly selected American Library Association
personal members (sample size: 3,000 members; responding: 1,987 or
67.1%, including 1,583 full-time members employed at the time of the
survey, which provided the subsample analyzed here) *showed that*, while
the majority of library directors in academic, public, school, and special
libraries were female (99 females vs. 77 men), this represented 11.2% of all

female librarians and 43.8% of all male librarians. This imbalance continued through the administrative structure, with 57.8% of the men holding positions at the director, assistant/associate director, and department head level compared to 32.7% of the women holding such positions. **(668)**

Ibid. . . . *showed that,* while women outnumbered men in all categories of library positions on an absolute basis, a higher proportion of men were found in director or associate/assistant director positions than their overall numbers would suggest, while a higher proportion of women than their numbers would suggest were found in public services, children's services, as school librarians or media specialists. Gender representation was fairly proportionate for department heads and in technical services. Specifically:

directors: 99 females compared to 77 males, representing 11.2% of the female respondents and 28.9% of the male respondents;

associate/assitant directors: 157 females compared to 27 males, representing 3.7% of the female respondents and 10.2% of the male respondents;

department heads: 157 females compared to 50 males, representing 17.8% of the female respondents and 18.7% of the male respondents;

public services (other): 120 females compared to 24 males, representing 13.5% of the female respondents and 9.0% of the male respondents;

technical services (other): 53 females compared to 23 males, representing 6.0% of the female respondents and 8.6% of the male respondents;

school librarians: 17 females compared to 1 male, representing 1.9% of the female respondents and 0.4% of the male respondents;

media specialists: 57 females compared to 6 males, representing 6.4% of the female respondents and 2.3% of the male respondents;

children's services: 37 females compared to 1 male, representing 4.2% of the female respondents and 0.4% of the male respondents. **(668)**

■ A study reported in 1981 of information on chief librarians generated in a 1975-76 survey of Canadian librarians in public, special, and academic libraries (study size: 96 chief librarians including 49 females and 47 males) *showed that* females earned an average of $16,444 while males earned an average of $20,896. Further, higher male salaries held true for each library type (small public, medium public, large public, special library, small university library, and college library) except large university library, where no women chiefs were represented. **(557)**

Ibid. . . . *showed that* career pattern for chief librarians was as follows:

started in their 20s and took no breaks (24 or 53.3% women; 22 or 56.4% men)

started in their 20s and took a break of less than 5 years (7 or 15.6% women; 0 men);

started in their 20s and took a break of more than 5 years (2 or 4.4% women; 1 or 2.6% men);

started in their 30s (12 or 26.7% women; 16 or 41% men). **(557)**

Ibid. . . . *showed that* women chief librarians tend to be younger than males. For example, the average age of female chief librarians was 44.5 years compared to 46.4 years for males. Further, 17 (34.7%) of the women were in their 30s compared to 12 (25.5%) of the males, while 13 (27.7%) of the males and 9 (18.4%) of the females were in their 40s. **(557)**

Ibid. . . . *showed that* length of career of chief librarians was as follows:

less than 10 years	15 (31.3%) women; 11 (23.4%) men
10-19 years	14 (29.2%) women; 21 (44.7%) men
20-29 years	10 (20.8%) women; 11 (23.4%) men
30 or more years	9 (18.7%) women; 4 (8.5%) men **(557)**

Ibid. . . . *showed that* females earned an average of $16,444 while males earned an average of $20,896. Further, higher male salaries held true for each library type (small public, medium public, large public, special library, small university library, and college library) except large university library, where no women chiefs were represented. **(557)**

■ A study reported in 1981 of a portion of the COSWL data involving the responses of 739 personal members (195 men; 544 women) of the American Library Association who were at the time of the study employed in libraries and who had received their professional library degrees prior to 1971 *showed that* 64.7% of the male library directors, 45.6% of male middle managers, and 32.6% of male librarians/other reported a career pattern involving different positions in different libraries, compared to

45.8% of female library directors, 44.9% of female middle managers, and 35.3% of female librarians/other so reporting. This was the most common career pattern for both groups. **(241)**

Ibid. . . . *showed that*, while more women (76 or 52.4%) than men (69 or 47.6%) were library directors, the percentage of men who were directors (35.4% of all men) was higher than the percentage of women who were directors (14% of all women). **(241)**

Ibid. . . . *showed that* fewer males than females reported limits to their mobility in terms of job seeking. 69.6% of male directors reported no mobility limits, 54.4% of male middle managers and 57.1% of male librarians/other reported no mobility limits, compared to 47.3% of female directors, 42.4% of female middle managers, and 42.5% of female librarians/other reporting no mobility limits. **(241)**

Academic

■ A survey reported in 1967 of selected head college librarians (sample size: 660; responding: 414 or 62.7%) *showed that* men tended to become head librarians at an earlier age than women librarians. Of the 85 librarians who were under 40 years of age, 65 (76.46%) were men. Only in the 50+ years old category do women have a higher percentage of head positions, 130 (68.42%) compared to 60 (31.58%) for men. **(177)**

Ibid. . . . *showed that* women head librarians tended to change positions less often than men. Of 173 head librarians who had been in their present positions for over 10 years, 112 (64.80%) were women. Of 82 head librarians who had been in their present positions for over 16 years, 60 (73.17%) were women. **(177)**

■ A 1972 study of U.S. medical school libraries and other large biomedical libraries (collection of 35,000+ volumes and staff of 3 or more) concerning the status of women professionals (survey size: 160 libraries; responding: 143; usable: 140 or 87.5%) *showed that*, of 133 filled head librarian positions, 54 (40.6%) were held by women while 79 (59.4%) were held by men. In terms of the total medical librarian population, 6% of the women were head librarians, while 30.3% of the men were head librarians. Representation of head medical librarians by gender in different kinds of medical libraries was as follows (based on the number of filled positions reported in parentheses):

medical school (97 positions)	34 (35.1%) women
society (14 positions)	8 (57.1%) women

continued

government (5 positions)   2 (40.0%) women
pharmaceutical (13 positions)   6 (46.2%) women
hospital (4 positions)   4 (100%) women   **(709)**

Ibid. . . . *showed that* the proportion of women head medical librarians had decreased since 1950. Specifically, while women held 40.6% of the top medical library positions overall in 1972, they held 83% (out of 106 top positions) in 1950. Similarly, for just medical school libraries, women held 35.1% of the top positions in 1972, while they held 86.1% (out of 72 top positions) in 1950.   **(709)**

Ibid. . . . *showed that* since 1950 the biggest gender change had taken place in the head positions of the larger medical libraries. In the 25 largest libraries women held 25% of the filled top positions in 1972, while in 1950 women held 57.1% of the top positions in these libraries. In the 25 smallest libraries women held 70.8% of the filled positions in 1972, while in 1950 women held 89.5% of the top positions in these libraries.   **(709)**

Ibid. . . . *showed that* overall, of 100 associate librarian positions reported filled, 74.0% were filled by women and 26.0% were filled by men. Further, combining both head and associate head positions indicated that overall 128 (14.3%) of the women in the sample held upper administrative positions while 105 (40.3%) of the males in the sample held upper administrative positions.   **(709)**

■ A 1977 survey of all libraries in U.S. medical schools and U.S. health science libraries holding over 40,000 volumes with staffs of 3 or more (survey size: 149 libraries; responding: 126 or 84.6%) *showed that*, of 118 head librarian positions filled at the time of the survey, men held 61.0% of the positions while women held 39.0% of the positions. In 1972, of 120 head librarian positions filled, men held 56.7% of the positions, while in 1950, of 88 head librarian positions filled, men held 17.0% of the positions. Overall, women constituted 77.3% of the librarians in the responding libraries.   **(727)**

Ibid. . . . *showed that*, of the 72 male head librarians, 10 (13.9%) held doctorates, while of 46 female head librarians, 3 (6.5%) held doctorates.
(727)

Ibid. . . . *showed that*, with the exception of the 25 largest libraries by collection size, the proportion of male head librarians had increased in both the larger and smaller libraries since 1950. For example, in the 25 largest libraries by staff size, women held 60% of 20 filled head librarian positions in 1950, 41.7% of 24 filled positions in 1972, and 34.8% of 23 filled positions in 1977. Likewise, in the 27 smallest libraries by staff size (3 libraries were tied for 25th position), women held 94.1% of 17 filled positions in 1950, 68.2% of 22 filled positions in 1972, and 56.0% of 25 filled positions in 1977. (In the 25 largest libraries by collection size women held 52.2% of 23 filled positions in 1950, 28.0% of 25 filled positions in 1972, and 30.4% of 23 filled positions in 1977.)   **(727)**

Ibid. . . . *showed that* overall the proportion of women head librarians had decreased since 1950. In 1950 women held 83.0% of 88 filled head positions, in 1972 they held 43.3% of 120 filled head positions, and in 1977 they held 39.0% of 118 filled head positions. For the 103 medical school libraries subset the progression was similiar. In 1950 women held 82.4% of 68 filled head positions, in 1972 they held 38.8% of 98 filled head positions, and in 1977 they held 34.4% of 96 filled head positions.   **(727)**

Ibid. . . . *showed that* between 1972 and 1977 men continued to receive a disproportionate share of the head librarian positions in medical libraries based on their numbers in the professional workforce. During this period 65.4% of the appointments to head librarian positions were male, although males constituted only 22.7% of the professional workforce in the 1977 sample.   **(727)**

Ibid. . . . *showed that,* of 28 female heads, 26 (92.9%) had only female associate librarians and 2 (7.1%) had only male associate librarians, while of 53 male heads, 37 (69.8%) had only female associate librarians, 10 (18.9%) had only male associate librarians, and 6 (11.3%) had 1 male and 1 female as associate librarians.   **(727)**

■ A 1980 survey of first-time-appointed academic library directors during the period 1970-80 (survey size: 230 directors; responding: 141 or 61.3%, including 98 males and 43 females) *showed that* ethnic background was as follows:

Asian-Americans accounted for 2 (1.4%) of the directors, including 2 (2.0%) of the males and none of the females;

Hispanics accounted for 2 (1.4%) of the directors, including 2 (2.0%) of the males and none of the females;

blacks accounted for 14 (10.0%) of the directors, including 7 (7.2%) of the males and 7 (9.3%) of the females;

whites accounted for 120 (85.1%) of the directors, including 85 (86.8%) of the males and 35 (81.4%) of the females;

3 individuals did not reply to the question. **(785)**

Special

■ A survey reported in 1971 of the professional law librarians listed as members of the American Association of Law Libraries (population: not given; response: "approximately 50%," no number given) *showed that*, of 286 female and 138 male head law librarians, the distribution of employing libraries was as follows:

	WOMEN	MEN
law school library	16%	39%
bar association library	9%	9%
law firm library	19%	12%
other firm library	9%	2%
city law library	2%	2%
county law library	15%	12%
state law library	12%	14%
federal law library	13%	8%
no response	5%	2%	**(383)**

Ibid. . . . *showed that*, of 426 female respondents, 286 (67.1%) were head law libarians, 76 (17.8%) were assistant head law librarians, 29 (6.8%) were catalogers, and 35 (8.2%) were "other." **(383)**

■ A 1972 study of U.S. medical school libraries and other large biomedical libraries (collection of 35,000+ volumes and staff of 3 or more) concerning the status of women professionals (survey size: 160 libraries; responding: 143; usable: 140 or 87.5%) *showed that*, of 133 filled head librarian positions, 54 (40.6%) were held by women while 79 (59.4%) were held by men. In terms of the total medical librarian population, 6% of the women were head librarians, while 30.3% of the men were head librarians. Representation of head medical librarians by gender in different kinds of medical libraries was as follows (based on the number of filled positions reported in parentheses):

medical school (97 positions)	34 (35.1%) women
society (14 positions)	8 (57.1%) women
government (5 positions)	2 (40.0%) women
pharmaceutical (13 positions)	6 (46.2%) women
hospital (4 positions)	4 (100%) women	**(709)**

Ibid. . . . *showed that* the proportion of women head medical librarians had decreased since 1950. Specifically, while women held 40.6% of the top medical library positions overall in 1972, they held 83% (out of 106 top positions) in 1950. Similarly, for just medical school libraries, women held 35.1% of the top positions in 1972, while they held 86.1% (out of 72 top positions) in 1950. **(709)**

Ibid. . . . *showed that* since 1950 the biggest gender change had taken place in the head positions of the larger medical libraries. In the 25 largest libraries women held 25% of the filled top positions in 1972, while in 1950 women held 57.1% of the top positions in these libraries. In the 25 smallest libraries women held 70.8% of the filled positions in 1972, while in 1950 women held 89.5% of the top positions in these libraries. **(709)**

Ibid. . . . *showed that* overall, of 100 associate librarian positions reported filled, 74.0% were filled by women and 26.0% were filled by men. Further, combining both head and associate head positions indicated that overall 128 (14.3%) of the women in the sample held upper administrative positions, while 105 (40.3%) of the males in the sample held upper administrative positions. **(709)**

■ A preliminary analysis reported in 1976 of a survey of American Association of Law Libraries members (survey size: "approximately 2,000" individuals; responding: "approximately 1,400" or 70%, of which responses from 888 respondents were analyzed at the time of the report) *showed that* 50% of the men and 50% of the women respondents were head librarians. This compares to an earlier survey of AALL members in 1970, when 50% of the men were head librarians. **(793)**

■ A 1977 survey of all libraries in U.S. medical schools and U.S. health science libraries holding over 40,000 volumes with staffs of 3 or more (survey size: 149 libraries; responding: 126 or 84.6%) *showed that*, of 118 head librarian positions filled at the time of the survey, men held 61.0% of the positions while women held 39.0% of the positions. In 1972, of 120 head librarian positions filled, men held 56.7% of the positions, while in 1950, of 88 head librarian positions filled, men held 17.0% of the positions. Overall, women constituted 77.3% of the librarians in the responding libraries. **(727)**

Ibid. . . . *showed that*, with the exception of the 25 largest libraries by collection size, the proportion of male head librarians had increased in both the larger and smaller libraries since 1950. For example, in the 25 largest libraries by staff size, women held 60% of 20 filled head librarian positions in 1950, 41.7% of 24 filled positions in 1972, and 34.8% of 23 filled positions in 1977. Likewise, in the 27 smallest libraries by staff size (3 libraries were tied for 25th position), women held 94.1% of 17 filled positions in 1950, 68.2% of 22 filled positions in 1972, and 56.0% of 25 filled positions in 1977. (In the 25 largest libraries by collection size women held 52.2% of 23 filled positions in 1950, 28.0% of 25 filled positions in 1972, and 30.4% of 23 filled positions in 1977.) **(727)**

Ibid. . . . *showed that*, of the 72 male head librarians, 10 (13.9%) held doctorates, while of 46 female head librarians, 3 (6.5%) held doctorates. **(727)**

Ibid. . . . *showed that* overall the proportion of women head librarians had decreased since 1950. In 1950 women held 83.0% of 88 filled head positions, in 1972 they held 43.3% of 120 filled head positions, and in 1977 they held 39.0% of 118 filled head positions. For the 103 medical school libraries subset the progression was similiar. In 1950 women held 82.4% of 68 filled head positions, in 1972 they held 38.8% of 98 filled head positions, and in 1977 they held 34.4% of 96 filled head positions. **(727)**

Ibid. . . . *showed that* between 1972 and 1977 men continued to receive a disproportionate share of the head librarian positions in medical libraries based on their numbers in the professional workforce. During this period 65.4% of the appointments to head librarian positions were male, although males constituted only 22.7% of the professional workforce in the 1977 sample. **(727)**

Ibid. . . . *showed that*, of 28 female heads, 26 (92.9%) had only female associate librarians and 2 (7.1%) had only male associate librarians, while of 53 male heads, 37 (69.8%) had only female associate librarians, 10 (18.9%) had only male associate librarians, and 6 (11.3%) had 1 male and 1 female as associate librarians. **(727)**

Gender Issues—Education

General

■ An analysis reported in 1974 of 660 library science and library science related dissertations completed between 1925 and 1972 *showed that*, for 435 doctoral recipients who received their degrees between 1953-72, there was a statistically significant relationship between sex and current type of position held (significant at the .001 level). Specifically, a higher proportion of males (29.3%) than females (14.3%) tended to work in academic libraries, while a higher proportion of females (65.7%) than males (58.1%) tended to join library school faculties. 3.8% of the females vs. 1.4% of the males worked in public libraries, 6.7% of the females vs. 0.5% of the males worked in school libraries, and 1.9% of the females vs. 2.7% of the males worked in special libraries. 7.6% of the females and 8.0% of the males worked in "other" positions. **(283)**

Ibid. . . . *showed that*, for 435 doctoral recipients who received their degrees between 1953-72, there was no statistically significant relationship between sex and mobility. Specifically, comparing location of job to location of school, 17.0% of the females and 9.5% of the males were in the same state, 27.4% of the females and 31.8% of the males were in contiguous states, while 55.6% of the females and 58.7% of the males were "geographically removed." **(283)**

Academic

■ A 1977 survey of all libraries in U.S. medical schools and U.S. health science libraries holding over 40,000 volumes with staffs of 3 or more (survey size: 149 libraries; responding: 126 or 84.6%) *showed that*, of the 72 male head librarians, 10 (13.9%) held doctorates, while of 46 female head librarians, 3 (6.5%) held doctorates. **(727)**

■ A comparison reported in 1983 of 2 surveys of Association of College and Research Libraries members concerning members' educational attainments (1973 survey—survey size: 300 members; responding: 259 or 86.3%; 1978 survey—survey size: 429 members; responding: 357 or 83.2%) *showed that*, based on the 1978 sample, the highest degree being held or pursued by gender was as follows (153 males responding; 192 females responding):

bachelor's degree: no males compared to 5 (2.6%) females;

second bachelor's degree: 2 (1.3%) males compared to 9 (4.7%) females;

master's degree: 62 (40.5%) males compared to 109 (56.8%) females;

second master's degree: 48 (31.4%) males compared to 46 (24.0%) females;

sixth-year certificate: 6 (3.9%) males compared to 5 (2.6%) females;

doctorate: 35 (22.9%) males compared to 18 (9.4%) females. **(799)**

Ibid. . . . *showed that*, based on the 1978 sample, males had a statistically significant higher level of education than females. For example, males were more likely to hold degrees above the first master's degree, while females were more likely to hold degrees at or below the level of the first master's degree. Specifically, 41.8% of the males had their highest degrees at or below the level of the first master's degree, while 64.1% of the females had such degrees (difference significant at the .05 level).   **(799)**

Ibid. . . . *showed that* overall a statistically significant greater proportion of females participated in workshops, short courses, and seminars than males (difference significant at the .05 level).   **(799)**

Ibid. . . . *showed that* overall more librarians had been enrolled in academic course work during the 12 months prior to the 1978 survey (34.4% respondents) than prior to the 1973 survey (22.2% respondents). Based on the 1978 survey, a statistically significant greater proportion of females had taken such courses than males (difference significant at the .05 level).
(799)

Gender Issues—Length of Service

General

■ A study reported in 1981 of information on chief librarians generated in a 1975-76 survey of Canadian librarians in public, special, and academic libraries (study size: 96 chief librarians including 49 females and 47 males) *showed that* length of career of chief librarians was as follows:

less than 10 years	15 (31.3%) women; 11 (23.4%) men
10-19 years	14 (29.2%) women; 21 (44.7%) men
20-29 years	10 (20.8%) women; 11 (23.4%) men
30 or more years	9 (18.7%) women; 4 (8.5%) men **(557)**

Gender Issues—Management

General

■ A study reported in 1979 of M.L.S. graduates from the University of Toronto between 1972 and 1977 and the University of Western Ontario between 1968-76 living in Canada (sample size: 300 males and 498 females; responding: 172 or 57.3% males and 204 or 40.9% females) *showed that*, by the second job, 27% of the males compared to 0% of the females were in administrative and related positions; by the third job, 41% of the males and 17% of the females were in administrative and related positions.
(553)

■ A 1980 survey of randomly selected American Library Association personal members (sample size: 3,000 members; responding: 1,987 or 67.1%, including 1,583 full-time members employed at the time of the survey, which provided the subsample analyzed here) *showed that* 38.5% of the males compared to 16.2% of the females supervised 5 or more professionals, while 45.1% of the males supervised 5 or more support staff compared to 25.8% females. **(668)**

■ A study of a portion of the COSWL data reported in 1981 involving the responses of 739 personal members (195 men; 544 women) of the American Library Association who were at the time of the study employed in libraries and who had received their professional library degrees prior to 1971 *showed that* fewer males than females reported limits to their mobility in terms of job seeking. 69.6% of male directors reported no mobility limits, 54.4% of male middle managers and 57.1% of male librarians/other reported no mobility limits, compared to 47.3% of female directors, 42.4% of female middle managers, and 42.5% of female librarians/other reporting no mobility limits. **(241)**

Academic

■ A 1972 study of U.S. medical school libraries and other large bio-medical libraries (collection of 35,000+ volumes and staff of 3 or more) concerning the status of women professionals (survey size: 160 libraries; responding: 143; usable: 140 or 87.5%) *showed that* over-all, of 100 associate librarian positions reported filled, 74.0% were filled by women and 26.0% were filled by men. Further, combining both head and associate head positions indicated that overall 128 (14.3%) of the women in the sample held upper administrative positions, while 105 (40.3%) of the males in the sample held upper administrative positions. **(709)**

■ A 1977 survey of all libraries in U.S. medical schools and U.S. health science libraries holding over 40,000 volumes with staffs of 3 or more (survey size: 149 libraries; responding: 126 or 84.6%) *showed that*, of the 98 filled associate librarian positions reported in the 1977 survey, 76 (77.6%) were held by women while 22 (22.4%) were held by men. **(727)**

Ibid. . . . *showed that*, of 28 female heads, 26 (92.9%) had only female associate librarians and 2 (7.1%) had only male associate librarians, while of 53 male heads, 37 (69.8%) had only female associate librarians, 10

(18.9%) had only male associate librarians, and 6 (11.3%) had 1 male and 1 female as associate librarians. **(727)**

Special

■ A survey reported in 1971 of the professional law librarians listed as members of the American Association of Law Libraries (population: not given; response: "approximately 50%," no number given) *showed that*, of 426 female respondents, 286 (67.1%) were head law libarians, 76 (17.8%) were assistant head law librarians, 29 (6.8%) were catalogers, and 35 (8.2%) were "other." **(383)**

■ A 1972 study of U.S. medical school libraries and other large biomedical libraries (collection of 35,000+ volumes and staff of 3 or more) concerning the status of women professionals (survey size: 160 libraries; responding: 143; usable: 140 or 87.5%) *showed that* overall, of 100 associate librarian positions reported filled, 74.0% were filled by women and 26.0% were filled by men. Further, combining both head and associate head positions indicated that overall 128 (14.3%) of the women in the sample held upper administrative positions, while 105 (40.3%) of the males in the sample held upper administrative positions. **(709)**

■ A 1977 survey of all libraries in U.S. medical schools and U.S. health science libraries holding over 40,000 volumes with staffs of 3 or more (survey size: 149 libraries; responding: 126 or 84.6%) *showed that*, of the 98 filled associate librarian positions reported in the 1977 survey, 76 (77.6%) were held by women while 22 (22.4%) were held by men. **(727)**

Ibid. . . . *showed that*, of 28 female heads, 26 (92.9%) had only female associate librarians and 2 (7.1%) had only male associate librarians, while of 53 male heads, 37 (69.8%) had only female associate librarians, 10 (18.9%) had only male associate librarians, and 6 (11.3%) had 1 male and 1 female as associate librarians. **(727)**

Gender Issues—Mobility

General

■ An analysis reported in 1974 of 660 library science and library science related dissertations completed between 1925 and 1972 *showed that*, for

435 doctoral recipients who received their degrees between 1953-72, there was no statistically significant relationship between sex and mobility. Specifically, comparing location of job to location of school, 17.0% of the females and 9.5% of the males were in the same state, 27.4% of the females and 31.8% of the males were in contiguous states, while 55.6% of the females and 58.7% of the males were "geographically removed."

(283)

■ A study reported in 1981 of a portion of the COSWL data involving the responses of 739 personal members (195 men; 544 women) of the American Library Association who were at the time of the study employed in libraries and who had received their professional library degrees prior to 1971 *showed that* fewer males than females reported limits to their mobility in terms of job seeking. 69.6% of male directors reported no mobility limits, 54.4% of male middle managers and 57.1% of male librarians/other reported no mobility limits, compared to 47.3% of female directors, 42.4% of female middle managers, and 42.5% of female librarians/other reporting no mobility limits. **(241)**

Academic

■ A survey reported in 1967 of selected head college librarians (sample size: 660; responding: 414 or 62.7%) *showed that* women head librarians tended to change positions less often than men. Of 173 head librarians who had been in their present positions for over 10 years, 112 (64.80%) were women. Of 82 head librarians who had been in their present positions for over 16 years, 60 (73.17%) were women. **(177)**

■ A 1975 survey of 530 (87% responding) academic librarians in 9 southern states out of a total academic librarian population of 1,964, investigating the relationship between job mobility and career advancement, *showed that* on the average women changed jobs every 5.2 years, while men changed jobs every 4.8 years. This was not a statistically significant difference. **(165)**

Ibid. . . . *showed that*, although job mobility was similar for men and women librarians, the reasons for job changes were not. 94% of the men left a prior position for career-related reasons, while only 75% of the women did. The remaining men and women left their prior positions for either personal or family reasons. **(165)**

Gender Issues—Personal Life

General

■ A study reported in 1981 of a portion of the COSWL data involving the responses of 739 personal members (195 men; 544 women) of the American Library Association who were at the time of the study employed in libraries and who had received their professional library degrees prior to 1971 *showed that*:

> 85.5% of male library directors
> 66.2% of male middle managers
> 56.1% of male librarian (other)

were married compared to:

> 52.6% of female library directors
> 47.9% of female middle managers
> 45.7% of female librarians (other)   **(241)**

Ibid. . . . *showed that*:

> 4.3% of male library directors
> 11.8% of male middle managers
> 7.0% of male librarians (other)

were divorced compared to:

> 17.1% of female directors
> 19.3% of female middle managers
> 18.1% of female librarians (other)

Further:

> 7.2% of male library directors
> 19.1% of male middle managers
> 35.1% of male librarians (other)

had never married compared to:

> 30.3% of female library directors
> 31.4% of female middle managers
> 34.7% of female librarians (other)   **(241)**

■ A study reported in 1981 of information on chief librarians generated in a 1975-76 survey of Canadian librarians in public, special, and academic libraries (study size: 96 chief librarians, including 49 females and 47 males) *showed that* among currently or previously married librarians 25 (78.1%)

of the men reported children, while 15 (53.6%) of the females reported children. **(557)**

Ibid. . . . *showed that* the marital status of 95 chief librarians was as follows: currently married (22 or 44.9% women; 31 or 67.4% men), previously married (7 or 14.3% women; 3 or 6.5% men), and single (20 or 40.8% women; 12 or 26.1% men). **(557)**

Gender Issues—Personality, etc.

Academic

■ A survey reported in 1975 to determine levels of job satisfaction, using a Maslow needs hierarchy, of 202 men and women library professionals from 23 college and university libraries in the greater New York metropolitan area *showed that*, in terms of needs fulfillment (degree to which job met needs), men and women showed similar levels of fulfillment in lower-order needs, i.e., social and security needs, but that women expressed statistically significant lower levels of fulfillment than men in meeting esteem and autonomy needs. **(103)**

Ibid. . . . *showed that*, in terms of needs deficiency (size of gap between actual and desired degree to which job fills needs), women had statistically significantly higher deficiencies than men in security, autonomy, esteem, and self-actualization. There was no statistically significant difference between men and women in the area of social needs. **(103)**

Ibid. . . . *showed that*, in terms of importance of needs (degree to which respondents considered the need important), both men and women ranked autonomy and self-actualization needs as most important. The judged importance of security, social, and esteem needs were similar for both men and women, while women considered autonomy and self-actualization as having less importance than men. **(103)**

Gender Issues—Professional Service

General

■ A 1980 survey of randomly selected American Library Association personal members (sample size: 3,000 members; responding: 1,987 or

67.1%, including 1,583 full-time members employed at the time of the survey, which provided the subsample analyzed here) *showed that* proportionately more males than females were involved in professional activities at the state, regional, and national level. Specifically, the involvement in professional activities by gender was as follows:

elected or appointed at the national level	31.7% males; 14.6% females
chair of committee section or division at the national level	28.2% males; 12.1% females
member of committee at the national level	63.2% males; 42.9% females
elected/appointed at the state/regional level	55.1% males; 38.7% females
chair of committee, section, division at state/regional level	49.9% males; 32.1% females
member of committee at state/regional level	71.9% males; 60.5% females **(668)**

■ A study of a portion of the COSWL data reported in 1981 involving the responses of 739 personal members (195 men; 544 women) of the American Library Association who were at the time of the study employed in libraries and who had received their professional library degrees prior to 1971 *showed that* at all comparable levels men were more likely than women to be elected or appointed to national association positions (e.g., male directors, 47.1% vs. female directors, 23.9%), were more likely to be elected or appointed to state or regional association positions (e.g., male directors, 82.6% vs. female directors, 73.3%), were more likely to author a book (e.g., male directors, 24.6% vs. female directors, 9.2%), and were more likely to author an article (e.g., male directors, 71.0% vs. female directors, 42.1%).   **(241)**

Academic

■ A 1972 study of U.S. medical school libraries and other large biomedical libraries (collection of 35,000+ volumes and staff of 3 or more) concerning the status of women professionals (survey size: 160 libraries; responding: 143; usable: 140 or 87.5%) *showed that*, during the time span 1968-69 through 1973-74, women held 47.7% of all Medical Library Association positions, constituted 60% of the officers, 43.3% of the board members, 52.5% of the committee chairs or cochairs, and 35.6% of the delegates. Further, during the period 1950 to 1972, 14 women (and 9 men) served as MLA presidents.   **(709)**

Special

■ A 1972 study of U.S. medical school libraries and other large biomedical libraries (collection of 35,000+ volumes and staff of 3 or more)
concerning the status of women professionals (survey size: 160 libraries;
responding: 143; usable: 140 or 87.5%) *showed that*, during the time span
1968-69 through 1973-74, women held 47.7% of all Medical Library
Association positions, constituted 60% of the officers, 43.3% of the board
members, 52.5% of the committee chairs or cochairs, and 35.6% of the
delegates. Further, during the period 1950 to 1972, 14 women (and 9 men)
served as MLA presidents.   **(709)**

Gender Issues—Salaries

General

■ A study reported in 1979 of M.L.S. graduates from the University of
Toronto between 1972 and 1977 and the University of Western Ontario
between 1968-76 living in Canada (sample size: 300 males and 498 females;
responding: 172 or 57.3% males and 204 or 40.9% females) *showed that*,
although male salaries reported at the time of the study were more than
$1,200 higher than female salaries reported at the time of the study, the
difference was not statistically significant.   **(553)**

Ibid. . . . *showed that* there were statistically significant differences between male and female salaries immediately after graduation [neither
salary levels nor difference between them was reported] (significant at the
.057 level). However, male graduates tended to be older than female
graduates to a statistically significant degree [neither age of graduates nor
significance levels were reported], and substantially more of the males
(53%) had been employed on a full-time basis before obtaining their
M.L.S. than females (45%).   **(553)**

■ A 1980 survey of randomly selected American Library Association
personal members (sample size: 3,000 members; responding: 1,987 or
67.1%, including 1,583 full-time members employed at the time of the
survey, which provided the subsample analyzed here) *showed that* the
median salary for full-time employed women was $14,700 compared to
$19,500 for full-time employed men (women's median salaries were 75% of
men's median salaries). This suggests a widening of the salary differentials
between men and women since 1970, when an ALA salary survey

indicated a median women's salary of $10,400 compared to a median men's salary of $13,500 (women's median salaries were 77% of men's median salaries).   **(668)**

Ibid. . . . *showed that*, when salaries were analyzed in terms of earning power (adjusted on the basis of the Consumer Price Index) for the period 1970-79, overall membership salaries showed a decline in purchasing power of 25%. For women the decline in purchasing power was 29%.

(668)

Ibid. . . . *showed that*, in academic, public, and school libraries, the average annual salary for women was less than that for men. Specifically:

average academic library salary	$14,850 women; $20,520 men
average public library salary	$14,236 women; $19,319 men
average school library salary	$14,725 women; $18,692 men **(668)**

Ibid. . . . *showed that*, in both academic and public libraries [school libraries had too few males in the sample to compare], "even in circumstances where women and men publish at the same rate, supervise the same number of professionals or non-professionals, received the MLS at the same time, or are the same age, women are likely to earn lower salaries than men." (No statistical values or significance levels given.)   **(668)**

■ A study reported in 1981 of information on chief librarians generated in a 1975-76 survey of Canadian librarians in public, special, and academic libraries (study size: 96 chief librarians, including 49 females and 47 males) *showed that* females earned an average of $16,444, while males earned an average of $20,896. Further, higher male salaries held true for each library type (small public, medium public, large public, special library, small university library, and college library) except large university library, where no women chiefs were represented.   **(557)**

Academic

■ A 1975 survey of 530 (87% responding) academic librarians in 9 southern states out of a total academic librarian population of 1,964, investigating the relationship between job mobility and career advancement, *showed that*, of the respondents who had changed jobs, 91% had subsequently received a salary increase. The size of the increase, however, was related to the reasons for the move. Of those librarians who had moved for career reasons, 24% made salary gains of $8,000 or more; of those who moved for noncareer reasons, only 16% received salary increases of $8,000 or more. **(165)**

Ibid. . . . *showed that* on the average women librarians who had left their last positions for career-related reasons increased their salaries by $1,861 less than men who had also moved for career reasons. Women who left their positions for noncareer reasons increased their salaries (average increase $3,586) by $2,742 less than men (average increase $6,328) who left their positions for noncareer reasons. These are both statistically significant differences (no significance level given). **(165)**

Special

■ A preliminary analysis reported in 1976 of a survey of American Association of Law Libraries members (survey size: "approximately 2,000" individuals; responding: "approximately 1,400" or 70%, of which responses from 888 respondents were analyzed at the time of the report) *showed that* men made more money than women. Specifically, 58% of the respondents earned $15,000/year or less (including 80% women; 20% men), while 8% of the respondents earned $30,000/year or more (including 26% women; 74% men). **(793)**

Grant Proposals

Academic

■ A 1980 survey of academic librarians in Alabama, Georgia, and Mississippi concerning faculty status (sample size: 416; responding: 271; usable: 267 or 64.2%) *showed that*, during the 1979-80 academic year, the research, publication, and grant proposal activity was as follows (for the entire group of 267; multiple responses allowed):

a book published	3.4% respondents
a book review published	7.5% respondents
a literature review or bibliography published	4.1% respondents
a research article published	15.3% respondents
a presentation at a professional meeting	12.0% respondents
a research proposal developed	19.5% respondents
a research proposal funded	8.3% respondents **(502)**

Ibid. . . . *showed that* 12.0% of the respondents received release time for proposal development, while 14.2% received release time for research and publication.   **(502)**

Job Hunting

General

■ A survey in 1970 of all libraries of all types in the 3-county Detroit metropolitan area conducted by the Wayne State University Department of Library Science (116 libraries responding, including 57% of the school libraries, 94% of the academic libraries, 80% of the special libraries, and 92% of the public libraries) *showed that* 75% of all libraries of all types reported no preference for any particular age level, while 25% indicated their greatest need was for librarians under 35 years of age; the need for black librarians was reported only by the large public and school library systems; and 4 school districts and 10 public libraries reported their greatest need was for male librarians.   **(086)**

■ The experience of a single new 1976 library school graduate without previous experience in the 1976 job market applying for specifically advertised professional-level library openings by submittting a job-specific cover letter and resume *showed that* the following was the response rate to 206 applications:

TYPE OF LIBRARY	# LIBRARIES	# RESPONDING	(%)
academic	106	87	82%
public	48	35	73%
special	34	24	71%
federal	7	4	57%
state	6	5	83%
cooperative	5	5	100%
TOTAL	206	160	78%
			(average)

TYPE OF POSITION			
administrative	80	65	81%
reference	66	50	75%
acquisitions/technical			
services	30	22	73%
circulation	22	17	77%
cataloging	5	3	60%
media/microforms	3	3	100%
TOTAL	206	160	78%
			(average)
			(109)

Ibid. . . . *showed that* the following was the average wait for a response:

TYPE OF LIBRARY	# LIBRARIES	3 RESPONDING
academic	87	17
public	35	17
special	24	14
federal	4	45
state	5	10
cooperative	5	12
TOTAL	106	17 (average)

TYPE OF POSITION		
administrative	65	18
reference	50	19
acquisitions/technical services	22	14
circulation	17	14
cataloging	3	7
media/microforms	3	17
TOTAL	160	17 (average)

(109)

Ibid. . . . *showed that*, of the 160 libraries requesting further information, 33 (21%) requested formal applications, 24 (15%) requested references and 19 (12%) requested transcripts. However, almost all the employers offering extensive consideration did ask for references. **(109)**

Ibid. . . . *showed that*, of the 106 positions for which responses were received, the average wait was as follows:

TYPE OF LIBRARY	# LIBRARIES	AVERAGE WAIT (DAYS)
academic	52	44
public	26	37
special	18	25
federal	4	45
state	3	47
cooperative	3	26
TOTAL	106	39 (average)

TYPE OF POSITION		
administrative	44	42
reference	33	40
acquisitions/technical services	17	35
circulation	8	31
cataloging	2	31

continued

TYPE OF POSITION	# LIBRARIES	AVERAGE WAIT (DAYS)
media/microforms	2	21
TOTAL	106	39 (average)

(109)

■ A survey reported in 1977 of the larger employers of librarians in the state of Indiana, including academic, public, special, and school libraries (31 institutions or systems queried; 30 responding) *showed that* the top-ranked criteria for hiring (ranked #1 by 20 respondents) was how the candidate handled the personal interview. Further, 18 ranked work experience second or third, and 20 ranked recommendations from former employers second or third. 27 ranked library school grades as fourth, fifth, or sixth in importance. **(285)**

■ A study of academic job advertisements at 5-year intervals (1959, 1964, 1969, 1974, and 1979) over a 20-year period taken from 3 library journals (*Library Journal, ALA Bulletin/American Libraries*, and *College and Research Libraries/College and Research Libraries News*), excluding jobs that were primarily administrative or technical in nature for a total of 1,254 jobs, *showed that* overall the types of jobs available were as follows:

cataloger	362 jobs,	28.9% of total
reference librarian	246 jobs,	19.6% of total
subject specialist	178 jobs,	14.2% of total
general librarian	177 jobs,	14.1% of total
technical services librarian	158 jobs,	12.6% of total
branch head	56 jobs,	4.5% ot total
circulation librarian	53 jobs,	4.2% of total
rare book/special collections librarian	18 jobs,	1.4% of total
bibliographic instruction librarian	6 jobs,	.5% of total

(515)

Ibid. . . . *showed that*, in 1959, 48 (26.0%) of the jobs advertised required an M.L.S., of which only 9 (4.9%) of the jobs required an ALA-accredited M.L.S., while by 1979, 244 (97.6%) of the jobs required an M.L.S., of which 193 (77.2%) required an ALA-accredited M.L.S. **(515)**

Ibid. . . . *showed that*, in 1959, 70 (37.8%) of the jobs advertised required library experience, of which 20 (10.8%) required specialized experience, while by 1979, 171 (68.4%) of the jobs required library experience, of which 138 (55.2%) required specialized experience. **(515)**

Ibid. . . . *showed that*, in 1959, 1 (.5%) job required a subject master's degree and no particular subject was specified, while by 1979 69 (27.6%) of the jobs required a subject master's degree, of which 40 (16.0%) required a specific subject area. **(515)**

Ibid. . . . *showed that* generally the number of qualifications for professional jobs had increased during the 20-year period. Specifically, the number of jobs requiring:

a foreign language increased from 38 (20.5%) of the jobs in 1959 to 88 (35.2%) of the jobs in 1979;

computer expertise increased from 0 in 1959 to 103 (41.2%) of the jobs in 1979;

subject background increased from 20 (10.8%) of the jobs in 1959 to 81 (32.4%) of the jobs in 1979;

AV knowledge increased from 1 (.5%) of the jobs in 1959 to 18 (7.2%) of the jobs in 1979;

teaching experience increased from 2 (1.1%) of the jobs in 1959 to 11 (4.4%) of the jobs in 1979;

specific library expertise increased from 10 (5.4%) of the jobs in 1959 to 52 (20.8%) of the jobs in 1979;

communicative ability increased from 2 (1.1%) of the jobs in 1959 to 34 (13.6%) of the jobs in 1979;

administrative ability increased from 1 (.5%) job in 1959 to 28 (11.2%) of the jobs in 1979. **(515)**

■ A review of the help-wanted ads in *American Libraries* and *Library Journal* for odd-numbered years from 1961 through 1979 plus 1980 for all aspects of librarianship at all levels *showed that* from 1967 on the number of M.L.S.'s granted exceeded jobs advertised as follows:

YEAR	TOTAL ADS IN AL & LJ	INDEX	M.L.S. DEGREES GRANTED	INDEX
1961	2,826	100	1,931	100
1963	3,159	112	2,363	122
1965	3,673	130	3,211	166
1967	4,401	156	4,489	233
1969	3,171	112	5,932	307
1971	1,505	53	7,001	363
1973	1,071	38	7,696	393
1975	1,105	39	8,091	419
1977	1,215	43	7,572	392
1979	1,384	49	5,906	306
1980	1,508	53	5,374	278

(110)

■ A study reported in 1981 of academic job openings listed in *Library Journal* during the period 1970-79 (2,531 openings) *showed that* 1,237 (49%) were public service positions, 897 (35%) were technical services openings, and 397 (16%) were administrative openings. **(495)**

Ibid. . . . *showed that* a cyclical pattern of job availability took place during the decade, beginning with a decline in 1970-72 (from 263 positions in 1970 to 167 in 1972) followed by an upswing in 1973-76 (from 229 positions in 1973 to 354 positions in 1976), which was followed by another decline in 1977-79 (from 317 positions in 1977 to 200 positions in 1979). **(495)**

Ibid. . . . *showed that* the regional distribution of job openings listed generally corresponded to the distribution of academic librarians employed in that region (based on 1970 statistics) in the Southeast, Southwest, and West, while the Northeast had fewer openings compared to the number of academic librarians employed in that area and the Midwest had more. Specifically:

Northeast	26% openings	32% present positions
Southwest	15% openings	16% present positions
Midwest	33% openings	26% present positions
Southwest	10% openings	10% present positions
West	16% openings	16% present positions **(495)**

Academic

■ A 1977 survey of the cataloging department heads in the library of each of the universities with American Library Association accredited graduate library programs (survey size: 60 libraries; responding: 42 or 70%) *showed that* 25 (60%) respondents reported a preference to hire their catalogers just out of library school, while 8 (19%) required new cataloging employees to have at least 2 years of experience. 4 (9%) respondents reported they hired both new and experienced catalogers, while 5 (12%) did not answer the question. **(761)**

■ A survey reported in 1978 of 407 academic and public libraries who had filled professional positions (61% [no number given] responding with 233 or 57% usable responses) *showed that* there was an average of 73 applicants for each academic library position and 47 for each public library position. Broken down by level: entry level averaged 92 applicants per position for academic libraries and 65 for public libraries, departmental level averaged 58 applicants per academic library position and 36 per public library position, administrative level averaged 73 applicants per academic position and 50 per public position. **(227)**

Ibid. . . . *showed that* in academic libraries there was an average of 110 applicants per reference position, 109 per audiovisual position, 69 per acquisitions, and 55 per cataloging position [conflicting data given concerning circulation], while in public libraries there was an average of 31 applicants per cataloging position and 26 per reference position, with no data available for other positions. **(227)**

Ibid. . . . *showed that* over 50% of the respondents ranked the following factors "very" or "most" important in candidates' obtaining an interview: vita (60%), experience (56%), letters of recommendation (54%), initial application letter accompanying vita (52%). **(227)**

Ibid. . . . *showed that* the following factors were "very" or "most" important in making the final selection: knowledgeability (88%), ability to articulate this knowledge (79%), community relationship (62%), personality (42%), and appearance (33%). **(227)**

Ibid. . . . *showed that* respondents reported hiring someone known to a search committee member prior to the search in 25% of the academic library cases and 21% of the public library cases. **(227)**

Ibid. . . . *showed that* 71% of the academic libraries reported affirmative action of "somewhat" or "considerable" importance in the hiring process, compared to 41% of the public libraries so reporting. In both groups 5% of the positions were filled with ethnic minorities, and both groups estimated that about 5% of the applicant pool consisted of ethnic minorities. **(227)**

Ibid. . . . *showed that* in academic libraries females were hired in 47% of the cases with the pool estimated at 48%, while in public libraries 37% of the positions were filled by females out of an estimated pool of 30%. **(227)**

Ibid. . . . *showed that* in 66% of the cases the hiring institution paid either unconditionally or conditionally for the interview costs. (The condition usually meant the costs were paid unless the applicant turned down an offered position.) **(227)**

Ibid. . . . *showed that* 25% of respondents felt that the applicant should request letters of recommendation, 33% preferred for the committee to request them in their own way, 16% preferred letters sent only upon committee request, and 10% preferred phone references in lieu of letters.
(227)

■ A study of academic job advertisements at 5-year intervals (1959, 1964, 1969, 1974, and 1979) over a 20-year period taken from 3 library journals (*Library Journal, ALA Bulletin/American Libraries*, and *College and Research Libraries/College and Research Libraries News*), excluding jobs which were primarily administrative or technical in nature for a total of 1,254 jobs, *showed that* the percentage of advertised positions offering faculty status, while fluctuating, did not substantially change over the 20-year period. Specifically, in 1959, 85 (45.9%) of the positions indicated faculty status, while in 1979, 112 (44.8%) of the positions indicated faculty status.
(515)

Ibid. . . . *showed that* overall the types of jobs available were as follows:

cataloger	362 jobs,	28.9% of total
reference librarian	246 jobs,	19.6% of total
subject specialist	178 jobs,	14.2% of total
general librarian	177 jobs,	14.1% of total
technical services librarian	158 jobs,	12.6% of total
branch head	56 jobs,	4.5% ot total
circulation librarian	53 jobs,	4.2% of total
rare book/special collections librarian	18 jobs,	1.4% of total
bibliographic instruction librarian	6 jobs,	.5% of total **(515)**

Ibid. . . . *showed that*, in 1959, 48 (26.0%) of the jobs advertised required an M.L.S., of which only 9 (4.9%) of the jobs required an ALA-accredited M.L.S., while by 1979, 244 (97.6%) of the jobs required an M.L.S., of which 193 (77.2%) required an ALA-accredited M.L.S.   **(515)**

Ibid. . . . *showed that*, in 1959, 70 (37.8%) of the jobs advertised required library experience, of which 20 (10.8%) required specialized experience, while by 1979, 171 (68.4%) of the jobs required library experience, of which 138 (55.2%) required specialized experience.   **(515)**

Ibid. . . . *showed that*, in 1959, 1 (.5%) job required a subject master's degree and no particular subject was specified, while by 1979 69 (27.6%) of the jobs required a subject master's degree, of which 40 (16.0%) required a specific subject area. **(515)**

■ A 1979 survey of members of the ACRL Discussion Group of Personnel Officers (sample size: 45; responding: 30) concerning entry-level requirements for professionals *showed that* 24 out of 27 agreed that previous nonprofessional experience was an important requirement for an entry-level position. The "majority" also indicated that the experience should be in an academic library. **(240)**

Ibid. . . . *showed that* 4 respondents reported that a foreign language was required for entry-level positions in their libraries, 16 reported that it was "very important" or "helpful," while only 1 respondent reported it was unimportant. The languages most often required were Romance languages (26 respondents) or German (22 respondents). **(240)**

Ibid. . . . *showed that* 20 respondents reported cataloging as requiring a foreign language, 11 reported "some reference positions" requiring foreign languages, and 7 reported subject specialists positions requiring a foreign language. **(240)**

■ A survey reported in 1980 of the membership of the Association of College and Research Libraries Discussion Group of Personnel Officers of research libraries concerning the importance of resume elements (population: 54; responding: 38 or 70.4%) *showed that* the 10 resume elements rated most highly by respondents out of 43 were the following (listed in descending order of importance):

1. previous experience in librarianship
2. current address
3. telephone number
4. dates of employment in previous positions
5. brief description of duties in previous positions
6. colleges and universities attended
7. years degrees awarded
8. foreign-language skills
9. full chronological accounting for time after completion of education
10. list of references (names and addresses) **(483)**

Public

■ A survey reported in 1978 of 407 academic and public libraries who had filled professional positions (61% [no number given] responding with 233 or 57% usable responses) *showed that* there was an average of 73 applicants for each academic library positions and 47 for each public library position. Broken down by level: entry level averaged 92 applicants per position for academic libraries and 65 for public libraries, departmental level averaged 58 applicants per academic library position and 36 per public library position, administrative level averaged 73 applicants per academic position and 50 per public position. **(227)**

Ibid. . . . *showed that* in academic libraries there was an average of 110 applicants per reference position, 109 per audiovisual position, 69 per acquisitions, and 55 per cataloging position [conflicting data given concerning circulation], while in public libraries there was an average of 31 applicants per cataloging position and 26 per reference position, with no data available for other positions. **(227)**

Ibid. . . . *showed that* over 50% of the respondents ranked the following factors "very" or "most" important in candidates' obtaining an interview: vita (60%), experience (56%), letters of recommendation (54%), initial application letter accompanying vita (52%). **(227)**

Ibid. . . . *showed that* the following factors were "very" or "most" important in making the final selection: knowledgeability (88%), ability to articulate this knowledge (79%), community relationship (62%), personality (42%), and appearance (33%). **(227)**

Ibid. . . . *showed that* respondents reported hiring someone known to a search committee member prior to the search in 25% of the academic library cases and 21% of the public library cases. **(227)**

Ibid. . . . *showed that* 71% of the academic libraries reported affirmative action of "somewhat" or "considerable" importance in the hiring process, compared to 41% of the public libraries so reporting. In both groups 5% of the positions were filled with ethnic minorities, and both groups estimated that about 5% of the applicant pool consisted of ethnic minorities. **(227)**

Ibid. . . . *showed that* in academic libraries females were hired in 47% of the cases with the pool estimated at 48%, while in public libraries 37% of positions were filled by females out of an estimated pool of 30%. **(227)**

Ibid. . . . *showed that* in 66% of the cases the hiring institution paid either unconditionally or conditionally for the interview costs. (The condition usually meant the costs were paid unless the applicant turned down an offered position.) **(227)**

Ibid. . . . *showed that* 25% of respondents felt that the applicant should request letters of recommendation, 33% preferred for the committee to request them in their own way, 16% preferred letters sent only upon committee request, and 10% preferred phone references in lieu of letters.

(227)

Library Education—Participation of Field in

General

■ A 1979 survey of Canadian librarians in 3 groups (librarians who were or had been executives of a library or library-related associations in Canada; library administrators and department heads in public or academic libraries located within 20 miles of a library school; and library school full-time faculty) concerning the interaction [no time period given] between the library field and library schools (survey size: 120 association librarians, 120 library administrators, and [65] library school faculty; responding: 78 or 65% association librarians, 90 or 75% library administrators, and 43 or 66% library school faculty) *showed that* the number of direct contact activities between library school students and both groups of library practitioners (interviews, observation visits, tours, guest lecturers in classes, field work supervisor, etc.) averaged 3.3 activities per practitioner, with the following breakdown:

0 activities per practitioner	10% practitioners
1-2 activities per practitioner	27% practitioners
3-4 activities per practitioner	31% practitioners
5-8 activities per practitioner	32% practitioners **(554)**

Ibid. . . . *showed that* interaction related to course preparation (e.g., what elements should be included in a course, course assignments, examples from experience, etc.) averaged .8 activities per both groups of practitioners, with the following breakdown:

0 activities per practitioner	54% practitioners
1 activity per practitioner	23% practitioners
2 activities per practitioner	15% practitioners
3 activities per practitioner	8% practitioners **(554)**

Ibid. . . . *showed that* interaction related to degree programs (e.g., serving on an accreditation team, curriculum committee, etc.) was as follows:

54% of the practitioners had volunteered suggestions or recommended topics for the curriculum;

11% had been asked to review a program;

10% had sat on a curriculum or other library school committee;

and 3 respondents had served as members of an accreditation team. **(554)**

Ibid. . . . *showed that* interaction related to research, publication, and association work was as follows:

20% of the practitioners reported interaction with library school faculty on research;

14% of the practitioners reported interaction with the library school faculty in publications;

56% of the practitioners reported interaction with the library school faculty in association work. **(554)**

Ibid. . . . *showed that* interaction involving reciprocal activities (e.g., practitioners seeking information or assistance from library school faculty on an informal or formal basis, enrollment in continuing education courses, etc.) averaged 3.1 activities per practitioner, with a breakdown as follows:

0 activities per practitioner	7% practitioners
1-2 activities per practitioner	36% practitioners
3-4 activities per practitioner	33% practitioners
5-7 activities per practitioner	24% practitioners **(544)**

Ibid. . . . *showed that* interaction with practitioners reported by library school faculty in terms of course planning and presentation was as follows:

63% of the instructors consulted with practitioners concerning 3 elements: course elements, course assignments, and illustrations of theory;

80% of the instructors consulted with practitioners concerning 2 of the 3 elements listed above. **(554)**

Ibid. . . . *showed that* interaction with practitioners reported by library school faculty in terms of association work was as follows: 93% of the faculty reported they were active on association committees, while 86% of the faculty reported they were active in working on association conferences and programs. **(554)**

Ibid. . . . *showed that* 44% of the faculty members reported that practitioners had called upon them for information or advice 10 or more times in the past 3 years. **(554)**

Minority Issues

General

■ A 1980 survey of randomly selected American Library Association personal members (sample size: 3,000 members; responding: 1,987 or 67.1%, including 1,583 full-time members employed at the time of the survey, which provided the subsample analyzed here) *showed that* 93.6% of the ALA members were "white," while ethnic minorities constituted 6.4% of the membership. According to the 1970 census, 8.1% of the librarians were members of ethnic minorities. The major ethnic groups were represented in ALA membership in the following proportions:

whites: 93.6% of the total membership, including 93.6% of the males and 93.7% of the females;

blacks: 3.3% of the total membership, including 1.6% of the males and 3.9% of the females;

Asian-Americans: 1.9% of the total membership, including 2.9% of the males and 1.6% of the females;

Hispanics: 0.5% of the total membership, including .5% of the males and .6% of the females. **(668)**

Ibid. . . . *showed that*, in school and public libraries, black librarians earned "significantly" higher salaries than white librarians. (No absolute dollar figures, statistical values, or significance levels given.) [The authors note that they suspect that black librarians are underrepresented in the sample and that this finding may be spurious.] **(668)**

Academic

■ A 1980 survey of first-time-appointed academic library directors during the period 1970-80 (survey size: 230 directors; responding: 141 or 61.3%, including 98 males and 43 females) *showed that* ethnic background was as follows:

Asian-Americans accounted for 2 (1.4%) of the directors, including 2 (2.0%) of the males and none of the females;

Hispanics accounted for 2 (1.4%) of the directors, including 2 (2.0%) of the males and none of the females;

blacks accounted for 14 (10.0%) of the directors, including 7 (7.2%) of the males and 7 (9.3%) of the females;

whites accounted for 120 (85.1%) of the directors, including 85 (86.8%) of the males and 35 (81.4%) of the females;

3 individuals did not reply to the question. **(785)**

Professional Development—Institutionally Encouraged

General

■ A study reported in 1969 of 138 working librarians chosen as a stratified random sample from the 1956 and 1961 graduating classes of ALA-approved library schools *showed that*, regarding taking further formal course work:

> 33.4% felt their superiors opposed it
> 31.2% felt their administrators opposed it
> 18.8% felt their governing boards opposed it

and regarding informal professional improvement activities:

> 15.2% felt their superiors opposed it
> 16.7% felt their administrators opposed it
> 8.8% felt their governing boards opposed it   **(073)**

Academic

■ A 1964 survey of 60 private liberal arts colleges (49 responding) *showed that* 13 institutions gave sabbatical leave to all librarians; 8 gave it to the head librarian only; 2 gave it to the head librarian, assistant librarian, and department head; and 26 had no definite policy or did not answer the question. Where sabbaticals are granted, the most usual pattern is full pay for 1 semester or half pay for 2 semesters.   **(170)**

■ A survey reported in 1968 of all ARL directors plus all other state university library directors concerning the degree to which librarians participate in traditional faculty activities (72 responding) *showed that* library directors strongly favored or encouraged: writing and publication (100%), campus committee and similar assignments (100%), professional service on local, state and national basis (100%), consulting work (99%), research (97%), surveys (96%), leaves of absence (92%), participation in nonlibrary professional association work (92%), participation in nonprofessional local activities (89%), and teaching (71%).
(182)

Ibid. . . . *showed that* all respondents reported giving time for professional activities and 99% said they pay [some] expenses. 78% of respondents said they paid some expenses to national meetings for staff not on programs or committees.   **(182)**

Ibid. . . . *showed that* respondents from 43% of the institutions reported that librarians have been given leave for study or foreign assignments within the last 3 years. **(182)**

Ibid. . . . *showed that*, for participation in nonlibrary professional work, time off is given by 85% of the institutions but expenses are paid "probably to a very limited extent" by only 47%. **(182)**

Ibid. . . . *showed that*, for participation in nonprofessional local activities, 39% of respondents reported that they neither gave time nor any expenses. In terms of time alone, 59% of respondents gave it, while 39% did not. **(182)**

Ibid. . . . *showed that* 76% of respondents reported allowing time for research and 83% provided some sort of financial assistance. About 60% reported that the research need not be related to library operations or problems. **(182)**

■ A survey reported in 1975 of a stratified random sample of libraries of accredited 4-year colleges and universities to include small, medium, and large institutions based on student enrollment (sample size: 150; usable responses: 141 or 94%) *showed that*, of the responding libraries, more than 80% reported that no formal in-service training was provided for the nonprofessional reference staff. However, 70% of responding libraries indicated that nonprofessionals could take classes during the working day (time had to made up in 1/2 of those cases), 51% of the libraries indicated that tuition waivers are given nonprofessionals taking classes, and 74% of the libraries reported that nonprofessionals could attend professional library meetings during the working day. **(105)**

■ A survey reported in 1976 of the libraries in the largest private and largest public college/university in each state of the continental U.S. (sample size: 100[sic]; responding: 79 or 79%) *showed that* 82% of the responding libraries had established procedures for [requesting permission to] attend professional meetings. "Over 90%" of the respondents make both time and money available for such attendance, although 79% of respondents require that the meetings be work-related. **(413)**

Ibid. . . . *showed that* 59% of the respondents had formal procedures for [requesting attendance] at professional workshops, although 80% provide time and money. 84% of the respondents indicated that these workshops must be work-related. **(413)**

Ibid. . . . *showed that* 75% of the respondents reported money was available for [professional] library staff to take formal classes (the number of classes that may be taken is limited), but only 50% allow release time for this activity (and the classes must be work-related) and only 16% "encourage" attendance at institutions other than their own.   **(413)**

Ibid. . . . *showed that* 39% of the respondents report availability of in-service training, while only 27 respondents (36%) provide supervisory training for [professional] staff members.   **(413)**

■ A 1981 survey of U.S. depository libraries, both academic and public (sample size: 221; responding: 171 or 77%) concerning their use of online data bases (DIALOG, ORBIT, and BRS), particularly with regard to government documents, *showed that* 66% of the documents librarians in responding institutions had received no online training, 19% had received training in DIALOG, 4% had received training in ORBIT, 4% had received training in BRS, and 7% had received training in some combination of all 3 online data bases.   **(317)**

Public

■ A survey reported in 1976 of current practices of a diverse group of selected "community aware" public libraries in 25 states (68 responding libraries) *showed that* the number of libraries already providing in-service training for professional staff in different areas was as follows (multiple responses allowed): in community contacts, 41 (60%); in community study 35 (51%); in human relations, 34 (50%); in group process, 25 (36%); and in community development, 19 (28%).   **(215)**

Ibid. . . . *showed that* the number of libraries reporting that further in-service programs were needed for professionals in different areas was as follows (multiple responses allowed): in community contacts (34%), in community study (50%), in human relations (44%), in group process (40%), and in community development (50%).   **(215)**

■ A 1981 survey of U.S. depository libraries, both academic and public (sample size: 221; responding: 171 or 77%) concerning their use of online data bases (DIALOG, ORBIT, and BRS), particularly with regard to government documents, *showed that* 66% of the documents librarians in responding institutions had received no online training, 19% had received training in DIALOG, 4% had received training in ORBIT, 4% had received training in BRS, and 7% had received training in some combination of all 3 online data bases.   **(317)**

School

■ A survey reported in 1963 of principals of elementary schools in 50 states (sample size: 730; responding: 424 or 58%) *showed that* 326 (76.9%) of the respondents reported that their schools had a collection of professional periodicals and books. An additional 23 principals reported a professional collection of books but no periodicals and 36 reported a professional collection of periodicals but no books.   **(277)**

Ibid. . . . *showed that* the book collections ranged from 5 to 500 with the median between 46-50, with the range of new books added each year 0 to 32 and a median of 5.   **(277)**

Professional Development—Reading

Academic

■ 2 surveys, 1 conducted in 1973 (sample size: 300; responding: 259 or 86.3%) and then repeated in 1978 (sample size: 429; responding: 357 or 83.2%) of ACRL (Association of College and Research Libraries) academic librarians concerning professional reading *showed that* in 1973 the average number of library journals read regularly in the preceeding 12-month period was 5.78 (95% confidence interval was 5.4 to 6.2 journals), while in 1978 the average number of library journals read regularly in the preceeding 12-month period was 5.9 (95% confidence interval was 5.6 to 6.2 journals). The average number of nonlibrary professional journals read regularly in the preceeding 12-month period was 1.0 for 1973 and 1.3 for 1978.   **(508)**

Ibid. . . . *showed that* the 4 most frequently read journals in each of the 2 surveys were as follows:

IN 1973	READ BY
American Libraries	90.0% of sample
College and Research Libraries	86.1% of sample
Library Journal	69.9% of sample
Library Resources and Technical Services	57.9% of sample
IN 1978	READ BY
American Libraries	92.2% of sample

continued

IN 1978   READ BY
College and Research Libraries   88.6% of sample
Library Journal   69.3% of sample
Journal of Academic Librarianship 44.0% of sample   **(508)**

Professional Organizations

General

■ A review reported in 1969 of official ALA Annual Conference attendance and total membership during the period 1950 through 1967 *showed that*, on the average for the whole period, 18.8% of the membership (4,648 individuals) attended Annual Conference and that for the last 5 years of that period over 25% of the membership (about 7,500 individuals) attended Annual Conference.   **(076)**

■ A 1978 survey of full-time faculty in 7 Canadian graduate library schools (population: 81 faculty; survey size: 71 faculty; responding: 59 or 83%) *showed that* the 5 most frequently reported professional groups to which respondents belonged were (multiple responses allowed):

Canadian Library Association   40 (67.8%) respondents
American Library Association   27 (45.8%) respondents
Association of American Library
    Schools   18 (30.5%) respondents
American Society for Information
    Science   18 (30.5%) respondents
Canadian Association of Library
    Schools   18 (30.5%) respondents
                                                          (551)

■ A 1980 survey of randomly selected American Library Association personal members (sample size: 3,000 members; responding: 1,987 or 67.1%, including 1,583 full-time members employed at the time of the survey, which provided the subsample analyzed here) *showed that* men appeared to be more heavily represented in ALA membership than their overall numbers in librarianship would suggest, although the female/male ratio for graduates of ALA-approved programs was fairly close to the female/male ratio in ALA membership. Specifically, women made up 75.8% of the ALA membership that was currently [at the time of the survey] employed full-time, while men made up 24.1% of such membership. This compared to the full population of U.S. librarians as reported in the 1970 census, in which the ratio was 84% female to 16% male, while the average ratio of females to males obtaining degrees from ALA-accredited programs during the period 1972-80 was 79% females to 21% males.
                                                          (668)

Ibid. . . . *showed that* the median age of ALA members was 40 for women and 42 for men, with 42.4% of the women and 41.0% of the men over 45 years of age. **(668)**

Ibid. . . . *showed that* 93.6% of the ALA members were "white," while ethnic minorities constituted 6.4% of the membership. According to the 1970 census, 8.1% of the librarians were members of ethnic minorities. The major ethnic groups were represented in ALA membership in the following proportions:

whites: 93.6% of the total membership, including 93.6% of the males and 93.7% of the females;

blacks: 3.3% of the total membership, including 1.6% of the males and 3.9% of the females;

Asian-Americans: 1.9% of the total membership, including 2.9% of the males and 1.6% of the females;

Hispanics: 0.5% of the total membership, including .5% of the males and .6% of the females. **(668)**

Ibid. . . . *showed that* ALA membership by library type was as follows:

academic libraries	31.8% total membership
public libraries	28.8% total membership
school libraries	13.6% total membership
special and other libraries	25.8% total membership

This compares to the 1970 Bureau of Labor Statistics "universe of librarians" as follows:

school libraries	45.2% total librarians	
public libraries	23.0% total librarians	
academic libraries	17.0% total librarians	
special and other libraries	14.8% total librarians	**(668)**

Ibid. . . . *showed that* of ALA members, men tended to be concentrated in academic libraries while women tended to be concentrated in public libraries. Specifically, the proportion of male and female ALA members in different types of libraries was as follows:

in school libraries: 3.5% of the male ALA members and 17.0% of the female ALA members;

in public libraries: 22.8% of the male ALA members and 30.7% of the female ALA members;

in academic libraries: 44.6% of the male ALA members and 27.7% of the female ALA members;

in special and other libraries: 25.7% of the male ALA
members and 22.4% of the female ALA members;

in nonlibrary/other: 3.4% of the male ALA members and 2.2%
of the female ALA members.   **(668)**

Ibid. . . . *showed that*, while the majority of library directors in academic,
public, school, and special libraries were female (99 females vs. 77 men),
this represented 11.2% of all female librarians and 43.8% of all male
librarians. This imbalance continued through the administrative structure,
with 57.8% of the men holding positions at the director, assistant/associate
director, and department head level, compared to 32.7% of the women
holding such positions.   **(668)**

Ibid. . . . *showed that*, while women outnumbered men in all categories of
library positions on an absolute basis, a higher proportion of men were
found in director or associate/assistant director positions than their overall
numbers would suggest, while a higher proportion of women than their
numbers would suggest were found in public services, children's services,
as school librarians or media specialists. Gender representation was fairly
proportionate for department heads and in technical services. Specifically:

directors: 99 females compared to 77 males, representing
11.2% of the female respondents and 28.9% of the male
respondents;

associate/assitant directors: 157 females compared to 27 males,
representing 3.7% of the female respondents and 10.2% of the
male respondents;

department heads: 157 females compared to 50 males,
representing 17.8% of the female respondents and 18.7% of
the male respondents;

public services (other): 120 females compared to 24 males,
representing 13.5% of the female respondents and 9.0% of the
male respondents;

technical services (other): 53 females compared to 23 males,
representing 6.0% of the female respondents and 8.6% of the
male respondents;

school librarians: 17 females compared to 1 male, representing
1.9% of the female respondents and 0.4% of the male
respondents;

media specialists: 57 females compared to 6 males, representing
6.4% of the female respondents and 2.3% of the male
respondents;

children's services: 37 females compared to 1 male,
representing 4.2% of the female respondents and 0.4% of the
male respondents. **(668)**

Ibid. . . . *showed that* 38.5% of the males compared to 16.2% of the
females supervised 5 or more professionals, while 45.1% of the males
supervised 5 or more support staff, compared to 25.8% females. **(668)**

Ibid. . . . *showed that*, in terms of publishing books, articles, and book
reviews, men published "roughly 3 times as many books and book reviews
and 4 times as many articles as women." Specifically:

books: 5.2% of the female respondents compared to 17.1% of
the male respondents had published books;

articles: 24.9% of the females compared to 52.5% of the males
had published articles;

book reviews: 18.8% of the females compared to 35.7% of the
males had published articles. **(668)**

Ibid. . . . *showed that* the median salary for full-time employed women
was $14,700 compared to $19,500 for full-time employed men (women's
median salaries were 75% of men's median salaries). This suggests a
widening of the salary differentials between men and women since 1970,
when an ALA salary survey indicated a median women's salary of $10,400
compared to a median men's salary of $13,500 (women's median salaries
were 77% of men's median salaries). **(668)**

Ibid. . . . *showed that*, when salaries were analyzed in terms of earning
power (adjusted on the basis of the Consumer Price Index) for the period
1970-79, overall membership salaries showed a decline in purchasing
power of 25%. For women the decline in purchasing power was 29%. **(668)**

Ibid. . . . *showed that* proportionately more males than females were
involved in professional activities at the state, regional, and national level.
Specifically, the involvement in professional activities by gender was as
follows:

elected or appointed
at the national level   31.7% males; 14.6% females
chair of committee
section or division at
the national level   28.2% males; 12.1% females

continued

member of committee at the national level	63.2% males; 42.9% females
elected/appointed at the state/regional level	55.1% males; 38.7% females
chair of committee, section, division at state/regional level	49.9% males; 32.1% females
member of committee at state/regional level	71.9% males; 60.5% females **(668)**

Ibid. . . . *showed that* the average annual librarian's salary by type of library was as follows:

academic librarian	$16,710 average salary
public librarian	$15,300 average salary
special librarian	$15,120 average salary
school librarian	$14,700 average salary

These salary rankings have remained fairly constant since at least 1970, when the ALA salary survey showed the following average annual librarian's salary by type of library:

academic librarian	$12,523 average salary
special librarian	$12,084 average salary
public librarian	$11,135 average salary
school librarian	$10,623 average salary **(668)**

Ibid. . . . *showed that*, in academic, public, and school libraries, the average annual salary for women was less than that for men. Specifically:

average academic library salary	$14,850 women; $20,520 men
average public library salary	$14,236 women; $19,319 men
average school library salary	$14,725 women; $18,692 men **(668)**

Ibid. . . . *showed that*, in both academic and public libraries [school libraries had too few males in the sample to compare], "even in circumstances where women and men publish at the same rate, supervise the same number of professionals or non-professionals, received the MLS at the same time, or are the same age, women are likely to earn lower salaries than men." (No statistical values or significance levels given.)   **(668)**

Ibid. . . . *showed that*, in school and public libraries, black librarians earned "significantly" higher salaries than white librarians. (No absolute dollar figures, statistical values, or significance levels given.) [The authors note that they suspect that black librarians are underrepresented in the sample and that this finding may be spurious.] **(668)**

■ A study reported in 1981 of a portion of the COSWL data involving the responses of 739 personal members (195 men; 544 women) of the American Library Association who were at the time of the study employed in libraries and who had received their professional library degree prior to 1971 *showed that* at all comparable levels men were more likely than women to be elected or appointed to national association positions (e.g., male directors, 47.1% vs. female directors, 23.9%), were more likely to be elected or appointed to state or regional association positions (e.g., male directors, 82.6% vs. female directors, 73.3%), were more likely to author a book (e.g., male directors, 24.6% vs. female directors, 9.2%) and were more likely to author an article (e.g., male directors, 71.0% vs. female directors, 42.1%). **(241)**

Academic

■ A survey reported in 1968 of all ARL directors plus all other state university library directors concerning the degree to which librarians participated in traditional faculty activities (72 responding) *showed that* library directors strongly favored or encouraged: writing and publication (100%), campus committee and similar assignments (100%), professional service on local, state, and national basis (100%) consulting work (99%), research (97%), surveys (96%), leaves of absence (92%), participation in nonprofessional local activities (89%), and teaching (71%). **(182)**

Ibid. . . . *showed that* all respondents reported giving time for professional activities and 99% said they pay [some] expenses. 78% of respondents said they paid some expenses to national meetings for staff not on programs or committees. **(182)**

Ibid. . . . *showed that*, for participation in nonlibrary professional work, time off was given by 85% of the institutions but expenses are paid "probably to a very limited extent" by only 47%. **(182)**

■ A 1972 study of U.S. medical school libraries and other large biomedical libraries (collection of 35,000+ volumes and staff of 3 or more) concerning the status of women professionals (survey size: 160 libraries;

responding: 143; usable: 140 or 87.5%) *showed that*, during the time span 1968-69 through 1973-74, women held 47.7% of all Medical Library Association positions, constituted 60% of the officers, 43.3% of the board members, 52.5% of the committee chairs or cochairs, and 35.6% of the delegates. Further, during the period 1950 to 1972, 14 women (and 9 men) served as MLA presidents.   **(709)**

Special

■ A 1972 study of U.S. medical school libraries and other large biomedi- cal libraries (collection of 35,000+ volumes and staff of 3 or more) concerning the status of women professionals (survey size: 160 libraries; responding: 143; usable: 140 or 87.5%) *showed that*, during the time span 1968-69 through 1973-74, women held 47.7% of all Medical Library Association positions, constituted 60% of the officers, 43.3% of the board members, 52.5% of the committee chairs or cochairs, and 35.6% of the delegates. Further, during the period 1950 to 1972, 14 women (and 9 men) served as MLA presidents.   **(709)**

■ A preliminary analysis reported in 1976 of a survey of Ameri- can Association of Law Libraries members (survey size: "approxi- mately 2,000" individuals; responding: "approximately 1,400" or 70%, of which responses from 888 respondents were analyzed at the time of the report) *showed that* the membership appeared to consist of 68% women and 32% men. An earlier survey of AALL members in 1970 suggested that the membership consisted of 53% women and 36% men.
                                        (793)

Ibid. . . . *showed that* 50% of the men and 50% of the women re- spondents were head librarians. This compares to an earlier survey of AALL members in 1970, when 50% of the men were head librarians.
                                        (793)

Ibid. . . . *showed that* the library size (in volumes) in which respondents worked was as follows:

small (50,000 volumes or less)	41% respondents	
medium (50-100,000 volumes)	22% respondents	
large (100-200,000 volumes)	22% respondents	
very large (200,000 volumes or more)	15% respondents	**(793)**

Ibid. . . . *showed that* the type of library in which respondents worked was as follows:

law school libraries	45% respondents
bar or lawyer association libraries	5% respondents
law firm libraries	21% respondents
non-law firm libraries	6% respondents
government libraries	23% respondents

This represented a 10% drop in members employed in law school libraries and a 13% increase in members employed in law firms [from the earlier 1970 survey of AALL members]. **(793)**

Ibid. . . . *showed that* education of respondents was as follows:

graduate degrees in library science	50% respondents
degree in law	26% respondents
both of the above	17% respondents
working on 1 of the above	9% respondents

Since an earlier survey of AALL members in 1970, the number of members with law degrees had increased from 40% to 43%, the members holding both degrees decreased from 23% to 17%, and the members holding neither degree decreased from 25% to 16%. Further, AALL members who had completed a formal course in law librarianship or legal bibliography had increased to 54% compared to the 1970 survey. **(793)**

Ibid. . . . *showed that*, of the 45% who work in law schools, 46% have faculty status and 36% have faculty rank. Of those with faculty rank:

23% were professors (including 68% males; 32% females);

33% were associate professors (including 65% males; 35% females);

and 26% were assistant professors (including 53% males; 47% females). **(793)**

Ibid. . . . *showed that* the experience of the respondents (as law librarians) was as follows:

3 years or less	36% respondents
4-7 years experience	26% respondents
8-10 years experience	13% respondents
over 10 years experience	26% respondents

This is a younger group than indicated by an earlier survey of AALL members in 1970, which indicated that 46% respondents had over 10 years of experience while 22% had 3 years or less of law library experience. **(793)**

Ibid. . . . *showed that* men made more money than women. Specifically, 58% of the respondents earned $15,000/year or less (including 80% women; 20% men), while 8% of the respondents earned $30,000/year or more (including 26% women; 74% men).   **(793)**

Publication—Opportunities and Requirements

Academic

■ A survey reported in 1968 of all ARL directors plus all other state university library directors concerning the degree to which librarians participate in traditional faculty activities (72 responding) *showed that* library directors strongly favored or encouraged: writing and publication (100%), campus committee and similar assignments (100%), professional service on local, state, and national basis (100%) consulting work (99%), research (97%), surveys (96%), leaves of absence (92%), participation in nonprofessional local activities (89%) and teaching (71%).   **(182)**

■ A study reported in 1975 of the degree to which 2-year college libraries (sample size: 26; responding: 23) in the state of Ohio conformed to the "Guidelines for Two-Year College Learning Resources Programs" established by the ACRL Board of Directors in 1972 *showed that* in the majority of cases the professional staff had faculty rank, status, benefits, and responsibilities, although in very few cases was advanced study, research, or publication required.   **(127)**

■ A survey reported in 1980 of Association of Research Libraries directors in academic libraries (population: 94; responding: 68 or 72%) concerning publication requirements for professional library staff *showed that* publication by librarians was required in 10 (15%) institutions, was encouraged in 41 (60%) institutions, and not encouraged in 17 (25%) institutions. Of those institutions requiring publication, 2 (20%) required publication in the field of librarianship only, while 8 (80%) allowed publication in all disciplines.   **(480)**

Ibid. . . . *showed that* 7 (10%) institutions allowed specific release time for working on publications, 28 (41%) allow librarians to apply for release time for publications, and 33 (49%) do not allow release time for work on publications.   **(480)**

Ibid. . . . *showed that* (multiple responses allowed) 18 (23%) institutions provide funding for research within the library, 40 (51%) reported research funding is available from the university, and 20 (26%) reported that research funding is not available. **(480)**

■ A 1980 survey of academic librarians in Alabama, Georgia, and Mississippi concerning faculty status (sample size: 416; responding: 271; usable: 267 or 64.2%) *showed that*, of the 220 respondents who reported having faculty status, 18.6% reported that research publication was required for promotion or tenure while 75.9% reported that it was not. (5.5% did not reply.) **(502)**

Ibid. . . . *showed that* 12.0% of the respondents received release time for proposal development while 14.2% received release time for research and publication. **(502)**

Ibid. . . . *showed that* during the 1979-80 academic year the research, publication, and grant proposal activity was as follows (for the entire group of 267; multiple responses allowed):

a book published	3.4% respondents
a book review published	7.5% respondents
a literature review or bibliography published	4.1% respondents
a research article published	15.3% respondents
a presentation at a professional meeting	12.0% respondents
a research proposal developed	19.5% respondents
a research proposal funded	8.3% respondents **(502)**

■ A survey reported in 1981 of Association of Research Libraries directors concerning the acceptability of nonlibrary/information science publications in the promotion and tenure of academic librarians (population: 108; responding: 82 or 75.9%) *showed that* subject publications appeared to be more acceptable in large academic libraries than in smaller ones. Specifically, 9 out of 50 (18.0%) libraries with professional staffs less than 100 reported that publications in subject fields carried less or no value compared to library/information science publications, while none of the 13 libraries with professional staffs in excess of 100 rated subject publications as having less than equal weight with library/information science publications. **(503)**

Ibid. . . . *showed that* 13 (15.9%) respondents reported that publication was essential for promotion and tenure at their institution, 67 (81.7%) reported that publication was not essential for promotion and tenure, and 2 (2.4%) did not reply.   **(503)**

Ibid. . . . *showed that* the importance of publications in subject fields compared to publications in library/information science for the promotion and tenure of librarians was reported as follows:

more importance	2 (2.4%) respondents
same importance	54 (65.9%) respondents
less importance	4 (4.9%) respondents
no importance	5 (6.1%) respondents
no answer	17 (20.7%) respondents **(503)**

■ A survey reported in 1981 of library directors in 4-year colleges and universities in 7 Rocky Mountain states (survey size: 76; responding: 64 or 84%) concerning faculty status of librarians *showed that* only 2 (5%) respondents reported 9-month contracts for librarians, while 7 (18%) respondents reported that the publishing requirements were the same for the librarians as for the teaching faculty.   **(492)**

Publishing—Directors

Academic

■ A 1980 survey of first-time-appointed academic library directors during the period 1970-80 (survey size: 230 directors; responding: 141 or 61.3%, including 98 males and 43 females) *showed that* the numbers of publications in the 10 years prior to appointment to a directorship were as follows:

Books (141 respondents): 109 (77.3%) respondents reported no books published, including 74 (75.5%) males and 35 (81.4%) females; 22 (15.6%) respondents reported publishing 1 book, including 17 (17.3%) males and 5 (11.6%) females; and 10 (7.1%) respondents reported publishing 2 or more books, including 7 (7.1%) males and 3 (7.0%) females;

Chapters in books (136 respondents): 108 (79.4%) respondents reported no chapters in books published, including 74 (77.9%) males and 34 (82.9%) females, while 28 (20.6%) respondents reported publishing from 1 to 10 chapters;

Articles (137 respondents): 62 (45.3%) respondents reported publishing no articles, including 40 (41.7%) males and 22 (53.7%) females; 44 (32.1%) respondents reported publishing from 1-5 articles, including 33 (34.4%) males and 11 (26.8%) females; and 27 (19.7%) respondents reported 6-80 articles published, including 19 (19.8%) males and 8 (19.5%) females;

Book reviews (132 respondents): 73 (55.3%) respondents reported publishing no book reviews, including 47 (52.8%) males and 26 (60.5%) females; 44 (25.8%) respondents reported publishing 1-10 reviews, including 21 (23.6%) males and 13 (30.2%) females; and 25 (18.9%) respondents reported publishing 11-500+ reviews, including 21 (23.6%) males and 4 (9.3%) females. **(785)**

Publishing—General Patterns

General

■ A study reported in 1973 based on the journal articles listed in the 1967 volume of *Library Literature* (4,418 journal articles in 247 journals) *showed that* 136 (55%) journals were listed in *Library Literature*'s regular list of library-oriented journals, while 111 (45%) journals were nonlibrary journals. Of the 4,418 articles, 1,162 (26%) were 1 page or less in length.
(610)

Ibid. . . . *showed that*, of 3,420 selected articles in 242 journals (excluding news and announcements about people and conferences, etc.), the 6 most frequently cited journals were as follows:

Library Journal (incl. *School Library Journal*)	575 (16.8%) articles
Publisher's Weekly	149 (4.4%) articles
Wilson Library Bulletin	131 (3.8%) articles
Medical Library Association Bulletin	94 (2.7%) articles
ALA Bulletin (American Libraries)	88 (2.6%) articles
Library of Congress Information Bulletin	86 (2.5%) articles **(610)**

Ibid. . . . *showed that*, of the 3,420 articles, the 3 most frequently occurring subject areas were: administration (625 or 18.3% articles), literatures (401 or 11.7% articles), and professional education (290 or 8.5% articles).
(610)

Ibid. . . . *showed that*, of both total and selected articles, 5% of the journals produced "about 50% of the articles," while 20% of the journals produced 80% of the articles. The bottom 50% of the journals contributed only 5% of the articles.   **(610)**

■ A 1976 survey of 33 English-language library journals published in North America that accepted unsolicited manuscripts *showed that* overall there was a 2-month delay between when an article was submitted and when the author was notified of acceptance or rejection. Further, if the article was accepted, there was generally a 5-month delay between acceptance and publication.   **(254)**

Ibid. . . . *showed that*, in 1975, 746 unsolicited articles were published out of a pool of 3,292 unsolicited submissions, for an overall acceptance rate of 22.7%.   **(254)**

Ibid. . . . *showed that*, in 1975, unsolicited manuscripts accounted for 746 (68.1%) of the total articles published (1,095 articles), while solicited manuscripts accounted for 349 (31.9%) of the total articles published.
                                                                              (254)

Ibid. . . . *showed that*, of the 33 journals, 6 were refereed:
  Bulletin of the Medical Library Association
  Information Processing and Management
  Journal of the American Society for Information Science
  College and Research Libraries
  Journal of Education for Librarianship
  Special Libraries   **(254)**

■ A 1977 analysis of journal citations in the automation chapter of the *Annual Review of Information Science and Technology* for the 10 previous years (1,263 citations, 800 journal citations) *showed that* the 3 most cited journals were: *Journal of Library Automation* (114 citations), *Program* (56 citations), *Library Resources and Technical Services* (55 citations).   **(330)**

■ A study reported in 1977 based on the application of the Flesch readability index to 15 library science journals *showed that* only 1 library science periodical (*Library Trends*) out of 15 studied was written at a difficulty level commensurate with an audience with a master's degree education.   **(002)**

Ibid. . . . *showed that* application of the Flesch readability index to 15 major library science periodicals revealed a statistically significant positive relationship between readability and number of periodical subscriptions (Pearson r = .69; r2 = .476).   **(002)**

■ A study reported in 1979 of the English-language literature of library administration (2,877 citations to materials cited in 364 refereed articles indexed in *Library Literature* between 1961-70) *showed that*, of the 94 most cited journals (those containing 2 or more citations), 41 (43.6%) were in the discipline of library science, 7 (7.4%) were in the discipline of administration science, while 46 (49.0%) were in other disciplines. **(566)**

Ibid. . . . *showed that*, of 1,613 authors (including both personal and corporate authors), 391 (24%) were cited twice or more, while 1,222 (76%) were cited only once. Further, corporate authors were dispropor-tionately highly represented among the cited works. 7 corporate authors cited twice or more accounted for 478 citations [average of 68.3 citations each], while 384 personal authors cited twice or more accounted for 1,300 citations [average of 3.4 citations each].   **(566)**

Ibid. . . . *showed that*, of 254 journal titles containing 1,149 article cita-tions, 2 (.8%) journal titles contained 289 (25%) of the articles, 8 (3.15%) journal titles contained 575 (50%) of the articles, and 246 journal titles contained the remaining 574 articles.   **(566)**

Ibid. . . . *showed that* the 8 most frequently cited journals in the area of library administration were as follows:

Library Journal	165 (14.4%) citations
College and Research Libraries	124 (10.8%) citations
ALA Bulletin [American Libraries]	94 (8.2%) citations
Library Quarterly	50 (4.4%) citations
Library Trends	48 (4.2%) citations
Special Libraries	36 (3.1%) citations
Wilson Library Bulletin	29 (2.5%) citations
Medical Library Association Bulletin	28 (2.4%) citations **(566)**

■ A study reported in 1980-81 of methods of research in library science based on English-language articles appearing in 39 journals published in North America, Great Britain, or by international bodies for selected years during the period 1935-75 (involving 1,272 research papers out of 6,567 total papers) *showed that*, while the number of research papers generated annually increased regularly after 1945, the ratio of research to other papers did not begin to increase until after 1965. Specifically, the number of research papers increased from 51 per year in 1935 to 387 per year in 1975, while the percentage of research papers in the total number of papers produced each year generally fluctuated between 14-16% through 1965, rising to 24% in 1970 and 31% in 1975. **(569)**

Ibid. . . . *showed that*, of 900 research papers generated between 1950 and 1975 clearly within the area of library science research, the 6 most frequently used methodologies were as follows (some papers reflected more than 1 methodology and were counted more than once):

surveys/experiments on libraries	284 (32%)	of total
historical methodologies	163 (18%)	of total
information system design	150 (17%)	of total
theoretical/analytic	127 (14%)	of total
secondary analysis	76 (8%)	of total
surveys on the public	53 (6%)	of total **(569)**

Ibid. . . . *showed that*, of 900 research papers generated between 1950 and 1975 clearly within the area of library science research, the distribution of organizations studied was as follows:

college/university libraries	129 (14%)	of total
libraries, other and general	129 (14%)	of total
printing, publishing, and allied trade firms	116 (13%)	of total
special libraries	94 (10%)	of total
public libraries	52 (6%)	of total
information centers/institutes	57 (6%)	of total
school libraries	14 (2%)	of total
other	84 (9%)	of total
not related to any organization	225 (25%)	of total **(569)**

Ibid. . . . *showed that*, of 115 research papers on library users generated between 1950 and 1975 clearly within the area of library science research, there were no papers on the aged patron, 1 paper on the handicapped patron, and 6 papers on "other disadvantaged" patrons. **(569)**

■ A study reported in 1981 of citations in English-language research papers dealing with library science research appearing in 39 North American, British, or international journals for selected years during the period 1950-75 (716 papers; 5,334 citations) *showed that* the number of citations per research paper was as follows:

no citations	151 (21%)	papers
1-4 citations	183 (26%)	papers

continued

5-9 citations	174 (24%)	papers	
10-14 citations	104 (15%)	papers	
15 or more citations	104 (15%)	papers	**(571)**

Ibid. . . . *showed that* the average and median number of citations per paper increased over time. In 1950 the number of citations averaged 3.9 with a mean of 1.7, while by 1975 the number of citations averaged 8.7 with a mean of 5.8. **(571)**

Ibid. . . . *showed that*, of 4,596 citations to subject/discipline areas (excluding citations to bibliographies and official documents), 78% were to the area of library and information science. However, library science researchers showed an increasing interest in fields other than library and information science. The number of papers with no citations to subject/discipline areas outside of the library and information science field was as follows:

1950	84% no out-of-field citations
1960	71% no out-of-field citations
1965	66% no out-of-field citations
1970	65% no out-of-field citations
1975	62% no out-of-field citations	**(571)**

Ibid. . . . *showed that*, of 4,946 citations (excluding official documents), the distribution by form of publication was as follows:

journals	2,323 (47%)	citations	
books	1,387 (28%)	citations	
reports	713 (14%)	citations	
proceedings	185 (4%)	citations	
collective works	238 (5%)	citations	
theses	100 (2%)	citations	**(571)**

Ibid. . . . *showed that* 25% of the citations were 7 years old or older at the time the citing article was published. **(571)**

Academic

■ A survey reported in 1977 of publishing by professional librarians in 10 of the larger Association for Research Libraries libraries over a 5-year period (academic 1969-70 through 1973-74 or calander 1970-74), involving authors for 1,106 publications, *showed that* the 3 most heavily used vehicles for publication by professional librarians were: national library journals (14% of the publications excluding book reviews), national subject journals (13% of the publications excluding book reviews), and articles in books (10% of the publications excluding book reviews). Book reviews constituted 33% of the total sample publications. **(256)**

Ibid. . . . *showed that* in any given year a relatively small proportion of the professional library staff published. For the 10 libraries the number of professional librarians publishing in any given year ranged from 3.6% to 11.4%, with the overall average for all staffs at 7.2%. **(256)**

Ibid. . . . *showed that* for the total 5-year period the average number of publications per publishing librarian (excluding book reviews) ranged from 1.4 to 6.0, with the overall average 3.3 publications in 5 years. The median number of publications per publishing librarian (excluding book reviews) ranged from 1 to 2.5, with the overall median 1 publication in 5 years.
(256)

■ A 1980 survey of academic librarians in Alabama, Georgia, and Mississippi concerning faculty status (sample size: 416; responding: 271; usable: 267 or 64.2%) *showed that* during the 1979-80 academic year the research, publication, and grant proposal activity was as follows (for the entire group of 267; multiple responses allowed):

a book published	3.4% respondents
a book review published	7.5% respondents
a literature review or bibliography published	4.1% respondents
a research article published	15.3% respondents
a presentation at a professional meeting	12.0% respondents
a research proposal developed	19.5% respondents
a research proposal funded	8.3% respondents **(502)**

■ A 1980 survey of first-time-appointed academic library directors during the period 1970-80 (survey size: 230 directors; responding: 141 or 61.3%, including 98 males and 43 females) *showed that* the numbers of publications in the 10 years prior to appointment to a directorship were as follows:

Books (141 respondents): 109 (77.3%) respondents reported no books published, including 74 (75.5%) males and 35 (81.4%) females; 22 (15.6%) respondents reported publishing 1 book, including 17 (17.3%) males and 5 (11.6%) females; and 10 (7.1%) respondents reported publishing 2 or more books, including 7 (7.1%) males and 3 (7.0%) females;

Chapters in books (136 respondents): 108 (79.4%) respondents reported no chapters in books published, including 74 (77.9%) males and 34 (82.9%) females, while 28 (20.6%) respondents reported publishing from 1 to 10 chapters;

Articles (137 respondents): 62 (45.3%) respondents reported publishing no articles, including 40 (41.7%) males and 22 (53.7%) females; 44 (32.1%) respondents reported publishing from 1-5 articles, including 33 (34.4%) males and 11 (26.8%) females; and 27 (19.7%) respondents reported 6-80 articles published, including 19 (19.8%) males and 8 (19.5%) females;

Book reviews (132 respondents): 73 (55.3%) respondents reported publishing no book reviews, including 47 (52.8%) males and 26 (60.5%) females; 44 (25.8%) respondents reported publishing 1-10 reviews, including 21 (23.6%) males and 13 (30.2%) females; and 25 (18.9%) respondents reported publishing 11-500+ reviews, including 21 (23.6%) males and 4 (9.3%) females. **(785)**

■ A survey reported in 1981 of Association of Research Libraries directors concerning the acceptability of nonlibrary/information science publications in the promotion and tenure of academic librarians (population: 108; responding: 82 or 75.9%) *showed that* the importance of publications in subject fields compared to publications in library/ information science for the promotion and tenure of librarians was reported as follows:

more importance	2 (2.4%)	respondents
same importance	54 (65.9%)	respondents
less importance	4 (4.9%)	respondents
no importance	5 (6.1%)	respondents
no answer	17 (20.7%)	respondents **(503)**

Ibid. . . . *showed that* subject publications appeared to be more acceptable in large academic libraries than in smaller ones. Specifically, 9 out of 50 (18.0%) libraries with professional staffs less than 100 reported that publications in subject fields carried less or no value compared to library/ information science publications while none of the 13 libraries with professional staffs in excess of 100 rated subject publications as having less than equal weight with library/information science publications. **(503)**

■ A study reported in 1982 of publication and citation patterns in *College and Research Libraries* during the 40 years between 1939-79, involving 1,775 articles, *showed that* between the first 5-year period (1939-44) and the last (1975-79) the percentage of articles without references [footnotes] dropped from 45 to 9, while the average number of references [footnotes] increased from an average of 2.89 per article to 15.46 per article. In the last 15 years the average number of references per article in *College and Research Libraries* "either approached or fell into the norm of 10 to 22 for scientific literature." **(511)**

Ibid. . . . *showed that* the topics treated during this period were as follows:

organization and administration	33.6% of total
general topics	18.7% of total
resources	14.3% of total
public services	13.7% of total
technical services	12.6% of total
automation/information retrieval	4.1% of total
library instruction	2.1% of total
photoreproduction	0.9% of total **(511)**

Ibid. . . . *showed that* the 3 most frequently cited journals by articles in *College and Research Libraries* were (5,205 citations):

College and Research Libraries	1,001 (19.23%) citations
Library Journal	550 (10.57%) citations
Library Quarterly	379 (7.28%) citations

10 journals (1.6% of the total number of journals cited) provided almost 55% of the total journal citations. **(511)**

Ibid. . . . *showed that*, of 11,658 citations to materials in *College and Research Libraries* articles, periodicals accounted for 5,205 (44.65%) citations, monographs accounted for 4,245 (36.41%) citations, and U.S. government publications accounted for 464 (3.98%) citations. **(511)**

Special

■ A 1978 study undertaken by the National Library of Medicine to investigate patterns and methods of communicating results of grant activities during the period 1970-77 (population: 344 grantees, including 35 library research grantees, 130 library project grantees, and 179 library improvement grantees; responding: 222 or 65%) *showed that*, based on a total of 783 communications reported, the average number of communications (both written and oral presentations) per grantee by type of grant was as follows:

library research grant 9.6 communications per grantee
library resource project 4.2 communications per grantee
library resource improvement .4 communications per grantee **(728)**

Ibid. . . . *showed that* the distribution of type of communication was as follows:

audiovisual	7 (.9%)	communications
book	20 (2.6%)	communications
chapter in book	25 (3.2%)	communications
thesis	30 (3.8%)	communications
newsletter or in-house report	99 (12.6%)	communications
report or proceeding	107 (13.7%)	communications
journal article	175 (22.3%)	communications
oral presentation	320 (40.9%)	communications **(728)**

Publishing—Gender Issues

General

■ A study reported in 1980 of authorship in 5 library periodicals over a 10-year period primarily in the 1970s (*College and Research Libraries, Library Journal, Library Quarterly, Library Trends*, and *RQ*) *showed that* authorship by gender was as follows:

College and Research Libraries (446 articles)	30.5% women; 69.5% men
Library Journal (872 articles)	37.5% women; 62.5% men
Library Quarterly (241 articles)	21.2% women; 78.8% men
Library Trends (422 articles)	32.7% women; 67.3% men
RQ (424 articles)	41.3% women; 58.7% men

Overall, in the profession women constituted 84% of the librarians and men 16% of the librarians. **(481)**

■ A 1980 survey of randomly selected American Library Association personal members (sample size: 3,000 members; responding: 1,987 or 67.1%, including 1,583 full-time members employed at the time of the survey, which provided the subsample analyzed here) *showed that*, in terms of publishing books, articles, and book reviews, men published "roughly 3 times as many books and book reviews and 4 times as many articles as women." Specifically:

books: 5.2% of the female respondents compared to 17.1% of the male respondents had published books;

articles: 24.9% of the females compared to 52.5% of the males had published articles;

book reviews: 18.8% of the females compared to 35.7% of the males had published articles. **(668)**

■ A study reported in 1981 of articles submitted to and published in *Library Resources and Technical Services* during the period 1957 through 1980 concerning author characteristics *showed that* the gender distribution for those published articles for which the author's gender could be determined was as follows:

1957-67 (580 articles)	36.7% women; 63.3% men
1968-77 (428 articles)	38.6% women; 61.4% men
1978-80 (109 articles)	45.0% women; 55.0% men **(763)**

Ibid. . . . *showed that*, of the papers submitted for publication during the period July 1979-June 1980 for which author gender could be determined, the majority of the papers accepted involved female authorship, while the majority of the papers rejected involved male authorship. Specifically, 33 papers were accepted (51.5% female authors; 48.5% male authors) and 49 papers were not accepted (42.9% female authors; 57.1% male authors). **(763)**

■ A study reported in 1982 of authorship of articles in the *Canadian Library Journal* during the period 1968 through 1980, involving 545 articles, *showed that*, for the 517 articles for which gender could be determined, women contributed 50.1% of the articles compared to 49.9% contributed by men. Nationally, women constituted 76.4% of the library professionals in Canada and men 23.6% based on the 1971 *Census of Canada*. Further, for the period 1968-77 (see citation 481), women contributed 48.1% of 416 articles compared to 51.9% contributed by men. For the period 1978-80 women contributed 58.4% of 101 articles compared to 41.6% contributed by men. **(298)**

Ibid. . . . *showed that*, for the 115 articles contributed by academic librarians for which gender could be determined, women contributed 34.8% of the articles compared to 65.2% contributed by men. Further, for the period 1968-77 (see citation 481), women contributed 33.3% of 99 articles compared to 66.7% contributed by men. **(298)**

Ibid. . . . *showed that*, for the 67 articles contributed by library science faculty for which gender could be determined, women contributed 43.3% of the articles compared to 56.7% of the articles contributed by men. According to *Teachers in Universities*, 1977-78, women constituted 48.4% of the Canadian library school faculty and men 51.6%. Further, for the period 1968-77 (see citation 481), women contributed 38.3% of the articles compared to 61.7% contributed by men. **(298)**

Academic

■ A study reported in 1980 of authorship in 5 library periodicals over a 10-year period primarily in the 1970s (*College and Research Libraries, Library Journal, Library Quarterly, Library Trends*, and *RQ*) *showed that* gender of authorship by academic librarians only was as follows:

College and Research	
Libraries (225 articles)	39.6% women; 60.4% men
Library Journal (163 articles)	25.1% women; 74.9% men
Library Quarterly (45 articles)	31.1% women; 68.9% men
Library Trends (101 articles)	24.7% women; 75.3% men
RQ (147 articles)	35.4% women; 64.6% men

Overall, 61.5% of the academic librarians were women, while 38.5% were men. **(481)**

■ A 1980 survey of first-time-appointed academic library directors during the period 1970-80 (survey size: 230 directors; responding: 141 or 61.3%, including 98 males and 43 females) *showed that* the number of publications in the 10 years prior to appointment of a directorship were as follows:

Books (141 respondents): 109 (77.3%) respondents reported no books published, including 74 (75.5%) males and 35 (81.4%) females; 22 (15.6%) respondents reported publishing 1 book, including 17 (17.3%) males and 5 (11.6%) females; and 10 (7.1%) respondents reported publishing 2 or more books, including 7 (7.1%) males and 3 (7.0%) females;

Chapters in books (136 respondents): 108 (79.4%) respondents reported no chapters in books published, including 74 (77.9%) males and 34 (82.9%) females, while 28 (20.6%) respondents reported publishing from 1 to 10 chapters;

Articles (137 respondents): 62 (45.3%) respondents reported

publishing no articles, including 40 (41.7%) males and 22 (53.7%) females; 44 (32.1%) respondents reported publishing from 1-5 articles, including 33 (34.4%) males and 11 (26.8%) females; and 27 (19.7%) respondents reported 6-80 articles published, including 19 (19.8%) males and 8 (19.5%) females;

Book reviews (132 respondents): 73 (55.3%) respondents reported publishing no book reviews, including 47 (52.8%) males and 26 (60.5%) females; 44 (25.8%) respondents reported publishing 1-10 reviews, including 21 (23.6%) males and 13 (30.2%) females; and 25 (18.9%) respondents reported publishing 11-500+ reviews, including 21 (23.6%) males and 4 (9.3%) females.   **(785)**

■ A study reported in 1982 of publication and citation patterns in *College and Research Libraries* during the 40 years between 1939-79, involving 1,775 articles, *showed that*, of 1,768 articles where gender of the principal author was known, males represented 78.85% of the authors and females 21.15%. This ratio was fairly stable, with male authorship ranging during the 8 5-year periods from 77% to 87%.   **(511)**

Special

■ A study reported in 1981 of authorship in 5 journals in special librarianship over a 10-year period (generally the decade of the 1970s) or over the life of the journal if it had not been published for a 10-year period *showed that* the gender of authors was as follows:

Journal of the American Society for Information Science (ASIS) (651 articles)	76.5% male; 23.5% female
Law Library Journal (313 articles)	58.8% male; 41.2% female
Bulletin of the Medical Library Association (657 articles)	43.1% male; 56.9% female
Online Review (150 articles)	40.7% male; 59.3% female
Special Libraries (747 articles)	52.5% male; 47.5% female

                                                       (496)

Ibid. . . . *showed that* a comparison of author gender with an earlier study of author gender in general library periodicals as well as with gender of special librarian and overall librarian populations (based on government figures published in *Library Manpower: A Study of Demand and Supply*, 1975) was as follows:

authors in Olsgaard study (see
   citation 481)   65.6% male; 34.4% female
authors in special library
   journals   56.3% male; 43.7% female
special librarian population   24.1% male; 75.9% female
overall librarian population   16.0% male; 84.0% female

(496)

■ A study reported in 1981 of approximately 10 years of articles published in the 1970s in 5 special library periodicals *showed that*:

of 313 authors in the *Law Library Journal* 58.8% of the authors were male;

of 651 authors in *Journal of the American Society for Information Science* 76.5% of the authors were male;

of 657 authors in *Bulletin of the Medical Library Association* 43.1% were male;

of 150 authors in *Online* (only 3 years considered) 40.7% were male;

and of 747 authors in *Special Libraries* 52.5% were male. **(372)**

Ibid. . . . *showed that* overall 56.3% of the authors in the 5 special library periodicals were male, compared to the national population of special librarians, which was 24.1% male. Further, 58.8% of the authors in the *Law Library Journal* were male, compared to 28.6% of the membership of the American Association of Law Libraries that was male. **(372)**

Ibid. . . . *showed that* there appeared to be no correlation between gender of editors and gender of authors; for example, the *Bulletin of the Medical Library Association* had 100% male editors, while 56.9% of its authors were female, compared to *Special Libraries*, which had 93% female editors, while 52.5% of its authors were male. **(372)**

Ibid. . . . *showed that* female authorship increased by 1.8% per year for *Law Library Journal*, by 2.66% per year for *Bulletin of the Medical Library Association*, and by 4.3% per year for *Special Libraries*. **(372)**

■ A study reported in 1982 of author characteristics in 5 special library journals (*Special Libraries, Journal of the American Society for Information Science, Law Library Journal, Bulletin of the Medical Library Association*, and *Online Review*) over a 10-year period (except for *Online*, which began in 1977) *showed that* 52.5% of the authors selected for publication in *Special Libraries* were male while 47.5% were female. A 10% sample of Special Libraries Association membership indicated that 20.8% were male and 79.2% were female.   **(438)**

Ibid. . . . *showed that* female authorship in *Special Libraries* increased 4.3% per year (during 1970-79) while increasing 1.8% per year (during 1969-78) in *Law Libraries Journal* and 2.7% per year (during 1969-78) in the *Bulletin of the Medical Library Association*.   **(438)**

Ibid. . . . *showed that* no correlation could be found between editor gender and sexual balance of authorship in the journals.   **(438)**

Publishing—Geographical Distribution

General

■ A study reported in 1980 of authorship in 5 library periodicals over a 10-year period primarily in the 1970s (*College and Research Libraries, Library Journal, Library Quarterly, Library Trends*, and *RQ*) *showed that* overall the number of authors from the Northeast and Midwest tended to be higher than the number of librarians in those areas would suggest, while the reverse was true of authors in the Southeast and Southwest. The number of authors from the West and the number of librarians in the West was roughly proportionate.   **(481)**

■ A study reported in 1981 of articles submitted to and published in *Library Resources and Technical Services* during the period 1957 through 1980 concerning author characteristics *showed that* the geographic distribution of the authorship of published articles when that could be determined (1957-67: 529 articles; 1968-77: 404 articles; and 1978-80: 105 articles) was as follows:

northeast authors accounted for 49.5%, 40.8%, and 37.1% of the 1957-67, 1968-77, and 1978-80 articles, respectively.

southeast authors accounted for 7.9%, 8.2%, and 12.4% of the 1957-67, 1968-77, and 1978-80 articles, respectively;

midwest authors accounted for 22.3%, 20.0%, and 28.6% of the 1957-67, 1968-77, and 1978-80 articles, respectively;

southwest authors accounted for 1.7%, 6.9%, and 5.7% of the 1957-67, 1968-77, and 1978-80 articles, respectively;

western authors accounted for 18.5%, 24.0%, and 16.2% of the 1957-67, 1968-77, and 1978-80 articles, respectively. **(763)**

Ibid. . . . *showed that* the papers submitted for publication during the period July 1979-June 1980 for which the author's geographic region could be determined (32 papers accepted; 46 papers not accepted) were distributed as follows:

northeastern authors accounted for 40.6% of the accepted articles and 34.8% of the rejected articles;

southeastern authors accounted for 18.8% of the accepted articles and 17.4% of the rejected articles;

midwestern authors accounted for 18.8% of the accepted articles and 19.6% of the rejected articles;

southwestern authors accounted for none of the accepted articles and 4.3% of the rejected articles;

western authors accounted for 21.9% of the accepted articles and 23.9% of the rejected articles. **(763)**

■ A study reported in 1982 of authorship of articles in the *Canadian Library Journal* during the period 1968 through 1980, involving 545 articles, *showed that*, for the 485 articles for which the author's location could be determined, the geographic distribution was as follows (percentage of Canadian librarians per province as reported in 1971 *Census of Canada* is also indicated):

Ontario	60.8% articles;	40.1% librarians
British Columbia	9.7% articles;	10.3% librarians
Saskatchewan	6.4% articles;	2.4% librarians
Manitoba	6.4% articles;	2.9% librarians
Alberta	6.2% articles;	6.0% librarians
Quebec	3.9% articles;	32.2% librarians
Nova Scotia	2.9% articles;	3.6% librarians
Newfoundland	2.1% articles;	0.8% librarians
New Brunswick	1.4% articles;	1.2% librarians
Northwest Territories	0.2% articles;	0.1% librarians
Prince Edward Island	0.0% articles;	0.3% librarians **(298)**

Special

■ A study of approximately 10 years of articles published in the 1970s in 5 special library periodicals *showed that* overall for the 5 special library periodicals 42.0% of the authors lived in the Northeast, 9.2% lived in the

Southeast, 25.9% lived in the Midwest, 6.0% lived in the Southwest, and 16.9% lived in the West.   **(372)**

Ibid. . . . *showed that* 28.1% of the authors published in the *Law Library Journal* lived in the West, although 19.3% of the membership of the American Association of Law Libraries lived in the West.   **(372)**

Publishing—Historical Patterns

Special

■ A study reported in 1982 of publishing activities of members of the American Association of Law Libraries in the *Law Library Journal* (volumes 59 through 72; 1966-79) *showed that* there was a steady increase in the percentage of contributions by law librarians, beginning with 48.4% of the contributions in 1966 and becoming 86.8% of the contributions by 1979.   **(374)**

Ibid. . . . *showed that* the percent of AALL members who were contributors remained fairly steady over this period, ranging from 1.4% of the total membership to 5.1% of the total membership and beginning with 3.8% of the total membership in 1966 and concluding with 1.4% of the total membership in 1979.   **(374)**

Publishing—Occupation

General

■ A study reported in 1980 of authorship in 5 library periodicals over a 10-year period primarily in the 1970s (*College and Research Libraries, Library Journal, Library Quarterly, Library Trends*, and *RQ*) *showed that* the occupations of authors ranged as follows for the 5 periodicals:

academic librarians	18.9% to 51.6%
public librarians	1.7% to 16.3%
other librarians	2.5% to 9.4%
library science faculty	16.6% to 30.4%
library science student	0.5% to 4.0%
other faculty	4.4% to 17.0%
other (nonlibrarian/nonfaculty)	11.3% to 28.9% **(481)**

■ A study reported in 1981 of articles submitted to and published in *Library Resources and Technical Services* during the period 1957 through

1980 concerning author characteristics *showed that* the occupations of authors for those published articles where it could be determined (1957-67: 575 articles; 1968-77: 447 articles; and 1978-80: 108 articles) were as follows:

academic librarians accounted for 46.4%, 54.8%, and 54.6% of the 1957-67, 1968-77, and 1978-80 articles, respectively.

public librarians accounted for 13.0%, 3.1%, and 3.7% of the 1957-67, 1968-77, and 1978-80 articles, respectively;

other librarians accounted for 16.9%, 16.3%, and 9.2% of the 1957-67, 1968-77, and 1978-80 articles, respectively;

library science faculty accounted for 14.1%, 16.5%, and 21.3% of the 1957-67, 1968-77, and 1978-80 articles, respectively;

library science students accounted for 1.0%, 1.3%, and 0.0% of the 1957-67, 1968-77, and 1978-80 articles, respectively;

other faculty accounted for 0.9%, 1.8%, and 0.9% of the 1957-67, 1968-77, and 1978-80 articles, respectively;

nonlibrarian/nonacademic individuals accounted for 8.5%, 6.9%, and 10.2% of the 1957-67, 1968-77, and 1978-80 articles, respectively. **(763)**

Ibid. . . . *showed that* the papers submitted for publication during the period July 1979-June 1980 for which author occupation could be determined (32 papers accepted; 42 not accepted) were distributed as follows:

academic librarians accounted for 37.5% of the accepted papers and 73.8% of the rejected papers;

public librarians accounted for 3.1% of the accepted papers and 2.4% of the rejected papers;

other librarians accounted for 15.6% of the accepted papers and 4.8% of the rejected papers;

library science faculty accounted for 25.0% of the accepted papers and 9.5% of the rejected papers;

library science students and other faculty submitted no papers;

nonlibrarian/nonacademic individuals accounted for 18.8% of the accepted papers and 9.5% of the rejected papers. **(763)**

■ A study reported in 1982 of authorship of articles in the *Canadian Library Journal* during the period 1968 through 1980, involving 545 articles, *showed that*, for the 477 articles for which author occupation could be determined, occupational distribution was as follows:

academic librarian	25.6% of total articles
public librarian	17.0% of total articles
other librarian	21.0% of total articles
library science faculty	14.5% of total articles
library science student	3.8% of total articles
other faculty	4.0% of total articles
nonlibrarian/nonacademic	14.3% of total articles

Further, for the 385 articles for which author occupation could be determined for the period 1968-77 (see citation 481), occupational distribution was as follows:

academic librarian	27.5% of total articles
public librarian	18.4% of total articles
other librarian	19.7% of total articles
library science faculty	12.7% of total articles
library science student	3.4% of total articles
other faculty	4.2% of total articles
nonlibrarian/nonacademic	14.0% of total articles **(298)**

Academic

■ A study reported in 1982 of publication and citation patterns in *College and Research Libraries* during the 40 years between 1939-79, involving 1,775 articles, *showed that* the 4 most frequent types of institutions with which authors were affiliated were:

academic libraries	1,042 articles (58.70%)
other (nonlibraries)	200 articles (11.27%)
library schools	152 articles (8.56%)
government libraries	111 articles (6.25%) **(511)**

■ A study reported in 1982 of authorship of articles in the *Canadian Library Journal* during the period 1968 through 1980, involving 545 articles, *showed that*, for the 112 articles by academic librarians whose position could be determined, the position distribution was as follows:

administrators	55.4% of total articles
supervised generalist	24.1% of total articles
branch/department head	13.4% of total articles
subject/technical specialist	7.1% of total articles **(298)**

Special

■ A study reported in 1981 of authorship in 5 journals in special librarianship over a 10-year period (generally the decade of the 1970s) or over the life of the journal if it had not been published for a 10-year period *showed that* the occupation of authors contributing articles broke down as follows:

academic	5.8% of total
library science faculty	10.3% of total
special librarians	41.6% of total
other librarians	3.3% of total
other faculty	5.4% of total
information supplier	4.7% of total
private/government	15.3% of total **(496)**

■ A study reported in 1981 of approximately 10 years of articles published in the 1970s in 5 special library periodicals *showed that* the occupation of authors in the *Law Library Journal* was as follows:

special librarians	62.6%
other faculty and graduate students	21.9%
nonlibrary private/government	9.3%
other librarians and library school students	2.5%
academic librarians	1.6%
information suppliers, brokers, etc.	1.1%
library science faculty	1.1% **(372)**

■ A study reported in 1982 of author characteristics in 5 special library journals (*Special Libraries, Journal of the American Society for Information Science, Law Library Journal, Bulletin of the Medical Library Association*, and *Online Review*) over a 10-year period (except for *Online* which began in 1977) *showed that* the 4 most frequent occupations of *Special Libraries* authors were: special librarian (43.8% authors), private/government librarians (16.4% authors), academic librarian (13.6% authors), and library science faculty (11.4% authors). **(438)**

Publishing—Other Author Characteristics

General

■ A study reported in 1979 of the English-language literature of library administration (2,877 citations to materials cited in 364 refereed articles indexed in *Library Literature* between 1961-70) *showed that*, of 1,613 authors (including both personal and corporate authors), 391 (24%) were cited twice or more while 1,222 (76%) were cited only once. Further, corporate authors were disproportionately highly represented among the cited works. 7 corporate authors cited twice or more accounted for 478 citations [average of 68.3 citations each], while 384 personal authors cited

twice or more accounted for 1,300 citations [average of 3.4 citations each].
(566)

Academic

■ A survey reported in 1977 of publishing by professional librarians in 10 of the larger Association for Research Libraries libraries over a 5-year period (academic 1969-70 through 1973-74 or calander 1970-74) involving authors for 1,106 publications *showed that* publishing did not seem to be much affected by years of professional experience. For example:

authors with 5 or fewer years of professional experience accounted for 18% of the publishing in the sample;

authors with 6-10 years of professional experience accounted for 17% of the publishing in the sample;

authors with 11-15 years of professional experience accounted for 16% of the publishing in the sample;

authors with 16-20 years of professional experience accounted for 20% of the publishing in the sample;

authors with 21-25 years of professional experience accounted for 10% of the publishing in the sample;

authors with more than 25 years of professional experience accounted for 14% of the publishing in the sample.

and authors whose years of professional experience could not be determined accounted for 5% of the publishing in the sample.   **(256)**

Ibid. . . . *showed that* publishing in terms of position held was as follows:

administrators	13% of sample publishing
branch or department librarians	43% of sample publishing
subject or technical specialists	29% of sample publishing
supervised generalists	15% of sample publishing
position not known	−1% of sample publishing **(256)**

Ibid. . . . *showed that* "almost 60%" of all publishing in the sample was by authors who had a subject master's degree, a Ph.D., or another higher degree. Further, although librarians with a Ph.D. were estimated to constitute only 3.6% of the survey population, they accounted for 25% of the publications.   **(256)**

■ A study reported in 1982 of publication and citation patterns in *College and Research Libraries* during the 40 years between 1939-79, involving 1,775 articles, *showed that*, of 1,709 articles where the institutional affiliation of the principal author was known, the 5 most frequently represented institutions were:

University of Illinois	73 articles; 44 authors
Columbia University	58 articles; 40 authors
Library of Congress	53 articles; 41 authors
Harvard University	47 articles; 26 authors
University of Chicago	37 articles; 27 authors **(511)**

Ibid. . . . *showed that* collaborative authorship had increased, with the number of articles having single authorship decreasing from 95.65% of the articles in the first 5-year period (1939-44) to 72.68% of the articles in the last 5-year period (1975-79).   **(511)**

Special

■ A study reported in 1981 of authorship in 5 journals in special librarianship over a 10-year period (generally the decade of the 1970s) or over the life of the journal if it had not been published for a 10-year period *showed that* the numbers of practicing librarians among the authors of each of the 5 special library journals were as follows:

Journal of the American Society for Information Science	at least 8.3%
Law Library Journal	at least 64.1%
Bulletin of the Medical Library Association	at least 71.2%
Online Review	at least 35.0%
Special Libraries	at least 57.4% **(496)**

Research

Academic

■ A survey reported in 1968 of all ARL directors plus all other state university library directors concerning the degree to which librarians participate in traditional faculty activities (72 responding) *showed that* library directors strongly favored or encouraged: writing and publication (100%), campus committee and similar assignments (100%), professional service on local, state, and national basis (100%), consulting work (99%), research (97%), surveys (96%), leaves of absence (92%), participation in nonprofessional local activities (89%), and teaching (71%).   **(182)**

Ibid. . . . *showed that* 2/3 of respondents reported that librarians are given time from their schedules to teach and 89% of respondents reported that librarians teach courses in their institutions. Further, librarians were reported as teaching library science and bibliography only slightly more than subjects outside of the library field.   **(182)**

Ibid. . . . *showed that* 76% of respondents reported allowing time for research and 83% provided some sort of financial assistance. About 60% reported that the research need not be related to library operations or problems.   **(182)**

Ibid. . . . *showed that* 86% of respondents reported giving time off for free consulting, while 74% would give the time when the consultant was paid. For surveys, 83% of respondents reported giving time off for free surveys, while 72% would give the time when the surveyor was paid.   **(182)**

■ A study reported in 1975 of the degree to which 2-year college libraries (sample size: 26; responding: 23) in the state of Ohio conformed to the "Guidelines for Two-Year College Learning Resources Programs" established by the ACRL Board of Directors in 1972 *showed that* in the majority of cases the professional staff had faculty rank, status, benefits, and responsibilities, although in very few cases was advanced study, research, or publication required.   **(127)**

■ A survey reported in 1976 of the libraries in the largest private and largest public college/university in each state of the continental U.S. (sample size: 100[sic]; responding: 79 or 79%) *showed that* less than 50% of the respondents reported providing time and funding for independent research on the part of [professional] library staff.   **(413)**

■ A survey reported in 1980 of Association of Research Libraries directors in academic libraries (population: 94; responding: 68 or 72%) concerning publication requirements for professional library staff *showed that* 7 (10%) institutions allowed specific release time for working on publications, 28 (41%) allow librarians to apply for release time for publications and 33 (49%) do not allow release time for work on publications.   **(480)**

Ibid. . . . *showed that* (multiple responses allowed) 18 (23%) institutions provide funding for research within the library, 40 (51%) reported research funding is available from the university, and 20 (26%) reported that research funding is not available. **(480)**

■ A 1980 survey of academic librarians in Alabama, Georgia, and Mississippi concerning faculty status (sample size: 416; responding: 271; usable: 267 or 64.2%) *showed that*, of the 220 respondents who reported having faculty status, 18.6% reported that research publication was required for promotion or tenure, while 75.9% reported that it was not. (5.5% did not reply.) **(502)**

Ibid. . . . *showed that* during the 1979-80 academic year the research, publication, and grant proposal activity was as follows (for the entire group of 267; multiple responses allowed):

a book published	3.4%	respondents
a book review published	7.5%	respondents
a literature review or bibliography published	4.1%	respondents
a research article published	15.3%	respondents
a presentation at a professional meeting	12.0%	respondents
a research proposal developed	19.5%	respondents
a research proposal funded	8.3%	respondents **(502)**

Ibid. . . . *showed that* 12.0% of the respondents received release time for proposal development, while 14.2% received release time for research and publication. **(502)**

■ A study reported in 1981 at Southern Illinois University, Carbondale, investigating teaching faculty perception of librarians (survey size: 507; responding: 386; usable: 384 or 75.7%) *showed that* 17% of the teaching faculty felt librarians should conduct research on practical topics related to improving service, 2% felt librarians should conduct research on scholarly library topics, 56% felt librarians should conduct research on both of the previously mentioned topics, 8% felt librarians should not conduct research, and 16% felt that librarians should decide whether they should conduct research on not. **(493)**

Ibid. . . . *showed that* 13% of the teaching faculty felt librarians should be given no research time, 21% felt librarians should be given 4 hours of research time per week, 31% felt librarians should be given 8 hours of research time per week, 8% felt librarians should be given 12 hours of research time per week, while 27% felt the amount of research time to be given depended upon the needs of the research project.   **(493)**

Ibid. . . . *showed that* 201 (57%) of the teaching faculty felt that librarians should have faculty rank and status whereas 148 (43%) felt librarians should not. Of these 148 (multiple responses allowed), 58% gave as their reason for denying librarians faculty rank and status "insufficient teaching," 40% gave "insufficient research and publication," 13% gave "insufficient service," and 27% gave "insufficient education." 37% gave a variety of other reasons.   **(493)**

■ A survey reported in 1981 of library directors in 4-year colleges and universities in 7 Rocky Mountain states (survey size: 76; responding: 64 or 84%) concerning faculty status of librarians *showed that*, although sabbatical leaves were reported possible for librarians in 33 (83%) institutions, research leaves were only available in 32 (80%) institutions and research funds were only available in 28 (70%) institutions.   **(492)**

■ A survey reported in 1983 of head librarians of accredited institutions of higher education in New York state, including 2-year colleges, 4-year colleges, universities, and graduate/professional schools (survey size: 264; responding: 188 or 71%) concerning faculty status for librarians *showed that*, of the total respondents, librarians had the following academic rights (multiple responses allowed):

eligible to serve on the campus governing board	76% of total
eligible for release time for professional activities	68% of total
eligible for sabbatical and other professional leaves	64% of total
eligible for tenure	58% of total
eligible for research funds	55% of total
given professorial titles	30% of total
given release time for research	20% of total
academic-year appointment	16% of total **(516)**

■ A survey reported in 1983 of the U.S. academic members of the Association of Research Libraries concerning faculty status for professionals (population: 89 libraries; responding: 89 or 100%, including 57 state and 32 private institutions) *showed that* the benefits and privileges given librarians in state institutions versus private institutions were as follows:

faculty rank	20 (35.1%) state; 1 (3.1%) private
indefinite tenure	34 (59.6%) state; 4 (12.5%) private
research funds	51 (89.5%) state; 13 (40.6%) private
travel funds	all libraries
research leave	47 (82.5%) state; 25 (78.1%) private
sabbatical leave	35 (61.4%) state; 10 (31.3%) private
tuition break	41 (71.9%) state; 28 (87.5%) private
option of 9-month appointment	15 (26.3%) state; 7 (21.9%) private **(788)**

Teaching and Consulting

Academic

■ A survey reported in 1968 of all ARL directors plus all other state university library directors concerning the degree to which librarians participate in traditional faculty activities (72 responding) *showed that* 2/3 of respondents reported that librarians are given time from their schedules to teach and 89% of respondents reported that librarians teach courses in their institutions. Further, librarians were reported as teaching library science and bibliography only slightly more than subjects outside of the library field.   **(182)**

Ibid. . . . *showed that* library directors strongly favored or encouraged: writing and publication (100%), campus committee and similar assignments (100%), professional service on local, state, and national basis (100%), consulting work (99%), research (97%), surveys (96%), leaves of absence (92%), participation in nonprofessional local activities (89%), and teaching (71%).   **(182)**

Ibid. . . . *showed that* 86% of respondents reported giving time off for free consulting, while 74% would give the time when the consultant was paid. For surveys, 83% of respondents reported giving time off for free surveys, while 72% would give the time when the surveyor was paid.   **(182)**

■ A 1969 survey of the 71 ARL libraries (57 responding; 55 or 77.5% usable) concerning librarians as teachers *showed that,* of the library staff members who also have teaching assignments in academic departments, 56.4% hold joint appointment; 20.0% do not hold joint appointments; and 23.6% of the responding libraries reported that the issue was "not applicable."   **(196)**

Ibid. . . . *showed that* 123 librarians (of whom 112 held faculty rank) were teaching 138 courses in 28 academic departments at the time of the study. ARL statistics for 1967-68 for the 55 libraries responding to the study indicated a total professional staff of 4,473 FTEs which means that 2.75% of the professional staff of these libraries were involved in formal teaching. 93 of the 138 courses taught by library staff were in library science.
                                                                      (196)

■ A 1976 survey of head law librarians in North American schools (sample size: 178; responding: 154 or 86.7%) *showed that* the number of law school libraries where professional staff besides the director taught courses (entire courses only) was as follows: 23 (16%) libraries reported staff teaching law school legal bibliography course only; 4 (3%) reported staff teaching library school legal bibliography or substantive courses; 3 (2%) reported staff teaching law school substantive courses only; 2 (1%) reported staff teaching both law school legal bibliography and substantive courses; 2 (1%) reported staff teaching both law and library school courses; 1 reported staff teaching courses in other schools; and 117 (76%) reported staff teaching no courses.   **(357)**

Ibid. . . . *showed that* 94 (61%) law school libraries reported that their professional staff other than the director were not involved in any organized teaching activities, including such things as partial lectures, tours, and the like.   **(357)**

■ A 1978 survey of law school libraries listed in the 1977 *AALS Directory of Law Teachers* (population: 167; responding: 158 or 95%) *showed that* 82 (52%) respondents felt it desirable that head law school librarians carry teaching responsibilities, 15 (10%) felt that head law school librarians should teach but only legal bibliography, 21 (13%) reported mixed feelings, and 40 (25%) felt that head law school librarians should not teach.
                                                                      (362)

■ A study reported in 1981 at Southern Illinois University, Carbondale, investigating teaching faculty perception of librarians (survey size: 507; responding: 386; usable: 384 or 75.7%) *showed that* 201 (57%) of the teaching faculty felt that librarians should have faculty rank and status whereas 148 (43%) felt librarians should not. Of these 148 (multiple responses allowed), 58% gave as their reason for denying librarians faculty rank and status "insufficient teaching," 40% gave "insufficient research and publication," 13% gave "insufficient service," and 27% gave "insufficient education." 37% gave a variety of other reasons.   **(493)**

Special

■ A 1976 survey of head law librarians in North American schools (sample size: 178; responding: 154 or 86.7%) *showed that* the number of law school libraries where professional staff besides the director taught courses (entire courses only) was as follows: 23 (16%) libraries reported staff teaching law school legal bibliography course only; 4 (3%) reported staff teaching library school legal bibliography or substantive courses; 3 (2%) reported staff teaching law school substantive courses only; 2 (1%) reported staff teaching both law school legal bibliography and substantive courses; 2 (1%) reported staff teaching both law and library school courses; 1 reported staff teaching courses in other schools; and 117 (76%) reported staff teaching no courses. **(357)**

Ibid. . . . *showed that* 94 (61%) law school libraries reported that their professional staff other than the director were not involved in any organized teaching activities, including such things as partial lectures, tours, and the like. **(357)**

■ A 1978 survey of law school libraries listed in the 1977 *AALS Directory of Law Teachers* (population: 167; responding: 158 or 95%) *showed that* 82 (52%) respondents felt it desirable that head law school librarians carry teaching responsibilities, 15 (10%) felt that head law school librarians should teach but only legal bibliography, 21 (13%) reported mixed feelings, and 40 (25%) felt that head law school librarians should not teach. **(362)**

BIBLIOGRAPHY OF ARTICLES

Note: This Bibliography cites all articles summarized in the six-volume set of *Handbooks.* Entries in the Bibliography are sequentially arranged by the citation reference numbers that correspond to the numbers appearing at the end of each research summary throughout the six volumes. The numbers in boldface located at the end of some citations refer only to those research summaries contained in this volume. Alphabetic access to the Bibliography is provided through the Author Index.

1   Pamela Kobelski and Jean Trumbore. "Student Use of On-line Bibliographic Services," *Journal of Academic Librarianship* 4:1 (March 1978), 14-18.

2   John V. Richardson, Jr. "Readability and Readership of Journals in Library Science," *Journal of Academic Librarianship* 3:1 (March 1977), 20-22. **(182, 183)**

3   Elizabeth Gates Kesler. "A Campaign against Mutilation," *Journal of Academic Librarianship* 3:1 (March 1977), 29-30.

4   Bruce Miller and Marilyn Sorum. "A Two Stage Sampling Procedure for Estimating the Proportion of Lost Books in a Library," *Journal of Academic Librarianship* 3:2 (May 1977), 74-80.

5   Jeffrey St. Clair and Rao Aluri. "Staffing the Reference Desk: Professionals or Nonprofessionals," *Journal of Academic Librarianship* 3:3 (July 1977), 149-153.

6   Valentine DeBruin. "Sometimes Dirty Things Are Seen on the Screen," *Journal of Academic Librarianship* 3:5 (November 1977), 256-266.

7   Herbert S. White. "The View from the Library School," *Journal of Academic Librarianship* 3:6 (January 1970), 321. **(55)**

8   Stella Bentley. "Collective Bargaining and Faculty Status," *Journal of Academic Librarianship* 4:2 (May 1978), 75-81.

9   Steven Seokho Chwe. "A Comparative Study of Job Satisfaction: Catalogers and Reference Librarians in University Libraries," *Journal of Academic Librarianship* 4:3 (July 1978), 139-143.

10   Jo Bell Whitlatch and Karen Kieffer. "Service at San Jose State University: Survey of Document Availability," *Journal of Academic Librarianship* 4:4 (September 1978), 196-199.

11   Joan Grant and Susan Perelmuter. "Vendor Performance Evaluation," *Journal of Academic Librarianship* 4:5 (November 1978), 366-367.

12   Robert Goehlert. "Book Availability and Delivery Service," *Journal of Academic Librarianship* 4:5 (November 1978), 368-371.

13   Linda L. Phillips and Ann E. Raup. "Comparing Methods for Teaching Use of Periodical Indexes," *Journal of Academic Librarianship* 4:6 (January 1979), 420-423.

14   Margaret Johnson Bennett, David T. Buxton and Ella Capriotti. "Shelf Reading in a Large, Open Stack Library," *Journal of Academic Librarianship* 5:1 (March 1979), 4-8.

15   Sarah D. Knapp and C. James Schmidt. "Budgeting To Provide Computer-Based Reference Services: A Case Study," *Journal of Academic Librarianship* 5:1 (March 1979), 9-13.

16   Herbert S. White. "Library Materials Prices and Academic Library Practices: Between Scylla and Charybdis," *Journal of Academic Librarianship* 5:1 (March 1979), 20-23.

17   Dorothy P. Wells. "Coping with Schedules for Extended Hours: A Survey of Attitudes and Practices," *Journal of Academic Librarianship* 5:1 (March 1979), 24-27.

18   Johanna E. Tallman. "One Year's Experience with CONTU Guidelines for Interlibrary Loan Photocopies," *Journal of Academic Librarianship* 5:2 (May 1979), 71-74.

19   Robert Goehlert. "The Effect of Loan Policies on Circulation Recalls," *Journal of Academic Librarianship* 5:2 (May 1979), 79-82.

20   James R. Dwyer. "Public Response to an Academic Library Microcatalog," *Journal of Academic Librarianship* 5:3 (July 1979), 132-141.

21   Paul Metz. "The Role of the Academic Library Director," *Journal of Academic Librarianship* 5:3 (July 1979), 148-152.

22   Anne B. Piternick. "Problems of Resource Sharing with the Community: A Case Study," *Journal of Academic Librarianship* 5:3 (July 1979), 153-158.

23   Shelley Phipps and Ruth Dickstein. "The Library Skills Program at the University of Arizona: Testing, Evaluation and Critique," *Journal of Academic Librarianship* 5:4 (September 1979), 205-214.

24   Michael Stuart Freeman. "Published Study Guides: What They Say about Libraries," *Journal of Academic Librarianship* 5:5 (November 1979), 252-255.

25   James H. Richards, Jr. "Missing Inaction," *Journal of Academic Librarianship* 5:5 (November 1979), 266-269.

26   Philip H. Kitchens. "Engineers Meet the Library," *Journal of Academic Librarianship* 5:5 (November 1979), 277-282.

27 Michael Rouchton. "OCLC Serials Records: Errors, Omissions, and Dependability," *Journal of Academic Librarianship* 5:6 (January 1980), 316-321.

28 Charles R. McClure. "Academic Librarians, Information Sources, and Shared Decision Making," *Journal of Academic Librarianship* 6:1 (March 1980), 9-15.

29 Marjorie E. Murfin. "The Myth of Accessibility: Frustration and Failure in Retrieving Periodicals," *Journal of Academic Librarianship* 6:1 (March 1980), 16-19.

30 Anthony W. Ferguson and John R. Taylor. "What Are You Doing? An Analysis of Activities of Public Service Librarians at a Medium-sized Research Library," *Journal of Academic Librarianship* 6:1 (March 1980), 24-29.

31 Regina Shelton. "Adaption: A One-Year Survey of Reserve Photocopying," *Journal of Academic Librarianship* 6:2 (May 1980), 74-76.

32 Dorothea M. Thompson. "The Correct Uses of Library Data Bases Can Improve Interlibrary Loan Efficiency," *Journal of Academic Librarianship* 6:2 (May 1980), 83-86.

33 Joan Repp and Julia A. Woods. "Student Appraisal Study and Allocation Formula: Priorities and Equitable Funding in a University Setting," *Journal of Academic Librarianship* 6:2 (May 1980), 87-90.

34 Elaine S. Friedman. "Patron Access to Online Cataloging Systems: OCLC in the Public Service Environment," *Journal of Academic Librarianship* 6:3 (July 1980), 132-139.

35 Edward C. Jestes. "Manual vs. Automated Circulation: A Comparison of Operating Costs in a University Library," *Journal of Academic Librarianship* 6:3 (July 1980), 144-150.

36 Kathleen A. Johnson and Barbara S. Plake. "Evaluation of PLATO Library Instructional Lessons: Another View," *Journal of Academic Librarianship* 6:3 (July 1980), 154-158.

37 Priscilla C. Yu. "International Gift and Exchange: The Asian Experience," *Journal of Academic Librarianship* 6:6 (January 1981), 333-338.

38 George W. Black, Jr. "Estimating Collection Size Using the Shelf List in a Science Library," *Journal of Academic Librarianship* (January 1981), 339-341.

39 Beth Macleod. "*Library Journal* and *Choice*: A Review of Reviews," *Journal of Academic Librarianship* 7:1 (March 1981), 23-28.

40 Frank Wm. Goudy. "HEA, Title II-C Grant Awards: A Financial Overview from FY 1978-79 through FY 1981-82," *Journal of Academic Librarianship* 8:5 (November 1982), 264-269.

41   Larry Hardesty and John Wright. "Student Library Skills and Attitudes and Their Change: Relationships to Other Selected Variables," *Journal of Academic Librarianship* 8:4 (September 1982), 216-220.

42   Penelope Pearson and Virginia Teufel. "Evaluating Undergraduate Library Instruction at the Ohio State University," *Journal of Academic Librarianship* 7:6 (January 1982), 351-357.

43   David S. Ferrioro. "ARL Directors as Proteges and Mentors," *Journal of Academic Librarianship* 7:6 (January 1982), 358-365.

44   Albert F. Maag. "So You Want to be a Director...," *Journal of Academic Librarianship* 7:4 (September 1981), 213-217.

45   Mary Noel Gouke and Sue Pease. "Title Searches in an Online Catalog and a Card Catalog: A Comparative Study of Patron Success in Two Libraries," *Journal of Academic Librarianship* 8:3 (July 1982), 137-143.

46   John K. Mayeski and Marilyn T. Sharrow. "Recruitment of Academic Library Managers: A Survey," *Journal of Academic Librarianship* 8:3 (July 1982), 151-154.

47   Linda K. Rambler. "Syllabus Study: Key to a Responsive Academic Library," *Journal of Academic Librarianship* 8:3 (July 1982), 155-159.

48   Marion T. Reid. "Effectiveness of the OCLC Data Base for Acquisitions Verification," *Journal of Academic Librarianship* 2:6 (January 1977), 303-326.

49   James D. Culley, Denis F. Healy and Kermit G. Cudd. "Business Students and the University Library: An Overlooked Element in the Business Curriculum," *Journal of Academic Librarianship* 2:6 (January 1977), 293-296.

50   Edward Kazlauskas. "An Exploratory Study: A Kenesic Analysis of Academic Library Service Points," *Journal of Academic Librarianship* 2:3 (July 1976), 130-134.

51   Helen Gothberg. "Immediacy: A Study of Communication Effect on the Reference Process," *Journal of Academic Librarianship* 2:3 (July 1976), 126-129.

52   John Vasi. "Building Libraries for the Handicapped: A Second Look," *Journal of Academic Librarianship* 2:2 (May 1976), 82-83.

53   Elliot S. Palais. "The Significance of Subject Dispersion for the Indexing of Political Science Journals," *Journal of Academic Librarianship* 2:2 (May 1976), 72-76.

54   Ruth Carol Cushman. "Lease Plans—A New Lease on Life for Libraries," *Journal of Academic Librarianship* 2:1 (March 1976), 15-19.

55 Charles R. McClure. "Subject and Added Entries as Access to Information," *Journal of Academic Librarianship* 2:1 (March 1976), 9-14.

56 Marilyn L. Miller and Barbara B. Moran. "Expenditures for Resources in School Library Media Centers FY '82-'83," *School Library Journal* 30:2 (October 1983), 105-114. **(80, 100)**

57 Karen Lee Shelley. "The Future of Conservation in Research Libraries," *Journal of Academic Librarianship* 1:6 (January 1976), 15-18.

58 Maryan E. Reynolds. "Challenges of Modern Network Development," *Journal of Academic Librarianship* 1:2 (May 1975), 19-22.

59 Marjorie E. Martin and Clyde Hendrick. "Ripoffs Tell Their Story: Interviews with Mutilators in a University Library," *Journal of Academic Librarianship* 1:2 (May 1975), 8-12.

60 Audrey Tobias. "The Yule Curve Describing Periodical Citations by Freshmen: Essential Tool or Abstract Frill?" *Journal of Academic Librarianship* 1:1 (March 1975), 14-16.

61 Allan J. Dyson. "Organizing Undergraduate Library Instruction," *Journal of Academic Librarianship* 1:1 (March 1975), 9-13.

62 David F. Kohl. "High Efficiency Inventorying through Predictive Data," *Journal of Academic Librarianship* 8:2 (May 1982), 82-84.

63 Eleanor Phinney. "Trends in Public Library Adult Services," *ALA Bulletin* 57:3 (March 1963), 262-266.

64 Zelia J. French. "Library-Community Self-studies in Kansas," *ALA Bulletin* 56:1 (January 1962), 37-41.

65 Guy Garrison. "Nonresident Library Fees in Suburban Chicago," *ALA Bulletin* 55:6 (June 1961), 1013-1017.

66 James E. Bryan. "The Christmas Holiday Jam," *ALA Bulletin* 55:6 (June 1961), 526-530.

67 Joint Libraries Committee on Fair Use in Photocopying, American Library Association. "Fair Use in Photocopying: Report on Single Copies," *ALA Bulletin* 55:6 (June 1961), 571-573.

68 Henry J. Dubester. "Stack Use of a Research Library," *ALA Bulletin* 55:10 (November 1961), 891-893.

69 Mary Virginia Gaver. "Teacher Education and School Libraries," *ALA Bulletin* 60:1 (January 1966), 63-72. **(61, 62)**

70 Richard Waters. "Free Space: Can Public Libraries Receive It?" *ALA Bulletin* 58:3 (March 1964), 232-234.

71 Frank L. Schick. "Professional Library Manpower," *ALA Bulletin* 58:4 (April 1964), 315-317.

72 Milbrey Jones. "Socio-Economic Factors in Library Service to Students," *ALA Bulletin* 58:11 (December 1964), 1003-1006.

73 Elizabeth W. Stone. "Administrators Fiddle while Employees Burn or Flee," *ALA Bulletin* 63:2 (February 1969), 181-187. **(166)**

74 Staff Organizations Round Table, American Library Association. "Opinions on Collective Bargaining," *ALA Bulletin* 63:6 (June 1969), 803-808. **(77)**

75 Library Administration Division, American Library Association. "Library Employment of Minority Group Personnel," *ALA Bulletin* 63:7 (July-August 1969), 985-987.

76 Eli M. Oboler. "The Case for ALA Regional Annual Conferences," *ALA Bulletin* 63:8 (September 1969), 1099-1101. **(170)**

77 Edward N. Howard. "Breaking the Fine Barrier," *ALA Bulletin* 63:11 (December 1969), 1541-1545.

78 Elin B. Christianson. "Variation of Editorial Material in Periodicals Indexed in *Reader's Guide*," *ALA Bulletin* 62:2 (February 1968), 173-182.

79 Insurance for Libraries Committee, American Library Association. "The Makings of a Nationwide Scandal," *ALA Bulletin* 62:4 (April 1968), 384-386.

80 George L. Gardiner. "Collective Bargaining: Some Questions Asked," *ALA Bulletin* 62:8 (September 1968), 973-976.

81 Barbara M. Conant. "Trials and Tribulations of Textbook Price Indexing," *ALA Bulletin* 61:2 (February 1967), 197-199.

82 Henry T. Drennan and Sarah R. Reed. "Library Manpower," *ALA Bulletin* 61:8 (September 1967), 957-965.

83 Jerry L. Walker. "Changing Attitudes toward the Library and the Librarian," *ALA Bulletin* 61:8 (September 1967), 977-981.

84 William R. Monat. "The Community Library: Its Search for a Vital Purpose," *ALA Bulletin* 61:11 (December 1967), 1301-1310.

85 Irene A. Braden. "Pilot Inventory of Library Holdings," *ALA Bulletin* 62:9 (October 1968), 1129-1131.

86 Genevieve Casey. "Library Manpower in the Detroit Metropolitan Region," *American Libraries* 1:8 (September 1970), 787-789. **(154)**

87 Nora Cambier, Barton Clark, Robert Daugherty and Mike Gabriel. "Books in Print 1969: An Analysis of Errors," *American Libraries* 1:9 (October 1970), 901-902.

88 Tom Childers and Beth Krevitt. "Municipal Funding of Library Services," *American Libraries* 3:1 (January 1972), 53-57.

89 Albert H. Rubenstein, David J. Werner, Gustave Rath, John A. Kernaghan, and Robert D. O'Keefe. "Search versus Experiment—the Role of the Research Librarian," *College and Research Libraries* 34:4 (July 1973), 280-286.

90 Frank F. Kuo. "A Comparison of Six Versions of Science Library Instruction," *College and Research Libraries* 34:4 (July 1973), 287-290.

91 Laurence Miller. "The role of Circulation Services in the Major University Library," *College and Research Libraries* 34:6 (November 1973), 463-471.

92 Ruth Hyman and Gail Schlachter. "Academic Status: Who Wants It?" *College and Research Libraries* 34:6 (November 1973), 472-478. (111)

93 Larry E. Harrelson. "Large Libraries and Information Desks," *College and Research Libraries* 35:1 (January 1974), 21-27.

94 Robert B. Downs. "Library Resources in the United States," *College and Research Libraries* 35:2 (March 1974), 97-108.

95 Richard J. Beeler. "Late-Study Areas: A Means of Extending Library Hours," *College and Research Libraries* 35:3 (May 1974), 200-203.

96 Rolland E. Stevens. "A Study of Interlibrary Loan," *College and Research Libraries* 35:5 (September 1974), 336-343.

97 Jay B. Clark. "An Approach to Collection Inventory," *College and Research Libraries* 35:5 (September 1974), 354-359.

98 Jan Baaske, Don Tolliver and Judy Westerberg. "Overdue Policies: A Comparison of Alternatives," *College and Research Libraries* 35:5 (September 1974), 354-359.

99 Clyde Hendrick and Marjorie E. Murfin. "Project Library Ripoff: A Study of Periodical Mutilation in a University Library," *College and Research Libraries* 35:6 (November 1974), 402-411.

100 Peter Marshall. "How Much, How Often?" *College and Research Libraries* 35:6 (November 1974), 453-456.

101 Robert Balay and Christine Andres. "Use of the Reference Service in a Large Academic Library," *College and Research Libraries* 36:1 (January 1975), 9-26.

102 Guy Walker. "Preservation Efforts in Larger U.S. Academic Libraries," *College and Research Libraries* 36:1 (January 1975), 39-44.

103 Susanne Patterson Wahba. "Job Satisfaction of Librarians: A Comparison between Men and Women," *College and Research Libraries* 36:1 (January 1975), 45-51. **(91, 149)**

104 Grant T. Skelley. "Characteristics of Collections Added to American Research Libraries 1940-1970: A Preliminary Investigation," *College and Reseach Libraries* 36:1 (January 1975), 52-60.

105 Laura M. Boyer and William C. Theimer, Jr. "The Use and Training of Nonprofessional Personnel at Reference Desks in Selected College and University Libraries," *College and Research Libraries* 36:3 (May 1975), 193-200. **(167)**

106 Robert J. Greene. "LENDS: An Approach to the Centralization/Decentralization Dilemma," *College and Research Libraries* 36:3 (May 1975), 201-207.

107 Frances L. Meals and Walter T. Johnson. "We Chose Microfilm," *College and Research Libraries* 21:3 (May 1960), 223-228.

108 George Caldwell. "University Libraries and Government Publications: A Survey," *College and Research Libraries* 22:1 (January 1961), 30-34.

109 Allen Story. "Leo in Libraryland," *American Libraries* 7:9 (October 1976), 569-571. **(154, 155, 156)**

110 Leslie R. Morris. "The Rise and Fall of the Library Job Market," *American Libraries* 12:9 (October 1981), 557-558. **(157)**

111 Richard De Gennaro. "Escalating Journal Prices: Time To Fight Back," *American Libraries* 8:1 (January 1977), 69-74.

112 Joe A. Hewitt. "The Impact of OCLC," *American Libaries* 7:5 (May 1976), 268-275.

113 Fritz Veit. "Book Order Procedures in the Publicly Controlled Colleges and Universities of the Midwest," *College and Research Libraries* 23:1 (January 1962), 33-40.

114 Keyes D. Metcalf. "Compact Shelving," *College and Research Libraries* 23:2 (March 1962), 103-111.

115 Natalie N. Nicholson and Eleanor Bartlett. "Who Uses University Libraries," *College and Research Libraries* 23:3 (May 1962), 217-259.

116 H. William Axford. "Rider Revisited," *College and Research Libraries* 23:4 (July 1962), 345-347.

117 E.J. Josey. "The Role of the College Library Staff in Instruction in the Use of the Library," *College and Research Libraries* 23:6 (November 1962), 492-498.

118 Edwin E. Williams. "Magnitude of the Paper-Deterioration Problems as Measured by a National Union Catalog Sample," *College and Research Libraries* 23:6 (November 1962), 499.

119 Stella Frank Mosborg. "Measuring Circulation Desk Activities Using a Random Alarm Mechanism," *College and Research Libraries* 41:5 (September 1980), 437-444.

120 Jean E. Koch and Judith M. Pask. "Working Papers in Academic Business Libraries," *College and Research Libraries* 41:6 (November 1980), 517-523.

121 Paul Metz. "Administrative Succession in the Academic Library," *College and Research Libraries* 39:5 (September 1978), 358-364. **(133)**

122 Libby Trudell and James Wolper. "Interlibrary Loan in New England," *College and Research Libraries* 39:5 (September 1978), 365-371.

123 Richard M. Dougherty. "The Evaluation of Campus Library Document Delivery Service," *College and Research Libraries* 34:1 (January 1973), 29-39.

124 Ung Chon Kim. "A Comparison of Two Out-of-Print Book Buying Methods," *College and Research Libraries* 34:5 (September 1973), 258-264.

125 Ann Gwyn, Anne McArthur and Karen Furlow. "Friends of the Library," *College and Research Libraries* 36:4 (July 1975), 272-282.

126 John J. Knightly. "Library Collections and Academic Curricula: Quantitative Relationships," *College and Research Libraries* 36:4 (July 1975), 295-301.

127 Alice S. Clark and Rita Hirschman. "Using the 'Guidelines': A Study of the State-Supported Two-Year College Libraries in Ohio," *College and Research Libraries* 36:5 (September 1975), 364-370. **(111, 178, 202)**

128 Virginia E. Yagello and Gerry Gutherie. "The Effect of Reduced Loan Periods on High Use Items," *College and Research Libraries* 36:5 (September 1975), 411-414.

129 George Piternick. "Library Growth and Academic Quality," *College and Research Libraries* 24:3 (May 1963), 223-229.

130 Robert N. Broadus. "An Analysis of Faculty Circulation in a University Library," *College and Research Libraries* 24:4 (July 1963), 323-325.

131 Perry D. Morrison. "The Personality of the Academic Librarian," *College and Research Libraries* 24:5 (September 1963), 365-368.

132 W.J. Bonk. "What is Basic Reference?" *College and Research Libraries* 25:3 (May 1964), 5-8.

133 Jean Legg "The Periodical Scene," *RQ* 7:3 (Spring 1968), 129-132.

134 Richard H. Perrine. "Catalog Use Difficulties," *RQ* 7:4 (Summer 1968), 169-174.

135 Thelma E. Larson. "A Survey of User Orientation Methods," *RQ* 8:3 (Spring 1969), 182-187.

136 Phil Hoehn and Jean Hudson. "Academic Library Staffing Patterns," *RQ* 8:4 (Summer 1969), 242-244.

137 T.H. Milby. "Two Approaches to Biology," *RQ* 11:3 (Spring 1972), 231-235.

138 James B. Way. "Loose Leaf Business Services," *RQ* 9:2 (Winter 1969), 128-133.

139 Mary Jane Swope and Jeffrey Katzer. "Why Don't They Ask Questions?" *RQ* 12:2 (Winter 1972), 161-165.

140 Robert M. Simmons. "Finding That Government Document," *RQ* 12:2 (Winter 1972), 167-171.

141 Lee Regan. "Status of Reader's Advisory Service," *RQ* 12:3 (Spring 1973), 227-233.

142 Bruce Cossar. "Interlibrary Loan Costs," *RQ* 12:3 (Spring 1973), 243-246.

143 Mary R. Turtle and William C. Robinson. "The Relationship between Time Lag and Place of Publication in *Library and Information Science Abstracts* and *Library Literature*," *RQ* 14:1 (Fall 1974), 28-31.

144 Rosemary Magrill and Charles H. Davis. "Public Library SDI; A Pilot Study," *RQ* 14:2 (Winter 1974), 131-137.

145 Steve Parker and Kathy Essary. "A Manual SDI System for Academic Libraries," *RQ* 15:1 (Fall 1975), 47-54.

146 Carl F. Orgren and Barbara J. Olson. "Statewide Teletype Reference Service," *RQ* 15:3 (Spring 1976), 203-209. **(12, 59, 70)**

147 Anne S. Mavor, Jose Orlando Toro and Ernest R. Deprospo. "An Overview of the National Adult Independent Learning Project," *RQ* 15:4 (Summer 1976), 293-308.

148 Danuta A. Nitecki. "Attitudes toward Automated Information Retrieval Services among RASD Members," *RQ* 16:2 (Winter 1976), 133-141.

149 Rhoda Garoogian. "Library Use of the New York Times Information Bank: A Preliminary Survey," *RQ* 16:1 (Fall 1976), 59-64.

150 Marcella Ciucki. "Recording of Reference/Information Service Activities: A Study of Forms Currently Used," *RQ* 16:4 (Summer 1977), 273-283.

151 Mollie Sandock. "A Study of University Students' Awareness of Reference Services," *RQ* 16:4 (Summer 1977), 284-296.

152 Kathleen Imhoff and Larry Brandwein. "Labor Collections and Services in Public Libraries throughout the United States, 1976," *RQ* 17:2 (Winter 1977), 149-158.

153 Cynthia Swenk and Wendy Robinson. "A Comparison of the Guides to Abstracting and Indexing Services Provided by Katz, Chicorel and Ulrich," *RQ* (Summer 1978), 317-319.

154 John P. Wilkinson and William Miller. "The Step Approach to Reference Service," *RQ* (Summer 1978), 293-299.

155 Gerald Johoda, Alan Bayer and William L. Needham. "A Comparison of On-Line Bibliographic Searches in One Academic and One Industrial Organization," *RQ* 18:1 (Fall 1978), 42-49.

156 Stephen P. Harter and Mary Alice S. Fields. "Circulation, Reference and the Evaluation of Public Library Service," *RQ* 18:2 (Winter 1978), 147-152.

157 Daniel Ream. "An Evaluation of Four Book Review Journals," *RQ* 19:2 (Winter 1979), 149-153.

158 Joseph W. Palmer. "Review Citations for Best-Selling Books," *RQ* 19:2 (Winter 1979), 154-158.

159 "An Evaluation of References to Indexes and Abstracts in Ulrich's 17th Edition," *RQ* 20:2 (Winter 1980), 155-159.

160 Victoria T. Kok and Anton R. Pierce. "The Reference Desk Survey: A Management Tool in an Academic Research Library," *RQ* 22:2 (Winter 1982), 181-187.

161 Sheila S. Intner. "Equality of Cataloging in the Age of AACR2," *American Libraries* 14:2 (February 1983), 102-103.

162 Joseph W. Palmer. "The Future of Public Library Film Service," *American Libraries* 13:2 (February 1982), 140-142.

163 Robert Grover and Mary Kevin Moore. "Print Dominates Library Service to Children," *American Libraries* 13:4 (April 1982), 268-269.

164 Richard H. Evensen and Mary Berghaus Levering. "Services Are 500% Better," *American Libraries* 10:6 (June 1979), 373.

165 Judith Schick. "Job Mobility of Men and Women Librarians and How It Affects Career Advancement," *American Libraries* 10:11 (December 1979), 643-647. (**83, 95, 98, 132, 133, 147, 153**)

166 Elizabeth Rountree. "Users and Nonusers Disclose Their Needs," *American Libraries* 10:8 (September 1979), 486-487.

167 George Bobinski. "A Survey of Faculty Loan Policies," *College and Research Libraries* 24:6 (November 1963), 483-486. add

168 L. Miles Raisig and Frederick G. Kilgour. "The Use of Medical Theses as Demonstrated by Journal Citations, 1850-1960," *College and Research Libraries* 25:2 (March 1964), 93-102.

169 George H. Fadenrecht. "Library Facilities and Practices in Colleges of Veterinary Medicine," *College and Research Libraries* 25:4 (July 1964), 308-335.

170 Donald Thompson. "Working Conditions in Selected Private College Libraries," *College and Research Libraries* 25:4 (July 1964), 261-294.**(109, 118, 120, 166)**

171 Benedict Brooks and Frederick G. Kilgour. "Catalog Subject Searches in the Yale Medical Library," *College and Research Libraries* 25:6 (November 1964), 483-487.

172 Patrick Barkey. "Patterns of Student Use of a College Library," *College and Research Libraries* 26:2 (March 1965), 115-118.

173 Genevieve Porterfield. "Staffing of Interlibrary Loan Service," *College and Research Libraries* 26:4 (July 1965), 318-320.

174 Harold Mathis. "Professional or Clerical: A Cross-Validation Study," *College and Research Libraries* 26:6 (November 1965), 525-531.

175 David H. Doerrer. 'Overtime' and the Academic Librarian," *College and Research Libraries* 27:3 (May 1966), 194-239.

176 Lois L. Luesing. "Church Historical Collections in Liberal Arts Colleges," *College and Research Libraries* 27:5 (July 1966), 291-317.

177 W.C. Blankenship. "Head Librarians: How Many Men? How Many Women?" *College and Research Libraries* 28:1 (January 1967), 41-48. **(128, 131, 132, 137, 147)**

178 Morrison C. Haviland. "Loans to Faculty Members in University Libraries," *College and Research Libraries* 28:3 (May 1967), 171-174.

179 R. Vernon Ritter. "An Investigation of Classroom-Library Relationships on a College Campus as Seen in Recorded Circulation and GPA's," *College and Research Libraries* 29:1 (January 1968), 3-4.

180 Peter Spyers-Duran. "Faculty Studies: A Survey of Their Use in Selected Libraries," *College and Research Libraries* 29:1 (January 1968), 55-61.

181 Raymond Kilpela. "The University Library Committee," *College and Research Libraries* 29:2 (March 1968), 141-143.

182 W. Porter Kellam and Dale L. Barker. "Activities and Opportunities of University Librarians for Full Participation in the Educational Enterprise," *College and Research Libraries* 29:5 (May 1968), 195-199. **(109, 166, 167, 175, 178, 201, 202, 205)**

183 Lloyd A. Kramer and Martha B. Kramer. "The College Library and the Drop-Out," *College and Research Libraries* 29:4 (July 1968), 310-312.

184 Carl Hintz. "Criteria for Appointment to and Promotion in Academic Rank," *College and Research Libraries* 29:5 (September 1968), 341-346. **(110, 122)**

185 Desmond Taylor. "Classification Trends in Junior College Libraries," *College and Research Libraries* 29:6 (September 1968), 351-356.

186 Raj Madan, Eliese Hetler and Marilyn Strong. "The Status of Librarians in Four-Year State Colleges and Universities," *College and Research Libraries* 29:5 (September 1968), 381-386. **(96, 110, 121)**

187 Victor Novak. "The Librarian in Catholic Institutions," *College and Research Libraries* 29:5 (September 1968), 403-410. **(96, 109, 118)**

188 Barbara H. Phipps. "Library Instruction for the Undergraduate," *College and Research Libraries* 29:5 (September 1968), 411-423.

189 Ashby J. Fristoe. "Paperbound Books: Many Problems, No Solutions," *College and Research Libraries* 29:5 (September 1968), 437-442.

190 Sidney Forman. "Innovative Practices in College Libraries," *College and Research Libraries* 29:6 (November 1968), 486-492.

191 Richard W. Trueswell. "Some Circulation Data from a Research Library," *College and Research Libraries* 29:6 (November 1968), 493-495.

192 Jane P. Kleiner. "The Information Desk: The Library's Gateway to Service," *College and Research Libraries* 29:6 (November 1968), 496-501.

193 J.E.G. Craig, Jr. "Characteristics of Use of Geology Literature," *College and Research Libraries* 3:3 (May 1969), 230-236.

194 Ronald A. Hoppe and Edward C. Simmel. "Book Tearing: The Bystander in the University Library," *College and Research Libraries* 3:3 (May 1969), 247-251.

195 Stephen L. Peterson. "Patterns of Use of Periodical Literature," *College and Research Libraries* 30:5 (September 1969), 422-430.

196 Mary B. Cassata. "Teach-in: The Academic Librarian's Key to Status," *College and Research Libraries* 31:1 (January 1970), 22-27 **(77, 110, 122, 205, 206)**

197 E.J. Josey. "Community Use of Junior College Libraries—A Symposium," *College and Research Libraries* 31:3 (May 1970), 185-198.

198 Virgil F. Massman. "Academic Library Salaries in a Seven-State Area," *College and Research Libraries* 3:6 (November 1969), 477-482. **(97, 105)**

199 James Krikelas. "Subject Searches Using Two Catalogs: A Comparative Evaluation," *College and Research Libraries* 30:6 (November 1969), 506-517.

200 James Wright. "Fringe Benefits for Academic Library Personnel," *College and Research Libraries* 31:1 (January 1970), 18-21. **(97, 111, 121)**

201 Howard Clayton. "Femininity and Job Satisfaction among Male Library Students at One Midwestern University," *College and Research Libraries* 31:6 (November 1970), 388-398. **(67)**

202 Philip V. Rzasa and John H. Moriarty. "The Types and Needs of Academic Library Users: A Case Study of 6,568 Responses," *College and Research Libraries* 31:6 (November 1970),403-409.

203 Bob Carmack and Trudi Loeber. "The Library Reserve System—Another Look," *College and Research Libraries* 32:2 (March 1971), 105-109.

204 C. James Schmidt and Kay Shaffer. "A Cooperative Interlibrary Loan Service for the State-Assisted University Libraries in Ohio," *College and Research Libraries* 32:3 (May 1971), 197-204.

205 Edward S. Warner. "A Tentative Analytical Approach to the Determination of Interlibrary Loan Network Effectiveness," *College and Research Libraries* 32:3 (May 1971), 217-221.

206 Irving Zelkind and Joseph Sprug. "Increased Control through Decreased Controls: A Motivational Approach to a Library Circulation Problem," *College and Research Libraries* 32:3 (May 1971), 222-226.

207 William E. McGrath. "Correlating the Subjects of Books Taken Out Of and Books Used Within an Open-Stack Library," *College and Research Libraries* 32:4 (July 1971), 280-285.

208 Thomas Kirk. "A Comparison of Two Methods of Library Instruction for Students in Introductory Biology," *College and Research Libraries* 32:6 (November 1971), 465-474.

209 Dawn McCaghy and Gary Purcell. "Faculty Use of Government Publications," *College and Research Libraries* 33:1 (January 1972), 7-12.

210 Joe A. Hewitt. "Sample Audit of Cards from a University Library Catalog," *College and Research Libraries* 33:1 (January 1972), 24-27.

211 William E. McGrath. "The Significance of Books Used According to a Classified Profile of Academic Departments," *College and Research Libraries* 33:3 (May 1972), 212-219.

212 Carlos A. Cuadra and Ruth J. Patrick. "Survey of Academic Library Consortia in the U.S.," *College and Research Libraries* 33:4 (July 1972), 271-283.

213 Marjorie Johnson. "Performance Appraisal of Librarians—A Survey," *College and Research Libraries* 33:5 (September 1972), 359-367.

214   Marvin E. Wiggins. "The Development of Library Use Instruction Programs," *College and Research Libraries* 33:6 (November 1972), 473-479.

215   Margaret E. Monroe. "Community Development as a Mode of Community Analysis," *Library Trends* 24:3 (January 1976), 497-514. **(168)**

216   Janet K. Rudd and Larry G. Carver. "Topographic Map Acquisition in U.S. Academic Libraries," *Library Trends* 29:3 Winter 1981), 375-390.

217   John Belland. "Factors Influencing Selection of Materials," *School Media Quarterly* 6:2 (Winter 1978), 112-119.

218   Virginia Witucke. "A Comparative Analysis of Juvenile Book Review Media," *School Media Quarterly* 8:3 (Spring 1980), 153-160.

219   M. Carl Drott and Jacqueline C. Mancall. "Magazines as Information Sources: Patterns of Student Use," *School Media Quarterly* 8:4 (Summer 1980), 240-250.

220   Jerry J. Watson and Bill C. Snider. "Book Selection Pressure on School Library Media Specialists and Teachers," *School Media Quarterly* 9:2 (Winter 1981), 95-101.

221   Jerry J. Watson and Bill C. Snider. "Educating the Potential Self-Censor," *School Media Quarterly* 9:4 (Summer 1981), 272-276. **(8)**

222   Lucy Anne Wozny. "Online Bibliographic Searching and Student Use of Information: An Innovative Teaching Approach," *School Library Media Quarterly* 11:1 (Fall 1982), 35-42.

223   Carol A. Doll. "School and Public Library Collection Overlap and the Implications for Networking," *School Library Media Quarterly* 11:3 (Spring 1983), 193-199.

224   Arthur Tannenbaum and Eva Sidhom. "User Environment and Attitudes in an Academic Microform Center," *Library Journal* 101:18 (October 15, 1976), 2139-2143.

225   Timothy Hays, Kenneth D. Shearer and Concepcion Wilson. "The Patron Is Not the Public," *Library Journal* 102:16 (September 15, 1977), 1813-1818.

226   Wilma Lee Woolard. "The Combined School and Public Library: Can It Work?" *Library Journal* 103:4 (February 15, 1978), 435-438.

227   David C. Genaway. "Bar Coding and the Librarian Supermarket: An Analysis of Advertised Library Vacancies," *Library Journal* 103:3 (February 1, 1978), 322-325. **(78, 79, 127, 159, 160, 162, 163)**

228   Hoyt Galvin. "Public Library Parking Needs," *Library Journal* 103:2 (November 15, 1978), 2310-2313.

229 Harold J. Ettelt. "Book Use at a Small (Very) Community College Library," *Library Journal* 103:2 (November 15, 1978), 2314-2315.

230 Frederick G. Kilgour. "Interlibrary Loans On-Line," *Library Journal* 104:4 (February 15, 1979), 460-463.

231 Paul Little. "The Effectiveness of Paperbacks," *Library Journal* 104:2 (November 15, 1979), 2411-2416.

232 Ken Kister. "Encyclopedias and the Public Library: A National Survey," *Library Journal* 104:8 (April 15, 1979), 890-893.

233 Arlene T. Dowell. "Discrepancies in CIP: How Serious Is the Problem," *Library Journal* 104:19 (November 1, 1979), 2281-2287.

234 Gary D. Byrd, Mary Kay Smith and Norene McDonald. "MINET in K.C.," *Library Journal* 104:17 (October 1, 1979), 2044-2047.

235 Ray L. Carpenter. "The Public Library Patron," *Library Journal* 104:3 (February 1, 1979), 347-351.

236 Cathy Schell. "Preventive Medicine: The Library Prescription," *Library Journal* 105:8 (April 15, 1980), 929-931.

237 Michael Gonzalez, Bill Greeley and Stephen Whitney. "Assessing the Library Needs of the Spanish-speaking," *Library Journal* 105:7 (April 1, 1980), 786-789.

238 Thomas Childers. "The Test of Reference," *Library Journal* 105:8 (April 15, 1980), 924-928.

239 Mary Noel Gouke and Marjorie Murfin. "Periodical Mutilization: The Insidious Disease," *Library Journal* 105:16 (September 15, 1980), 1795-1797.

240 Sheila Creth and Faith Harders. "Requirements for the Entry Level Librarian," *Library Journal* 105:18 (October 15, 1980), 2168-2169. (7, 8, 78, 90, 94, 106, 108, 161)

241 Kathleen M. Heim and Leigh S. Estabrook. "Career Patterns of Librarians," *Drexel Library Quarterly* 17:3 (Summer 1981), 35-51. (130, 137, 145, 147, 148, 150, 175)

242 Margaret Peil. "Library Use by Low-Income Chicago Families," *Library Quarterly* 33:4 (October 1963), 329-333.

243 Herbert Goldhor and John McCrossan. "An Exploratory Study of the Effect of a Public Library Summer Reading Club on Reading Skills," *Library Quarterly* 36:1 (June 1966), 14-24.

244 Robert Sommer. "Reading Areas in College Libraries," *Library Quarterly* 38:3 (July 1968), 249-260.

245 Isaac T. Littleton. "The Literature of Agricultural Economics: Its Bibliographic Organization and Use," *Library Quarterly* 39:2 (April 1969), 140-152.

246   G. Edward Evans. "Book Selection and Book Collection Usage in Academic Libraries," *Library Quarterly* 40:3 (July 1970), 297-308.

247   Marilyn Werstein Greenberg. "A Study of Reading Motivation of Twenty-Three Seventh-Grade Students," *Library Quarterly* 40:3 (July 1970), 309-317.

248   Ben-Ami Lipetz. "Catalog Use in a Large Research Library," *Library Quarterly* 42:1 (January 1972), 129-130.

249   John Aubry. "A Timing Study of the Manual Searching of Catalogs," *Library Quarterly* 42:4 (October 1972), 399-415.

250   Kenneth H. Plate and Elizabeth W. Stone. "Factors Affecting Librarians' Job Satisfaction: A Report of Two Studies," *Library Quarterly* 44:2 (April 1974), 97-109.

251   Elizabeth Warner McElroy. "Subject Variety in Adult Reading: I. Factors Related to Variety in Reading," *Library Quarterly* 38:1 (April 1968), 154-167.

252   James C. Baughman. "A Structural Analysis of the Literature of Sociology," *Library Quarterly* 44:4 (October 1974), 293-308.

253   Edd E. Wheeler. "The Bottom Lines: Fifty Years of Legal Footnoting in Review," *Law Library Journal* 72:2 (Spring 1979), 245-259.

254   Daniel O'Connor and Phyllis Van Orden. "Getting into Print," *College and Research Libraries* 39:5 (September 1978), 389-396. (182)

255   Howard Fosdick. "Library Education in Information Science: Present Trends," *Special Libraries* 69:3 (March 1978), 100-108. (10)

256   Paula de Simone Watson. "Publication Activity among Academic Librarians," *College and Research Libraries* 38:5 (September 1977), 375-384. (186, 200)

257   Susan Andriette Ariew. "The Failure of the Open Access Residence Hall Library," *College and Research Libraries* 39:5 (September 1978), 372-380.

258   Mary Ellen Soper. "Characteristics and Use of Personal Collections," *Library Quarterly* (October 1976), 397-415.

259   Ronald R. Powell. "An Investigation of the Relationships Between Quantifiable Reference Service Variables and Reference Performance in Public Libraries," *Library Quarterly* 48:1 (January 1978), 1-19.

260   Mary Jo Lynch. "Reference Interviews in Public Libraries," *Library Quarterly* 48:2 (April 1978), 119-142.

261   William A. Satariano. "Journal Use in Sociology: Citation Analysis versus Readership Patterns," *Library Quarterly* 48:3 (July 1978), 293-300.

262 Paul Metz. "The Use of the General Collection in the Library of Congress," *Library Quarterly* 49:4 (October 1979), 415-434.

263 Michael Halperin and Maureen Strazdon. "Measuring Students' Preferences for Reference Service: A Conjoint Analysis," *Library Quarterly* 50:2 (April 1980), 208-224.

264 Herbert S. White. "Factors in the Decisions by Individuals and Libraries To Place or Cancel Subscriptions to Scholarly and Research Journals," *Library Quarterly* 50:3 (July 1980), 287-309.

265 George D'Elia. "The Development and Testing of a Conceptual Model of Public Library User Behavior," *Library Quarterly* 50:4 (October 1980), 410-430.

266 Donald A. Hicks. "Diversifying Fiscal Support by Pricing Public Library Services: A Policy Impact Analysis," *Library Quarterly* 50:4 (October 1980), 453-474.

267 Theodora Hodges and Uri Block. "Fiche or Film for COM Catalogs: Two Use Tests," *Library Quarterly* 52:2 (April 1982), 131-144.

268 Terry L. Weech and Herbert Goldhor. "Obtrusive versus Unobtrusive Evaluation of Reference Service in Five Illinois Public Libraries: A Pilot Study," *Library Quarterly* 52:4 (October 1982), 305-324.

269 Stephen E. Wiberley, Jr. "Journal Rankings From Citation Studies: A Comparison of National and Local Data From Social Work," *Library Quarterly* 52:4 (October 1982), 348-359.

270 George D'Elia and Sandra Walsh. "User Satisfaction with Library Service— A Measure of Public Library Performance?" *Library Quarterly* 53:2 (April 1983), 109-133.

271 Edward A. Dyl. "A Note on Price Discrimination by Academic Journals," *Library Quarterly* 53:2 (April 1983), 161-168.

272 Michael R. Kronenfeld and James A. Thompson. "The Impact of Inflation on Journal Costs," *Library Journal* 106:7 (April 1,1981), 714-717.

273 George D'Elia and Mary K. Chelton. "Paperback Books," *Library Journal* 107:16 (September 15, 1982), 1718-1721.

274 Patsy Hansel and Robert Burgin. "Hard Facts about Overdues," *Library Journal* 108:4 (February 15, 1983), 349-352.

275 Robert Dale Karr. "Becoming a Library Director," *Library Journal* 108:4 (February 15, 1983), 343-346. (66).

276 Mary V. Gaver. "The Science Collection—New Evidence To Consider," *Junior Libraries* (later *School Library Journal*) 7:6 (February 1961), 4-7.

277 Dorothy G. Petersen. "Teachers' Professional Reading," *School Library Journal* 9:8 (April 1963), 24-27. (169)

278 Linda Kraft. "Lost Herstory: The Treatment of Women in Children's Encyclopedias," *School Library Journal* 19:5 (January 1973), 26-35.

279 John Stewig and Margaret Higgs. "Girls Grow Up: A Study of Sexism in Children's Literature," *School Library Journal* 19:5 (January 1973), 44-49.

280 W. Bernard Lukenbill. "Fathers in Adolescent Novels," *School Library Journal* 20:6 (February 1974), 26-30.

281 Jacqueline C. Mancall and M. Carl Drott. "Tomorrow's Scholars: Patterns of Facilities Use," *School Library Journal* 20:7 (March 1980), 99-103.

282 John McCrossan. "Education of Librarians Employed in Small Public Libraries," *Journal of Education for Librarianship* 7:4 (Spring 1967), 237-245. **(79, 83, 87, 88, 99, 107)**

283 Gail Schlachter and Dennis Thomison. "The Library Science Doctorate: A Quantitative Analysis of Dissertations and Recipients," *Journal of Education for Librarianship* 15:2 (Fall 1974), 95-111. **(16, 18, 20, 21, 22, 23, 24, 27, 33, 47, 48, 64, 84, 85, 127, 129, 143, 147)**

284 Constance Rinehart and Rose Mary Magrill. "Characteristics of Applicants for Library Science Teaching Positions," *Journal of Education for Librarianship* 16:3 (Winter 1976), 173-182. **(28, 37, 38, 49)**

285 George W. Whitbeck. "Grade Inflation in the Library School—Myth or Reality," *Journal of Education for Librarianship* 17:4 (Spring 1977), 214-237. **(7, 52, 93, 156)**

286 Charles H. Davis. "Computer Programming for Librarians," *Journal of Education for Librarianship* 18:1 (Summer 1977), 41-52. **(50, 52)**

287 Helen M. Gothberg. "A Study of the Audio-Tutorial Approach to Teaching Basic Reference," *Journal of Education for Librarianship* 18:3 (Winter 1978), 193-202. **(70)**

288 J. Periam Danton. "British and American Library School Teaching Staffs: A Comparative Inquiry," *Journal of Education for Librarianship* 19:2 (Fall 1978), 97-129. **(25, 30, 31, 35, 39, 44, 50)**

289 Lucille Whalen. "The Role of the Assistant Dean in Library Schools," *Journal of Education for Librarianship* 20:1 (Summer 1979), 44-54. **(3, 4)**

290 A. Neil Yerkey. "Values of Library School Students, Faculty and Librarians: Premises for Understanding," *Journal of Education for Librarianship* 21:2 (Fall 1980), 122-134. **(39, 68, 69)**

291 Judith B. Katz. "Indicators of Success: Queens College Department of Library Science," *Journal of Education for Librarianship* 19:2 (Fall 1978), 130-139. **(5, 53, 54, 56)**

292 Lawrence Auld, Kathleen H. Heim and Jerome Miller. "Market Receptivity for an Extended M.L.S.," *Journal of Education for Librarianship* 21:3 (Winter 1981), 235-245. **(89, 104, 105)**

293 John Richardson, Jr. and Peter Hernon. "Theory vs. Practice: Student Preferences," *Journal of Education for Librarianship* 21:4 (Spring 1981), 287-300. **(7, 66, 67, 69, 70)**

294 Richard I. Blue and James L. Divilbiss. "Optimizing Selection of Library School Students," *Journal of Education for Librarianship* 21:4 (Spring 1981), 301-312. **(6)**

295 David H. Jonassen and Gerald G. Hodges. "Student Cognitive Styles: Implications for Library Educators," *Journal of Education for Librarianship* 22:3 (Winter 1982), 143-153. **(68, 71)**

296 Mary Kingsbury. "How Library Schools Evaluate Faculty Performance," *Journal of Education for Librarianship* 22:4 (Spring 1982), 219-238. **(36, 37)**

297 John W. Lee and Raymond L. Read. "The Graduate Business Student and the Library," *College and Research Libraries* 33:5 (September 1972), 403-407.

298 Carol Steer. "Authors Are Studied," *Canadian Library Journal* 39:3 (June 1982), 151-155. **(42, 190, 191, 195, 198)**

299 Rashid Tayyeb. "Implementing AACR 2—A National Survey," *Canadian Library Journal* 39:6 (December 1982), 373-376.

300 Dick Matzek and Scott Smith. "Online Searching in the Small College Library—The Economics and the Results," *Online* (March 1982), 21-29.

301 Mary Lee Bundy. "Metropolitan Public Library Use," *Wilson Library Bulletin* 41:9 (May 1967), 950-961.

302 John Shipman. "Signifying Renewal as Well as Change: One Library's Experience with the Center for Research Libraries," *Library Acquisitions: Practice and Theory* 2:5 (1978), 243-248.

303 Nathan R. Einhorn. "The Inclusion of the Products of Reprography in the International Exchange of Publications," *Library Acquisitions: Practice and Theory* 2:5 (1978), 227-236

304 Nancy J. Williamson. "Education for Acquisitions Librarians: A State of the Art Review," *Library Acquisitions: Practice and Theory* 2:3-4 (1978), 199-208. **(8)**

305 Janet L. Flowers. "Time Logs for Searchers: How Useful?" *Library Acquisitions: Practice and Theory* 2:2 (1978), 77-83.

306 D.N. Wood. "Current Exchange of Serials at the British Library Lending Division," *Library Acquisitions: Practice and Theory* 3:2 (1979), 107-113.

307 Robert Goehlert. "Journal Use Per Monetary Unit: A Reanalysis of Use Data," *Library Acquisitions: Practice and Theory* 3:2 (1979), 91-98.

308 Margaret Landesman and Christopher Gates. "Performance of American Inprint Vendors: A Comparison at the University of Utah," *Library Acquisitions: Practice and Theory* 4:3-4 (1980), 187-192.

309 Kenton Pattie and Mary Ernst. "Chapter II Grants: Libraries Gain," *School Library Journal* 29:5 (January 1983), 17-19.

310 John Erlandson and Yvonne Boyer. "Acquistions of State Documents," *Library Acquisitions: Practice and Theory* 4:2 (1980), 117-127.

311 George V. Hodowanec. "Analysis of Variables Which Help To Predict Book and Periodical Use," *Library Acquisitions: Practice and Theory* 4:1 (1980), 75-85.

312 Darrell L. Jenkins. "Acquiring Acquisitions Librarians," *Library Acquisitions: Practice and Theory* 5:2 (1981), 81-87.

313 Steven E. Maffeo. "Invoice Payment by Library Acquisitions: A Controlled Time Study," *Library Acquisitions: Practice and Theory* 5:2 (1981), 67-71.

314 Joyce G. McDonough, Carol Alf O'Connor and Thomas A. O'Connor. "Moving the Backlog: An Optimum Cycle for Searching OCLC," *Library Acquisitions: Practice and Theory* 6:3 (1982), 265-270.

315 Paul B. Wiener. "Recreational Reading Services in Academic Libraries: An Overview," *Library Acquisitions: Practice and Theory* 6:1 (1982), 59-70.

316 Peter Hernon. "Use of Microformatted Government Publications," *Microform Review* 11:4 (Fall 1982), 237-252.

317 Charles R. McClure. "Online Government Documents Data Base Searching and the Use of Microfiche Documents Online by Academic and Public Depository Librarians," *Microfilm Review* 10:4 (Fall 1981), 245-259. **(168, 169)**

318 Peter Hernon and George W. Whitbeck. "Government Publications and Commercial Microform Publishers: A Survey of Federal Depository Libraries," *Microform Review* 6:5 (September 1977), 272-284.

319 Robert F. Jennings and Hathia Hayes. "The Use of Microfiche Copies of Children's Trade Books in Selected Fourth-Grade Classrooms," *Microform Review* 3:3 (July 1974), 189-193.

320 E.R. Norten. "New Books in Microform: A Survey," *Microform Review* 1:4 (October 1972), 284-288.

321 Renata Tagliacozzo, Manfred Kochen and Lawrence Rosenberg. "Orthographic Error Patterns of Author Names in Catalog Searches," *Journal of Library Automation* 3:2 (June 1970), 93-101.

322 Lorne R. Buhr. "Selective Dissemination of MARC: A User Evaluation," *Journal of Library Automation* 5:1 (March 1972), 39-50.

323 Gerry D. Guthrie and Steven D. Slifko. "Analysis of Search Key Retrieval on a Large Bibliographic File," *Journal of Library Automation* 6:2 (June 1972), 96-100.

324 Alan L. Landgraf and Frederick G. Kilgour. "Catalog Records Retrieved by Personal Author Using Derived Search Keys," *Journal of Library Automation* 6:2 (June 1973), 103-108.

325 Martha E. Williams. "Data Element Statistics for the MARC II Data Base," *Journal of Library Automation* 6:2 (June 1976), 89-100.

326 Michael D. Cooper and Nancy A. DeWath. "The Cost of On-Line Bibliographic Searching," *Journal of Library Automation* 9:3 (September 1976), 195-209.

327 Edward John Kazlauskas. "The Application of the Instrumental Development Process to a Module on Flowcharting," *Journal of Library Automation* 9:3 (September 1976), 234-244. **(70)**

328 Lawrence K. Legard and Charles P. Bourne. "An Improved Title Word Search Key for Large Catalog Files," *Journal of Library Automation* 9:4 (December 1976), 318-327.

329 Ryan E. Hoover. "Patron Appraisal of Computer-Aided On-Line Bibliographic Retrieval Services," *Journal of Library Automation* 9:4 (December 1976), 335-350.

330 T.D.C. Kuch. "Analysis of the Literature of Library Automation through Citations in the *Annual Review of Information Science and Technology*," *Journal of Library Automation* 10:1 (March 1977), 82-84. **(182)**

331 Isobel Jean Mosley. "Cost-Effectiveness Analysis of the Automation of a Circulation System," *Journal of Library Automation* 10:3 (September 1977), 240-254.

332 Michael D. Cooper and Nancy A. DeWath. "The Effect of User Fees on the Cost of On-Line Searching in Libraries," *Journal of Library Automation* 10:4 (December 1977), 304-319.

333 James W. Bourg, Douglas Lacy, James Llinas and Edward T. O'Neill. "Developing Corporate Author Search Keys," *Journal of Library Automation* 11:2 (June 1978), 106-125.

334 Cynthia C. Ryans. "A Study of Errors Found in Non-MARC Cataloging in a Machine-Assisted System," *Journal of Library Automation* 11:2 (June 1978), 125-132.

335 Joselyn Druschel. "Cost Analysis of an Automated and Manual Cataloging and Book Processing System," *Journal of Library Automation* 14:1 (March 1981), 24-49.

336 Kunj B. Bastogi and Ichiko T. Morita. "OCLC Search Key Usage Patterns in a Large Research Library," *Journal of Library Automation* 14:2 (June 1981), 90-99.

337 Georgia L. Brown. "AACR 2: OCLC's Implementation and Database Conversion," *Journal of Library Automation* 14:3 (September 1981), 161-173.

338 James R. Martin. "Automation and the Service Attitudes of ARL Circulation Managers," *Journal of Library Automation* 14:3 (September 1981), 190-194.

339 University of Oregon Library. "A Comparison of OCLC, RLG/RLIN and WLN," *Journal of Library Automation* 14:3 (September 1981), 215-217.

340 Terence Crowley. "Comparing Fiche and Film: A Test of Speed," *Journal of Library Automation* 14:4 (December 1981), 292-294.

341 Public Service Satellite Consortium. "Cable Library Survey Results," *Journal of Library Automation* 14:4 (December 1981), 304-313.

342 Dennis Reynolds. "Entry of Local Data on OCLC: The Options and Their Impact on the Processing of Archival Tapes," *Information Technology and Libraries* 1:1 (March 1982), 5-14.

343 Joseph Ford. "Network Service Centers and Their Expanding Role," *Information Technology and Libraries* 1:1 (March 1982), 28-35.

344 Carolyn A. Johnson. "Retrospective Conversion of Three Library Collections," *Information Technology and Libraries* 1:2 (June 1982), 133-139.

345 Lynn L. Magrath. "Computers in the Library: The Human Element," *Information Technology and Libraries* 1:3 (September 1982), 266-270.

346 Izabella Taler. "Automated and Manual ILL: Time Effectiveness and Success Rate," *Information Technology and Libraries* 1:3 (September 1982), 277-280.

347 Martha E. Williams, Stephen W. Barth and Scott E. Preece. "Summary of Statistics for Five Years of the MARC Data Base," *Journal of Library Automation* 12:4 (December 1979), 314-337.

348 Susan U. Golden and Gary A. Golden. "Access to Periodicals: Search Key versus Keyword," *Information Technology and Libraries* 2:1 (March 1983), 26-32.

349 Ray R. Larson and Vicki Graham. "Monitoring and Evaluating MELVYL," *Information Technology and Libraries* 2:1 (March 1983), 93-104.

350 Barbara E. Carr. "Improving the Periodicals Collection through an Index Correlation Study," *Reference Services Review* 9:4 (October/December 1981), 27-31.

351 I.N. Sengupta. "Impact of Scientific Serials on the Advancement of Medical Knowledge: An Objective Method of Analysis," *International Library Review* 4:2 (April 1972), 169-195.

352 June L. Stewart. "The Literature of Politics: A Citation Analysis," *International Library Review* 2:3 (July 1970), 329-353.

353 I.N. Sengupta. "The Literature of Microbiology," *International Library Review* 6:3 (July 1974), 353-369.

354 I.N. Sengupta. "The Literature of Pharmacology," *International Library Review* 6:4 (October 1974), 483-504.

355 A.W. Hafner. "Citation Characteristics of Physiology Literature, 1970-72," *International Library Review* 8:1 (January 1976), 85-115.

356 Hans Hanan Wellisch. "Script Conversion Practices in the World's Libraries," *International Library Review* 8:1 (January 1976), 55-84.

357 Christine Anderson Brock and Gayle Smith Edelman. "Teaching Practices of Academic Law Librarians," *Law Library Journal* 71:1 (February 1978), 96-107. **(118, 119, 206, 207)**

358 Charles B. Wolfe. "Current Problems Facing State Law Libraries," *Law Library Journal* 71:1 (February 1978), 108-114).

359 Mindy J. Myers. "The Impact of Lexis on the Law Firm Library: A Survey," *Law Library Journal* 71:1 (February 1978), 158-169.

360 Nancy P. Johnson. "Legal Periodical Usage Survey: Method and Application," *Law Library Journal* 71:1 (February 1978), 177-186.

361 Ann M. Carter. "Budgeting in Private Law Firm Libraries," *Law Library Journal* 71:1 (February 1978), 187-194.

362 James F. Bailey, III and Oscar M. Trelles, II. "Autonomy, Librarian Status, and Librarian Tenure in Law School Libraries: The State of the Art, 1978," *Law Library Journal* 71:3 (August 1978), 425-462. **(97, 100, 112, 116, 118, 119, 120, 123, 125, 206, 207)**

363 Frank Wm. Goudy. "Funding Local Public Libraries: FY 1966 to FY 1980," *Public Libraries* 21:2 (Summer 1982), 52-54.

364 Guy Garrison. "A Look At Research on Public Library Problems in the 1970's," *Public Libraries* 19:1 (Spring 1980), 4-8. **(19)**

365 Terry L. Weech. "School and Public Library Cooperation—What We Would Like To Do, What We Do," *Public Libraries* 18:2 (Summer 1979), 33-34.

366 Patricia L. Piper and Cecilia Hing Ling Kwan. "Cataloging and Classification Practices in Law Libraries: Results of a Questionnaire," *Law Library Journal* 71:3 (August 1978), 481-483.

367 Christian M. Boissonnas. "The Quality of OCLC Bibliographic Records: The Cornell Law Library Experience," *Law Library Journal* 72:1 (Winter 1979), 80-85.

368 Kent Schrieffer and Linnea Christiani. "Ballots at Boalt," *Law Library Journal* 72:3 (Summer 1979), 497-512.

369 Ermina Hahn. "Survey of Technical Services Practices at Fifty Large Law School Libraries," *Law Library Journal* 73:3 (Summer 1980), 715-725.

370 Lana Caswell Garcia. "Legal Services Law Librarianship—An Investigation of Salary and Benefits in a Pioneer Field," *Law Library Journal* 73:3 (Summer 1980), 731-733. **(103)**

371 Reynold J. Kosek. "Faculty Status and Tenure for Nondirector, Academic Law Librarians" a section within "Status of Academic Law Librarians," *Law Library Journal* 73:4 (Fall 1980), 892-905. **(112, 113, 117, 123, 126)**

372 Martha C. Adamson and Gloria J. Zamora. "Authorship Characteristics in *Law Library Journal*: A Comparative Study," *Law Library Journal* 74:3 (Summer 1981), 527-533. **(41, 193, 196, 199)**

373 David G. Badertscher. "An Examination of the Dynamics of Change in Information Technology as Viewed from Law Libraries and Information Centers," *Law Library Journal* 75:2 (Spring 1982), 198-211.

374 Donald J. Dunn. "The Law Librarian's Obligation To Publish," *Law Library Journal* 75:2 (Spring 1982), 225-231. **(196)**

375 Audio-Visual Committee, American Association of Law Libraries. "Summary of Audio-Visual Materials Used in Legal Education: Audio-Visual Committee Report—June 1967," *Law Library Journal* 60:3 (August 1967), 272-276.

376 Cameron Allen. "Duplicate Holding Practices of Approved American Law School Libraries." *Law Library Journal* 62:2 (May 1969), 191-200.

377 Margaret Shediac. "Private Law Libraries Special Interest Section 1980 Salary Survey," *Law Library Journal* 74:2 (Spring 1981), 444-457.**(102, 103)**

378 Bettie H. Scott. "Price Index for Legal Publications," *Law Library Journal* 75:1 (Winter 1982), 171-174.

379 Silvia A. Gonzalez. "County Law Library Survey," *Law Library Journal* 74:3 (Summer 1981), 654-691. **(103)**

380 Silvia A. Gonzalez. "Survey of State Law Libraries," *Law Library Journal* 74:1 (Winter 1981), 160-201. **(103)**

381 Silvia A. Gonzalez. "Survey of Court Law Libraries," *Law Library Journal* 74:2 (Spring 1981), 458-494. **(103)**

382 David A. Thomas. "1980 Statistical Survey of Law School Libraries and Librarians," *Law Library Journal* 74:2 (Spring 1981), 359-443.**(99, 102)**

383 Marija Hughes. "Sex-Based Discrimination in Law Libraries," *Law Library Journal* 64:1 (February 1971), 13-22. **(127, 140, 146)**

384 Oscar M. Trelles. "Law Libraries and Unions," *Law Library Journal* 65:2 (May 1972), 158-180.

385 Claudia Sumler, Kristine Barone and Art Goetz. "Getting Books Faster and Cheaper: A Jobber Acquisitions Study," *Public Libraries* 19:4 (Winter 1980), 103-105.

386 Vernon A. Rayford. "A Black Librarian Takes a Look at Discrimination: by a Law School Library Survey," *Law Library Journal* 65:2 (May 1972), 183-189. **(127)**

387 Audio-Visual Committee, American Association of Law Libraries. "The Use of Audio-Visual Teaching Aids and Library Microforms in American Legal Education," *Law Library Journal* 66:1 (February 1973), 84-87.

388 Cameron Allen. "Whom We Shall Serve: Secondary Patrons of the University Law School Library," *Law Library Journal* 66:2 (May 1973), 160-171.

389 O. James Werner. "The Present Legal Status and Conditions of Prison Law Libraries," *Law Library Journal* 66:3 (August 1973), 259-269. **(80)**

390 George S. Grossman. "Clinical Legal Education and the Law Library," *Law Library Journal* 67:1 (February 1974), 60-78.

391 Kurt Schwerin and Igor I. Kavass. "Foreign Legal Periodicals in American Law Libraries 1973 Union List," *Law Library Journal* 67:1 (February 1974), 120-126.

392 Bethany J. Ochal. "County Law Libraries," *Law Library Journal* 67:2 (May 1974), 177-234.

393 Peter Enyingi. "Subject Cataloging Practices in American Law Libraries: A Survey," *Law Library Journal* 68:1 (February 1975), 11-17.

394 Sandra Sadow and Benjamin R. Beede. "Library Instruction in American Law Schools," *Law Library Journal* 68:1 (February 1975), 27-32.

395 Michael L. Richmond. "Attitudes of Law Librarians to Theft and Mutilation Control Methods," *Law Library Journal* 68:1 (February 1975), 60-81.

396   Ellin B. Christianson. "Mergers in the Publishing Industry, 1958-1970," *Journal of Library History, Philosophy and Comparative Librarianship* 7:1 (January 1972), 5-32.

397   Eugene E. Graziano. "Interlibrary Loan Analysis: Diagnostic for Scientific Serials Backfile Acquisitions," *Special Libraries* 53:5 (May/June 1962), 251-257.

398   John E. James. "Library Technician Program: The Library Technician Graduates' Point of View," *Special Libraries* 62:6 (July/August 1971), 268-278.**(50, 54, 55)**

399   James M. Matarazzo. "Scientific Journals: Page or Price Explosion?" *Special Libraries* 63:2 (February 1972), 53-58.

400   Julie L. Moore. "Bibliographic Control of American Doctoral Dissertations," *Special Libraries* 63:7 (July 1972), 285-291.

401   Robert T. Bottle and William W. Chase. "Some Characteristics of the Literature on Music and Musicology," *Special Libraries* 63:10 (October 1972), 469-476.

402   William P. Koughan and John A. Timour. "Are Hospital Libraries Meeting Physicians' Information Needs?" *Special Libraries* 64:5/6 (May/June 1972), 222-227.

403   Jean M. Ray. "Who Borrows Maps from a University Library Map Collection —And Why?" *Special Libraries* 65:3 (March 1974), 104-109.

404   Ching-Chih Chen. "How Do Scientists Meet Their Information Needs?" *Special Libraries* 65:7 (July 1974), 272-280.

405   Katherine C. Owen. "Productive Journal Titles in the Pharmaceutical Industry," *Special Libraries* 65:10/11 (October/November 1974), 430-439.

406   Stanley A. Elman. "Cost Comparison of Manual and On-Line Computerized Literature Searching," *Special Libraries* 66:1 (January 1975), 12-18.

407   Jerome P. Fatcheric. "Survey of Users of a Medium-Sized Technical Library," *Special Libraries* 66:5/6 (May/June 1975), 245-251.

408   Bahaa El-Hadidy. "Bibliographic Control among Geoscience Abstracting and Indexing Services," *Special Libraries* 66:5/6 (May/June 1975), 260-265.

409   Ruth W. Wender. "Hospital Journal Title Usage Study," *Special Libraries* 66:11 (November 1975), 532-537.

410   Thelma Freides. "Bibliographic Gaps in the Social Science Literature," *Special Libraries* 67:2 (February 1976), 68-75.

411   Eileen E. Hitchingham. "MEDLINE Use in a University without a School of Medicine," *Special Libraries* 67:4 (April 1976), 188-194.

412   David Hull and Henry D. Fearnley. "The Museum Library in the United States: A Sample," *Special Libraries* 67:7 (July 1976), 289-298. **(80, 88, 101)**

413   Amelia Breiting, Marcia Dorey and Deirdre Sockbeson. "Staff Development in College and University Libraries," *Special Libraries* 67:7 (July 1976), 305-309. **(167, 168, 202)**

414   Arley L. Ripin and Dorothy Kasman. "Education for Special Librarianship: A Survey of Courses Offered in Accredited Programs," *Special Libraries* 67:11 (November 1976), 504-509. **(13)**

415   George W. Black, Jr. "Selected Annaul Bound Volume Production," *Special Libraries* 67:11 (November 1976), 534-536.

416   Howard Fosdick. "An SDC-Based On-Line Search Service: A Patron Evaluation Survey and Implications," *Special Libraries* 68:9 (September 1977), 305-312.

417   Diane M. Nelson. "Methods of Citation Analysis in the Fine Arts," *Special Libraries* 68:11 (November 1977), 390-395.

418   Annette Corth. "Coverage of Marine Biology Citations,"*Special Libraries* 68:12 (December 1977), 439-446.

419   Jean K. Martin. "Computer-Based Literature Searching: Impact on Interlibrary Loan Service," *Special Libaries* 69:1 (January 1978), 1-6.

420   Jean M. Ray. "Who Borrows Maps from a University Library Map Collection —and Why? Report II," *Special Libraries* 69:1 (January 1978), 13-20.

421   Robert Goehlert. "Periodical Use in an Academic Library: A Study of Economists and Political Scientists," *Special Libraries* 69:2 (February 1978), 51-60.

422   Sandra J. Springer, Robert A. Yokel, Nancy M. Lorenzi, Leonard T. Sigell and E. Don Nelson. "Drug Information to Patient Care Areas via Television: Preliminary Evaluation of Two Years' Experience," *Special Libraries* 69:4 (April 1978), 155-163.

423   Martha J. Bailey. "Requirement for Middle Managerial Positions," *Special Libraries* 69:9 (September 1978), 323-331. **(3, 78, 82, 86, 87, 106)**

424   Carolyn L. Warden. "An Industrial Current Awareness Service: A User Evaluation Study," *Special Libraries* 69:12 (December 1978), 459-467.

425   Charles H. Davis. "Programming Aptitude as a Function of Undergraduate Major," *Special Libraries* 69:12 (December 1978), 482-485. **(53)**

426   Jean Mace Schmidt. "Translation of Periodical Literature in Plant Pathology," *Special Libraries* 70:1 (January 1979), 12-17.

427 Susan Dingle-Cliff and Charles H. Davis. "Collection Overlap in Canadian Addictions Libraries," *Special Libraries* 70:2 (February 1979), 76-81.

428 John J. Knightly. "Overcoming the Cirterion Problem in the Evaluation of Library Performance," *Special Libraries* 70:4 (April 1979), 173-178.

429 Ruth W. Wender. "Counting Journal Title Usage in the Health Sciences," *Special Libraries* 70:5/6 (May/June 1975), 219-226.

430 John Steuben. "Interlibrary Loan of Photocopies of Articles under the New Copyright Law," *Special Libraries* 70:5/6 (May/June 1979), 227-232.

431 John Kok and Edward G. Strable. "Moving Up: Librarians Who Have Become Officers of Their Organization," *Special Libraries* 71:1 (January 1980), 5-12. **(81, 128)**

432 Rebecca J. Jensen, Herbert D. Asbury and Radford G. King. "Costs and Benefits to Industry of Online Literature Searches," *Special Libraries* 71:7 (July 1980), 291-299.

433 C. Margaret Bell. "The Applicability of OCLC and Inforonics in Special Libraries," *Special Libraries* 71:9 (September 1980), 398-404.

434 A. Neil Yerkey. "The Psychological Climate of Librarianship: Values of Special Librarians," *Special Libraries* 72:3 (July 1981), 195-200. **(69)**

435 Virgil P. Diodato. "Author Indexing," *Special Libraries* 72:4 (October 1981), 361-369.

436 Judith M. Pask. "Bibliographic Instruction in Business Libraries," *Special Libraries* 72:4 (October 1981), 370-378.

437 Ann T. Dodson, Paul P. Philbin and Kunj B. Rastogi. "Electronic Interlibrary Loan in the OCLC Library: A Study of its Effectiveness," *Special Libraries* 73:1 (January 1982), 12-20.

438 Gloria J. Zamora and Martha C. Adamson. "Authorship Characteristics in *Special Libraries*: A Comparative Study," *Special Libraries* 73:2 (April 1982), 100-107. **(42, 194, 199)**

439 Robert K. Poyer. "Time Lag in Four Indexing Services," *Special Libraries* 73:2 (April 1982), 142-146.

440 Pauline R. Hodges. "Keyword in Title Indexes: Effectiveness of Retrieval in Computer Searches," *Special Libraries* 74:1 (January 1983), 56-60.

441 D.K. Varma. "Increased Subscription Costs and Problems of Resource Allocation," *Special Libraries* 74:1 (January 1983), 61-66.

442 Michael Halperin and Ruth A. Pagell. "Searchers' Perceptions of Online Database Vendors," *Special Libraries* 74:2 (April 1973), 119-126.

443 Michael E.D. Koenig. "Education for Special Librarianship," *Special Librar-ies* 74:2 (April 1983), 182-196. **(13, 14, 59, 108, 109)**

444 Powell Niland and William H. Kurth. "Estimating Lost Volumes in a University Library Collection," *College and Research Libraries* 37:2 (March 1976), 128-136.

445 Rush G. Miller. "The Influx of Ph.D.s into Librarianship: Intrusion or Transfusion?" *College and Research Libraries* 37:2 (March 1976), 158-165. **(16, 17, 21, 33, 85, 86, 97, 98)**

446 Steven Leach. "The Growth Rates of Major Academic Libraries: Rider and Purdue Reviewed," *College and Research Libraries* 37:6 (November 1976), 531-542.

447 T. Saracevic, W.M. Shaw, Jr. and P.B. Kantor. "Causes and Dynamics of User Frustration in an Academic Library," *College and Research Libraries* 38:1 (January 1977), 7-18.

448 R.W. Meyer and Rebecca Panetta. "Two Shared Cataloging Data Bases: A Comparison," *College and Research Libraries* 38:1 (January 1977), 19-24.

449 Peter Hernon and Maureen Pastine. "Student Perceptions of Academic Librarians," *College and Research Libraries* 38:2 (March 1977), 129-139.

450 Catherine V. Von Schon. "Inventory 'By Computer'," *College and Research Libraries* 38:2 (March 1977), 147-152.

451 David C. Genaway and Edward B. Stanford. "Quasi-Departmental Librar-ies," *College and Research Libraries* 38:3 (May 1977), 187-194.

452 Elizabeth W. Matthews. "Trends Affecting Community College Library Administrators," *College and Research Libraries* 38:3 (May 1977), 210-217.

453 Lawrence J. Perk. "Secondary Publications in Education: A Study of Duplication," *College and Research Libraries* 38:3 (May 1977), 221-226.

454 Geraldine Murphy Wright. "Current Trends in Periodical Collections," *College and Research Libraries* 38:3 (May 1977), 234-240.

455 Lawrence J. Perk and Noelle Van Pulis. "Periodical Usage in an Education-Psychology Library," *College and Research Libraries* 38:4 (July 1977), 304-308. **(5)**

456 Egill A. Halldorsson and Marjorie E. Murfin. "The Performance of Profes-sionals and Nonprofessionals in the Reference Interview," *College and Research Libraries* 38:5 (September 1977), 385-395.

457 Susan A. Lee. "Conflict and Ambiguity in the Role of the Academic Library Director," *College and Research Libraries* 38:5 (September 1977), 396-403.

458 Glenn R. Wittig. "Dual Pricing of Periodicals," *College and Research Libraries* 38:5 (September 1977), 412-418.

459 Miriam A. Drake. "Attribution of Library Costs," *College and Research Libraries* 38:6 (November 1977), 514-519.

460 Harry M. Kriz. "Subscriptions vs. Books in a Constant Dollar Budget," *College and Research Libraries* 39:2 (March 1978), 105-109.

461 Charles J. Popovich. "The Characteristics of a Collection for Research in Business/Management," *College and Research Libraries* 39:2 (March 1978), 117.

462 Jean A. Major. "The Visually Impaired Reader in the Academic Library," *College and Research Libraries* 39:3 (May 1978), 191-196.

463 Herbert S. White and Karen Momenee. "Impact of the Increase in Library Doctorates," *College and Research Libraries* 39:3 (May 1978), 207-214. (17, 24, 25, 28, 29, 31, 34, 38, 39, 84, 91)

464 James Michalko and Toby Heidtmann. "Evaluating the Effectiveness of an Electronic Security System," *College and Research Libraries* 39:4 (July 1978), 263-267.

465 William M. McClellan. "Judging Music Libraries," *College and Research Libraries* 39:4 (July 1978), 281-286.

466 Rita Hoyt Smith and Warner Granade. "User and Library Failures in an Undergraduate Library," *College and Research Libraries* 39:6 (November 1978), 467-473.

467 Linda Ann Hulbert and David Stewart Curry. "Evaluation of an Approval Plan," *College and Research Libraries* 39:6 (November 1978), 485-491.

468 Julia F. Baldwin and Robert S. Rudolph. "The Comparative Effectiveness of a Slide/Tape Show and a Library Tour," *College and Research Libraries* 40:1 (January 1979), 31-35.

469 Melissa D. Trevvett. "Characteristics of Interlibrary Loan Requests at the Library of Congress," *College and Research Libraries* 40:1 (January 1979), 36-43.

470 Elaine Zaremba Jennerich and Bessie Hess Smith. "A Bibliographic Instruction Program in Music," *College and Research Libraries* 40:3 (May 1979), 226-233.

471 William J. Maher and Benjamin F. Shearer. "Undergraduate Use Patterns of Newspapers on Microfilm," *College and Research Libraries* 40:3 (May 1979), 254-260.

472 Larry Hardesty, Nicholas P. Lovrich, Jr. and James Mannon. "Evaluating Library-Use Instruction," *College and Research Libraries* 40:4 (July 1979), 309-317.

473 Seymour H. Sargent. "The Uses and Limitations of Trueswell," *College and Research Libraries* 40:5 (September 1979), 416-425.

474 Patricia Stenstrom and Ruth B. McBride." Serial Use by Social Science Faculty: A Survey," *College and Research Libraries* 40:5 (September 1979), 426-431.

475 Elaine C. Clever. "Using Indexes as 'Memory Assists'," *College and Research Libraries* 40:5 (September 1979), 444-449.

476 William E. McGrath, Donald J. Simon and Evelyn Bullard. "Ethnocentricity and Cross-Disciplinary Circulation," *College and Research Libraries* 40:6 (November 1979), 511-518.

477 Michael Gorman and Jami Hotsinpiller. "ISBD: Aid or Barrier to Understanding," *College and Research Libraries* 40:6 (November 1979), 519-526.

478 Jinnie Y. Davis and Stella Bentley. "Factors Affecting Faculty Perceptions of Academic Libraries," *College and Research Libraries* 40:6 (November 1979), 527-532.

479 Dennis J. Reynolds. "Regional Alternatives for Interlibrary Loan: Access to Unreported Holdings," *College and Research Libraries* 41:1 (January 1980), 33-42.

480 Ronald Rayman and Frank William Goudy. "Research and Publication Requirements in University Libraries," *College and Research Libraries* 41:1 (January 1980), 43-48. **(112, 124, 178, 179, 202, 203)**

481 John N. Olsgaard and Jane Kinch Olsgaard. "Authorship in Five Library Periodicals," *College and Research Libraries* 41:1 (January 1980), 49-53. **(40, 189, 191, 194, 196)**

482 Albert F. Maag. "Design of the Library Director Interview: The Candidate's Perspective," *College and Research Libraries* 41:2 (March 1980), 112-121.

483 Thomas M. Gaughan. "Resume Essentials for the Academic Librarian," *College and Research Libraries* 41:2 (March 1980), 122-127. **(161)**

484 Harold B. Shill. "Open Stacks and Library Performance," *College and Research Libraries* 41:3 (May 1980), 220-225.

485 Robert L. Turner, Jr. "Femininity and the Librarian—Another Test," *College and Research Libraries* 41:3 (May 1980), 235-241. **(68)**

486 Ray L. Carpenter. "College Libraries: A Comparative Analysis in Terms of the ACRL Standards," *College and Research Libraries* 42:1 (January 1981), 7-18.

487 George V. Hodowanec. "An Acquisition Rate Model for Academic Libraries," *College and Research Libraries* 39:6 (September 1978), 439-442.

488 Roland Person. "Long-Term Evaluation of Bibliographic Instruction: Lasting Encouragement," *College and Research Libraries* 42:1 (January 1981), 19-25.

489 Laslo A. Nagy and Martha Lou Thomas. "An Evaluation of the Teaching Effectiveness of Two Library Instructional Videotapes," *College and Research Libraries* 42:1 (January 1981), 26-30.

490 David N. King and John C. Ory. "Effects of Library Instruction on Student Research: A Case Study," *College and Research Libraries* 42:1 (January 1981), 31-41.

491 Herbert S. White. "Perceptions by Educators and Administrators of the Ranking of Library School Programs," *College and Research Libraries* 42:3 (May 1981), 191-202. **(63, 64)**

492 Russ Davidson, Connie Capers Thorson and Margo C. Trumpeter. "Faculty Status for Librarians in the Rocky Mountain Region: A Review and Analysis," *College and Research Libraries* 42:3 (May 1981), 203-213. **(113, 119, 121, 124, 180, 204)**

493 M. Kathy Cook. "Rank, Status, and Contribution of Academic Librarians as Perceived by the Teaching Faculty at Southern Illinois University, Carbondale," *College and Research Libraries* 42:3 (May 1981), 214-223. **(114, 203, 204, 206)**

494 John N. Olsgaard and Jane Kinch Olsgaard. "Post-MLS Educational Requirements for Academic Librarians," *College and Research Libraries* 42:3 (May 1981), 224-228. **(86, 87, 107)**

495 Ronald Rayman. "Employment Opportunities for Academic Librarians in the 1970's: An Analysis of the Past Decade," *College and Research Libraries* 42:3 (May 1981), 229-234. **(77, 158)**

496 Martha C. Adamson and Gloria J. Zamora. "Publishing in Library Science Journals: A Test of the Olsgaard Profile," *College and Research Libraries* 42:3 (May 1981), 235-241. **(41, 192, 193, 199, 201)**

497 Charles Sage, Janet Klass, Helen H. Spalding and Tracey Robinson. "A Queueing Study of Public Catalog Use," *College and Research Libraries* 42:4 (July 1981), 317-325.

498 Doris Cruger Dale. "Cataloging and Classsification Practices in Community College Libraries," *College and Research Libraries* 42:4 (July 1981), 333-339.

499 Dana Weiss. "Book Theft and Book Mutilation in a Large Urban University Library," *College and Research Libraries* 42:4 (July 1981), 341-347.

500 Raymond L. Carpenter. "Two-Year College Libraries: A Comparative Analysis in Terms of the ACRL Standards," *College and Research Libraries* 42:5 (September 1981), 407-415.

501 Paul D. Luyben, Leonard Cohen, Rebecca Conger and Selby U. Gration. "Reducing Noise in a College Library," *College and Research Libraries* 42:5 (September 1981), 470-481.

502 Prabha Sharma. "A Survey of Academic Librarians and Their Opinions Related to Nine-Month Contracts and Academic Status Configurations in Alabama, Georgia and Mississippi," *College and Research Libraries* 42:6 (November 1981), 561-570. **(99, 113, 124, 153, 154, 179, 186, 203)**

503 Priscilla Geahigan, Harriet Nelson, Stewart Saunders and Lawrence Woods. "Acceptability of Non-Library/Information Science Publications in the Promotion and Tenure of Academic Librarians," *College and Research Libraries* 42:6 (November 1981), 571-575. **(114, 124, 179, 180, 187)**

504 Barbara Moore, Tamara J. Miller and Don L. Tolliver. "Title Overlap: A Study of Duplication in the University of Wisconsin System Libraries," *College and Research Libraries* 43:1 (January 1982), 14-21.

505 Gary A. Golden, Susan U. Golden and Rebecca T. Lenzini. "Patron Approaches to Serials: A User Study," *College and Research Libraries* 43:1 (January 1982), 22-30.

506 Thomas T. Surprenant. "Learning Theory, Lecture, and Programmed Instruction Text: An Experiment in Bibliographic Instruction," *College and Research Libraries* 43:1 (January 1982), 31-37.

507 Larry Hardesty, Nicholas P. Lovrich, Jr. and James Mannon. "Library-Use Instruction: Assessment of the Long-Term Effects," *College and Research Libraries* 43:1 (January 1982), 38-46.

508 Robert Swisher and Peggy C. Smith. "Journals Read by ACRL Academic Librarians, 1973 and 1978," *College and Research Libraries* 43:1 (January 1982), 51-58. **(169, 170)**

509 William Caynon. "Collective Bargaining and Professional Development of Academic Librarians," *College and Research Libraries* 43:2 (March 1982), 133-139.

510 Barbara J. Smith. "Background Characteristics and Education Needs of a Group of Instruction Librarians in Pennsylvania," *College and Research Libraries* 43:3 (May 1982), 199-207.

511 Gloria S. Cline. "*College and Research Libraries*: Its First Forty Years," *College and Research Libraries* 43:3 (May 1982), 208-232. **(188, 192, 198, 201)**

512 John B. Harer and C. Edward Huber. "Copyright Policies in Virginia Academic Library Reserve Rooms," *College and Research Libraries* 43:3 (May 1982), 233-241.

513 Laurie S. Linsley. "Academic Libraries in an Interlibrary Loan Network," *College and Research Libraries* 43:4 (July 1982), 292-299.

514 Timothy D. Jewell. "Student Reactions to a Self-Paced Library Skills Workbook Program: Survey Evidence," *College and Research Libraries* 43:5 (September 1982), 371-378.

515 Mary Baier Wells. "Requirements and Benefits for Academic Librarians: 1959-1979," *College and Research Libraries* 43:6 (November 1982), 450-458. **(82, 90, 93, 96, 98, 99, 105, 106, 114, 156, 157, 160, 161)**

516 Marjorie A. Benedict, Jacquelyn A. Gavryck and Hanan C. Selvin. "Status of Academic Librarians in New York State," *College and Research Libraries* 44:1 (January 1983), 12-19. **(114, 115, 122, 125, 204)**

517 Carol Truett. "Services to Developmental Education Students in the Community College: Does the Library Have a Role?" *College and Research Libraries* 44:1 (January 1983), 20-28.

518 Gene K. Rinkel and Patricia McCandless. "Application of a Methodology Analyzing User Frustration," *College and Research Libraries* 44:1 (January 1983), 29-37.

519 Jo Bell Whitlatch. "Library Use Patterns Among Full- and Part-Time Faculty and Students," *College and Research Libraries* 44:2 (March 1983), 141-152.

520 Madeleine Stern. "Characteristics of the Literature of Literary Scholarship," *College and Research Libraries* 44:4 (July 1983), 199-209.

521 Philip Schwarz. "Demand-Adjusted Shelf Availability Parameters: A Second Look," *College and Research Libraries* 44:4 (July 1983), 210-219.

522 Paul M. Anderson and Ellen G. Miller. "Participative Planning for Library Automation: The Role of the User Opinion Survey," *College and Research Libraries* 44:4 (July 1983), 245-254.

523 Raymond W. Barber and Jacqueline C. Mancall. "The Application of Bibliometric Techniques to the Analysis of Materials for Young Adults," *Collection Management* 2:3 (Fall 1978), 229-245.

524 Kenneth C. Kirsch and Albert H. Rubenstein. "Converting from Hard Copy to Microfilm: An Administrative Experiment," *Collection Management* 2:4 (Winter 1978), 279-302.

525 Herbert Goldhor. "U.S. Public Library Adult Non-Fiction Book Collections in the Humanities," *Collection Management* 3:1 (Spring 1979), 31-43.

526 Sally F. Williams. "Construction and Application of a Periodical Price Index," *Collection Management* 2:4 (Winter 1978), 329-344.

527 Mary Jane Pobst Reed. "Identification of Storage Candidates among Monographs," *Collection Management* 3:2/3 (Summer/Fall 1979), 203-214.

528 Ung Chon Kim. "Participation of Teaching Faculty in Library Book Selection," *Collection Management* 3:4 (Winter 1979), 333-352.

529 Glenn R. Lowry. "A Heuristic Collection Loss Rate Determination Methodology: An Alternative to Shelf-Reading," *Collection Management* 4:1/2 (Spring/Summer 1982), 73-83.

530 Stewart Saunders. "Student Reliance on Faculty Guidance in the Selection of Reading Materials: The Use of Core Collections," *Collection Management* 4:4 (Winter 1982), 9-23.

531 Ralph M. Daehn. "The Measurement and Projection of Shelf Space," *Collection Management* 4:4 (Winter 1982), 25-39.

532 Igor I. Kavass. "Foreign and International Law Collections in Selected Law Libraries of the United States: Survey, 1972-73," *International Journal of Law Libraries* 1:3 (November 1973), 117-133.

533 Robert J. Garen. "Library Orientation on Television," *Canadian Library Journal* 24:2 (September 1967), 124-126.

534 D.W. Miller. "Non-English Books in Canadian Public Libraries," *Canadian Library Journal* 27:2 (March/April 1970), 123-129.

535 Robert H. Blackburn. "Canadian Content in a Sample of Photocopying," *Canadian Library Journal* 27:5 (September/October 1970), 332-340.

536 Peter H. Wolters and Jack E. Brown. "CAN/SDI System: User Reaction to a Computer Information Retrieval System for Canadian Scientists and Technologists," *Canadian Library Journal* 28:1 (January/ February), 20-23.

537 M. Jamil Qureshi. "Academic Status, Salaries and Fringe Benefits in Community College Libraries of Canada," *Canadian Library Journal* 28:1 (January/February 1971), 41-45. **(97, 110, 121)**

538 George J. Snowball. "Survey of Social Sciences and Humanities Monograph Circulation by Random Sampling of the Stack," *Canadian Library Journal* 28:5 (September/October 1971), 352-361.

539 Roop K. Sandhu and Harjit Sandhu. "Job Perception of University Librarians and Library Students," *Canadian Library Journal* 28:6 (November/ December 1971), 438-445.

540 Brian Dale and Patricia Dewdney. "Canadian Public Libraries and the Physically Handicapped," *Canadian Library Journal* 29:3 (May/June 1972), 231-236.

541 R.G. Wilson. "Interlibrary Loan Experiments at the University of Calgary," *Canadian Library Journal* 30:1 (January/February 1973), 38-40.

542 Peter Simmons. "Studies in the Use of the Card Catalogue in a Public Library," *Canadian Library Journal* 31:4 (August 1974), 323-337.

543 L.J. Amey and R.J. Smith. "Combination School and Public Libraries: An Attitudinal Study," *Canadian Library Journal* 33:3 (June 1976), 251-261.

544 John Wilkinson. "The Library Market for Canadian Juvenile Fiction: A Further Analysis," *Canadian Library Journal* 34:1 (February 1977), 5-15.

545 Larry Orten and John Wiseman. "Library Service to Part-time Students," *Canadian Library Journal* 34:1 (February 1977), 23-27.

546 Esther L. Sleep. "Whither the ISSN? A Practical Experience," *Canadian Library Journal* 34:4 (August 1977), 265-270.

547 Sarah Landy. "Why Johnny Can Read...but Doesn't," *Canadian Library Journal* 34:5 (October 1977), 379-387.

548 Sharon Mott. "An Edmonton High School Reduces Book Losses," *Canadian Library Journal* 35:1 (February 1978), 45-49.

549 Fotoula Pantazis. "Library Technicians in Ontario Academic Libraries," *Canadian Library Journal* 35:2 (April 1978), 77-91. **(55)**

550 Dorothy Ryder. "Canadian Reference Sources—A 10 Year Overview," *Canadian Library Journal* 35:4 (August 1978), 289-293.

551 Laurent-G. Denis. "Full-time Faculty Survey Describes Educators," *Canadian Library Journal* 36:3 (June 1979), 107-121. **(4, 14, 25, 26, 27, 29, 30, 34, 45, 50, 62, 170)**

552 Marie Foster. "Philosophy of Librarianship," *Canadian Library Journal* 36:3 (June 1979), 131-137. **(67)**

553 Kenneth H. Plate and Jacob P. Seigel. "Career Patterns of Ontario Librarians," *Canadian Library Journal* 36:3 (June 1979), 143-148. **(129, 144, 151)**

554 Mavis Cariou. "Liaison Where Field and Faculty Meet," *Canadian Library Journal* 36:3 (June 1979), 155-163. **(12, 13, 60, 61, 163, 164)**

555 Norman Horrocks. "Encyclopedias and Public Libraries: A Canadian Survey," *Canadian Library Journal* 38:2 (April 1981), 79-83.

556 Stephen B. Lawton. "Diffusion of Automation in Post-Secondary Institutions," *Canadian Library Journal* 38:2 (April 1980), 93-97.

557 Mary Ann Wasylycia-Coe. "Profile: Canadian Chief Librarians by Sex," *Canadian Library Journal* 38:3 (June 1981), 159-163. **(128, 131, 136, 144, 149, 152)**

558 Margaret Currie, Elaine Goettler and Sandra McCaskill. "Evaluating the Relationship between Library Skills and Library Instruction," *Canadian Library Journal* 39:1 (February 1982), 35-37.

559 Esther L. Sleep. "Periodical Vandalism: A Chronic Condition," *Canadian Library Journal* 39:1 (February 1982), 39-42.

560 Kenneth Setterington. "The Ph.D. in Library Administration: A Report of Research," *Library Research* (after Spring 1983 called *Library and Information Science Research*) 5:2 (Summer 1983), 177-194. **(19, 20, 27, 35, 65)**

561   Robert F. Rose. "Identifying a Core Collection of Business Periodicals for Academic Libraries," *Collection Management* 5:1/2 (Spring/Summer 1983), 73-87.

562   Raymond Kilpela. "A Profile of Library School Deans, 1960-81," *Journal of Education for Librarianship* 23:3 (Winter 1983), 173-191. **(14, 15, 16, 20, 45, 46, 47, 65, 66)**

563   Charlene Renner and Barton M. Clark. "Professional and Nonprofessional Staffing Patterns in Departmental Libraries," *Library Research* 1 (1979), 153-170.

564   Jacqueline C. Mancall and M. Carl Drott. "Materials Used by High School Students in Preparing Independent Study Projects: A Bibliometric Approach," *Library Research* 1 (1979), 223-236.

565   Alan R. Samuels. "Assessing Organizational Climate in Public Libraries," *Library Research* 1 (1979), 237-254.

566   Diane Mittermeyer and Lloyd J. Houser. "The Knowledge Base for the Administration of Libraries," *Library Research* 1 (1979), 255-276. **(183, 200)**

567   Michael V. Sullivan, Betty Vadeboncoeur, Nancy Shiotani and Peter Stangl. "Obsolescence in Biomedical Journals: Not an Artifact of Literature Growth," *Library Research* 2 (1980-81), 29-46.

568   Robert V. Williams. "Sources of the Variability in Level of Public Library Development in the United States: A Comparative Analysis," *Library Research* 2 (1980-81), 157-176.

569   Bluma C. Peritz. "The Methods of Library Science Research: Some Results from a Bibliometric Survey," *Library Research* 2 (1980-81), 251-268. **(184)**

570   Nancy Van House DeWath. "Fees for Online Bibliographic Search Services in Publicly-Supported Libraries," *Library Research* 3 (1981), 29-45.

571   Bluma C. Peritz. "Citation Characteristics in Library Science: Some Further Results from a Bibliometric Survey," *Library Research* 3 (1981), 47-65.**(184, 185)**

572   Gary Moore. "Library Long-Range Planning: A Survey of Current Practices," *Library Research* 3 (1981), 155-165.

573   Larry Hardesty. "Use of Library Materials at a Small Liberal Arts College," *Library Research* 3 (1981), 261-282.

574   Stewart Saunders, Harriet Nelson and Priscilla Geahigan. "Alternatives to the Shelflist Measure for Determining the Size of a Subject Collection," *Library Research* 3 (1981), 383-391.

575   P. Robert Paustian. "Collection Size and Interlibrary Loan in Large Academic Libraries," *Library Research* 3 (1981), 393-400.

576   Daniel O. O'Connor. "Evaluating Public Libraries Using Standard Scores: The Library Quotient," *Library Research* 4 (1982), 51-70.

577 Snunith Shoham. "A Cost-Preference Study of the Decentralization of Academic Library Services," *Library Research* 4 (1982), 175-194.

578 A.S. Pickett. "San Franscisco State College Library Technical Services Time Study," *Library Resources and Technical Services* 4:1 (Winter 1960), 45-46.

579 Rosamond H. Danielson. "Cornell's Area Classification: A Space-Saving Device for Less-Used Books," *Library Resources and Technical Services* 5:2 (Spring 1961), 139-141.

580 Miriam C. Maloy. "Reclassification for the Divisional Plan," Library Resources and Technical Services 6:3 (Summer 1962), 239-242.

581 Andre Nitecki. "Costs of a Divided Catalog," *Library Resources and Technical Services* 6:4 (Fall 1962), 351-355.

582 Donald V. Black. "Automatic Classification and Indexing, for Libraries?" *Library Resources and Technical Services* 9:1 (Winter 1965), 35-52.

583 Perry D. Morrison. "Use of Library of Congress Classsification Decisions in Academic Libraries—An Empirical Study," *Library Resources and Technical Services* 9:2 (Spring 1965), 235-242.

584 Manuel D. Lopez. "Subject Catalogers Equal to the Future?" *Library Resources and Technical Services* 9:3 (Summer 1965), 371-375.

585 Ashby J. Fristoe. "The Bitter End," *Library Resources and Technical Services* 10:1 (Winter 1966), 91-95.

586 Ole V. Groos. "Less-Used Titles and Volumes of Science Journals: Two Preliminary Notes," *Library Resources and Technical Services* 10:3 (Summer 1966), 289-290.

587 Paula M. Strain. "A Study of the Usage and Retention of Technical Periodicals," *Library Resources and Technical Services* 10:3 (Summer 1966), 295-304.

588 William R. Nugent. "Statistics of Collection Overlap at the Libraries of the Six New England State Universities," *Library Resources and Technical Services* 12:1 (Winter 1968), 31-36.

589 Walter R. Stubbs and Robert N. Broadus. "The Value of the Kirkus Service for College Libraries," *Library Resources and Technical Services* 13:2 (Spring 1969), 203-205.

590 Barton R. Burkhalter and LaVerne Hoag. "Another Look at Manual Sorting and Filing: Backwards and Forwards," *Library Resources and Technical Services* 14:3 (Summer 1970), 445-454.

591 "More on DC Numbers on LC Cards: Quantity and Quality," *Library Resources and Technical Services* 14:4 (Fall 1970), 517-527.

592 Carol A. Nemeyer. "Scholarly Reprint Publishing in the United States: Selected Findings from a Recent Survey of the Industry," *Library Resources and Technical Services* 15:1 (Winter 1971), 35-48.

593 Betty J. Mitchell and Carol Bedoian. "A Systematic Approach to Performance Evaluation of Out-of-Print Book Dealers: The San Fernando Valley State College Experience," *Library Resources and Technical Services* 15:2 (Spring 1971), 215-222.

594 Barbara Schrader and Elaine Orsini. "British, French and Australian Publications in the National Union Catalog: A Study of NPAC's Effectiveness," *Library Resources and Technical Services* 15:3 (Summer 1971), 345-353.

595 Joel Levis. "Canadian Publications in the English Language: CBI vs. *Canadiana*," *Library Resources and Technical Services* 15:3 (Summer 1971), 354-358.

596 Zubaidah Isa. "The Entry-Word in Indonesian Names and Titles," *Library Resources and Technical Services* 15:3 (Summer 1971), 393-398.

597 Richard J. Hyman. "Access to Library Collections: Summary of a Documentary and Opinion Survey on the Direct Shelf Approach and Browsing," *Library Resources and Technical Services* 15:4 (Fall 1971), 479-491.

598 Robert L. Mowery. "The Cryptic Other," *Library Resources and Technical Services* 16:1 (Winter 1972), 74-78.

599 Ann Craig Turner. "Comparative Card Production Methods," *Library Resources and Technical Services* 16:3 (Summer 1972), pp. 347-358.

600 Edmund G. Hamann. "Expansion of the Public Card Catalog in a Large Library," *Library Resources and Technical Services* 16:4 (Fall 1972), 488-496.

601 Ernest R. Perez. "Acquisitions of Out-of-Print Materials," *Library Resources and Technical Services* 17:1 (Winter 1973), 42-59.

602 E. Dale Cluff and Karen Anderson. "LC Card Order Experiment Conducted at University of Utah Marriott Library," *Library Resources and Technical Services* 17:1 (Winter 1973), 70-72.

603 Betty J. Mitchell. "Methods Used in Out-of-Print Acquisition; A Survey of Out-of-Print Book Dealers," *Library Resources and Technical Services* 17:2 (Spring 1973), 211-215.

604 George Piternick. "University Library Arrearages," *Library Resources and Technical Services* 13:1 (Winter 1969), 102-114.

605 Nancy E. Brodie. "Evaluation of a KWIC Index for *Library Literature*," *Journal of the American Society for Information Science* 21:1 (January-February 1970), 22-28.

606 William S. Cooper. "The Potential Usefulness of Catalog Access Points Other than Author, Title and Subject," *Journal of the American Society for Information Science* 21:2 (March-April 1970), 112-127.

607 Barbara F. Frick and John M. Ginski. "Cardiovascular Serial Literature: Characteristics, Productive Journals, and Abstracting/Indexing Coverage," *Journal of the American Society for Information Science* 21:5 (September-October 1970), 338-344.

608 Ching-Chih Chen. "The Use Patterns of Physics Journals in a Large Academic Research Library," *Journal of the American Society for Information Science* 23:4 (July-August 1972), 254-265.

609 Janet Friedlander. "Clinician Search for Information," *Journal of the American Society for Information Science* 24:1 (January-February 1973), 65-69.

610 Tefko Saracevic and Lawrence J. Perk. "Ascertaining Activities in a Subject Area through Bibliometric Analysis," *Journal of the American Society for Information Science* 24:3 (March-April 1973), 120-134. **(181, 182)**

611 Ruth Kay Maloney. "Title versus Title/Abstract Text Searching in SDI Systems," *Journal of the American Society for Information Science* 25:6 (November-December 1974), 370-373.

612 Gladys B. Dronberger and Gerald T. Kowitz. "Abstract Readability as a Factor in Information Systems," *Journal of the American Society for Information Science* 26:2 (March-April 1975), 108-111.

613 Jerry R. Byrne. "Relative Effectiveness of Titles, Abstracts and Subject Headings for Machine Retrieval from the COMPENDEX Services," *Journal of the American Society for Information Science* 26:4 (July-August 1975), 223-229.

614 Joseph D. Smith and James E. Rush. "The Relationship between Author Names and Author Entries in a Large On-Line Union Catalog as Retrieved Using Truncated Keys," *Journal of the American Society for Information Science* 28:2 (March 1977), 115-120.

615 Marcia J. Bates. "Factors Affecting Subject Catalog Search Success," *Journal of the American Society for Information Science* 28:3 (May 1977), 161-169.

616 Terry Noreault, Matthew Koll and Michael J. McGill. "Automatic Ranked Output from Boolean Searches in SIRE," *Journal of the American Society for Information Science* 28:6 (November 1977), 333-339.

617 Chai Kim and Eui Hang Shin. "Sociodemographic Correlates of Intercounty Variations in the Public Library Output," *Journal of the American Society for Information Science* 28:6 (November 1977), 359-365.

618 Harold E. Bamford, Jr. "Assessing the Effect of Computer Augmentation on Staff Productivity," *Journal of the American Society for Information Science* 30:3 (May 1979), 136-142.

619 Charles H. Davis and Deborah Shaw. "Collection Overlap as a Function of Library Size: A Comparison of American and Canadian Public Libraries," *Journal of the American Society for Information Science* 30:1 (January 1979), 19-24.

620 M. Carl Drott and Belver C. Griffith. "An Empirical Examination of Bradford's Law and the Scattering of Scientific Literature," *Journal of the American Society for Information Science* 29:5 (September 1978), 238-246.

621 James D. Anderson. "*Ad hoc* and Selective Translations of Scientific and Technical Journal Articles: Their Characteristicsand Possible Predictability," *Journal of the American Societyfor Information Science* 29:3 (May 1978), 130-135.

622 Richard C. Anderson, Francis Narin and Paul McAllister. "Publication Ratings versus Peer Ratings of Universities," *Journal of the American Society for Information Science* 29:2 (March 1978), 91-103. (**63, 65, 76**)

623 Dennis R. Eichesen. "Cost-Effectiveness Comparison of Manual and On-line Retrospective Bibliographic Searching," *Journal of the American Society for Information Science* 29:2 (March 1978), 56-66.

624 Topsy N. Smalley. "Comparing *Psychological Abstracts* and *Index Medicus* for Coverage of the Journal Literature in a Subject Area in Psychology," *Journal of the American Society for Information Science* 31:3 (May 1980), 144-146.

625 Paul R. McAllister, Richard C. Anderson and Francis Narin. "Comparison of Peer and Citation Assessment of the Influence of Scientific Journals," *Journal of the American Society for Information Science* 31:3 (May 1980), 148-152.(**76**)

626 Jerry Specht. "Patron Use of an Online Circulation System in Known-Item Searching," *Journal of the American Society for Information Science* 31:5 (September 1980), 335-346.

627 Guilbert C. Hentschke and Ellen Kehoe. "Serial Acquisition as a Capital Budgeting Problem," *Journal of the American Society for Information Science* 31:5 (September 1980), 357-362.

628 G. Edward Evans and Claudia White Argyres. "Approval Plans and Collection Development in Academic Libraries," *Library Resources and Technical Services* 18:1 (Winter 1974), 35-50.

629 Doris E. New and Retha Zane Ott. "Interlibrary Loan Analysis as a Collection Development Tool," *Library Resources and Technical Services* 18:3 (Summer 1974), 275-283.

630 H. William Axford. "The Validity of Book Price Indexes for Budgetary Projections," *Library Resources and Technical Services* 19:1 (Winter 1975), 5-12.

631 Geza A. Kosa. "Book Selection Tools for Subject Specialists in a Large Research Library: An Analysis," *Library Resources and Technical Services* 19:1 (Winter 1975), 13-18.

632 George P. D'Elia. "The Determinants of Job Satisfaction among Beginning Librarians," *Library Quarterly* 49:3 (July 1979), 283-302.

633 Tim LaBorie and Michael Halperin. "Citation Patterns in Library Science Dissertations," *Journal of Education for Librarianship* 16:4 (Spring 1976), 271-283. **(17, 18)**

634 Anne Woodsworth and Victor R. Neufeld. "A Survey of Physician Self-education Patterns in Toronto. Part 1: Use of Libraries," *Canadian Library Journal* 29:1 (January-February 1972), 38-44.

635 Richard Eggleton. "The ALA Duplicates Exchange Union—A Study and Evaluation," *Library Resources and Technical Services* 19:2 (Spring 1975), 148-163.

636 Katherine H. Packer and Dagobert Soergel. "The Importance of SDI for Current Awareness in Fields with Severe Scatter of Information," *Journal of the American Society for Information Science* 30:3 (May 1979), 125-135.

637 Doris M. Carson. "The Act of Cataloging," *Library Resources and Technical Services* 20:2 (Spring 1976), 149-153.

638 Robert L. Mowery. "The Cutter Classification: Still at Work," *Library Resources and Technical Services* 20:2 (Spring 1976), 154-156.

639 Kelly Patterson, Carol White and Martha Whittaker. "Thesis Handling in University Libraries," *Library Resources and Technical Services* 21:3 (Summer 1977), 274-285.

640 Sandra L. Stokley and Marion T. Reid. "A Study of Performance of Five Book Dealers Used by Louisiana State University Library," *Library Resources and Technical Services* 22:2 (Spring 1978), 117-125.

641 Hans H. Wellisch. "Multiscript and Multilingual Bibliographic Control: Alternatives to Romanization," *Library Resources and Technical Services* 22:2 (Spring 1978), 179-190.

642 Bert R. Boyce and Mark Funk. "Bradford's Law and the Selection of High Quality Papers," *Library Resources and Technical Services* 22:4 (Fall 1978), 390-401.

643 Susan Dingle-Cliff and Charles H. Davis. "Comparison of Recent Acquisitions and OCLC Find Rates for Three Canadian Special Libraries," *Journal of the American Society for Information Science* 32:1 (January 1981), 65-69.

644 Rose Mary Juliano Longo and Ubaldino Dantas Machado. "Characterization of Databases in the Agricultural Sciences," *Journal of the American Society for Information Science* 32:2 (March 1981), 83-91.

645 Edward S. Warner. "The Impact of Interlibrary Access to Periodicals on Subscription Continuation/Cancellation Decision Making," *Journal of the American Society for Information Science* 32:2 (March 1981), 93-95.

646 Charles T. Payne and Robert S. McGee. "Comparisons of LC Proofslip and MARC Tape Arrival Dates at the University of Chicago Library," *Journal of Library Automation* 3:2 (June 1970), 115-121.

647 Wanda V. Dole and David Allerton. "University Collections: A Survey of Costs," *Library Acquistions: Practice and Theory* 6:2 (1982), 25-32.

648 Silvia A. Gonzalez. "1976 Statistical Survey of Law Libraries Serving a Local Bar," *Law Library Journal* 70:2 (May 1977), 222-237. **(101)**

649 Carole J. Mankin and Jacqueline D. Bastille. "An Analysis of the Differences between Density-of-Use Ranking and Raw-Use Ranking of Library Journal Use," *Journal of the American Society for Information Science* 32:3 (May 1981), 224-228.

650 Katherine W. McCain and James E. Bobick. "Patterns of Journal Use in a Departmental Library: A Citation Analysis," *Journal of the American Society for Information Science* 32:4 (July 1981), 257-267.

651 Manfred Kochen, Victoria Reich and Lee Cohen. "Influence on [sic] Online Bibliographic Services on Student Behavior," *Journal of the American Society for Information Science* 32:6 (November 1981), 412-420.

652 Mark P. Carpenter and Francis Narin. "The Adequacy of the *Science Citation Index* (SCI) as an Indicator of International Scientific Activity," *Journal of the American Society for Information Science* 32:6 (November 1981), 430-439.

653 Chai Kim. "Retrieval Languages of Social Sciences and Natural Sciences: A Statistical Investigation," *Journal of the American Society for Information Science* 33:1 (January 1982), 3-7.

654 Ann H. Schabas. "Postcoordinate Retrieval: A Comparison of Two Indexing Languages," *Journal of the American Society for Information Science* 33:1 (January 1982), 32-37.

655 Miranda Lee Pao. "Collaboration in Computational Musicology," *Journal of the American Society for Information Science* 33:1 (January 1982), 38-43.

656 Robert K. Poyer. "*Science Citation Index*'s Coverage of the Preclinical Science Literature," *Journal of the American Society for Information Science* 33:5 (September 1982), 333-337.

657 Stephen M. Lawani and Alan E. Bayer. "Validity of Citation Criteria for Assessing the Influence of Scientific Publications: New Evidence with Peer Assessment," *Journal of the American Society for Information Science* 34:1 (January 1983), 59-66. **(75)**

658 Edward G. Summers, Joyce Matheson and Robert Conry. "The Effect of Personal, Professional and Psychological Attributes, and Information Seeking Behavior on the Use of Information Sources by Educators," *Journal of the American Society for Information Science* 34:1 (January 1983), 75-85.

659 Bluma C. Peritz. "A Note on 'Scholarliness' and 'Impact,'" *Journal of the American Society for Information Science* 34:5 (September 1983), 360-362. (76)

660 Michael D. Cooper. "Response Time Variations in an Online Search System," *Journal of the American Society for Information Science* 34:6 (November 1983), 374-380.

661 Richard S. Marcus. "An Experimental Comparison of the Effectiveness of Computers and Humans as Search Intermediaries," *Journal of the American Society for Information Science* 34:6 (November 1983), 381-404.

662 Michael J. Simonds, "Work Attitudes and Union Membership," *College and Research Libraries* 36:2 (March 1975), 136-142.

663 Jerold Nelson. "Faculty Awareness and Attitudes toward Academic Library Reference Services: A Measure of Communication," *College and Research Libraries* 34:5 (September 1973), 268-275.

664 Andre Nitecki, "Polish Books in America and the Farmington Plan," *College and Research Libraries* 27:6 (November 1966), 439-449.

665 Leslie R. Morris. "Projections of the Number of Library School Graduates," *Journal of Education for Librarianship* 22:4 (Spring 1982), 283-291. (21, 58, 59, 72)

666 Thomas J. Galvin and Allen Kent. "Use of a University Library Collection," *Library Journal* 102:20 (November 1977), 2317-2320. [For further and more complete information see Allen Kent, et al. *Use of Library Materials: The University of Pittsburgh Study.* New York: Marcel Dekker, 1979.]

667 Allen Kent. "Library Resource Sharing Networks: How To Make a Choice," *Library Acquisitions: Practice and Theory* 2 (1978), 69-76. [For further and more complete information see Allen Kent, et al. *Use of Library Materials: The University of Pittsburgh Study.* New York: Marcel Dekker, 1979.]

668 Leigh S. Estabrook and Kathleen M. Heim. "A Profile of ALA Personal Members," *American Libraries* 11:11 (December 1980), 654-659. [For a fuller and more complete description of this study see Kathleen M. Heim and Leigh S. Estabrook. *Career Profiles and Sex Discrimination in the Library Profession.* Chicago: American Library Association, 1983.](56, 95, 129, 130, 135, 145, 150, 152, 165, 170, 171, 172, 173, 174, 175, 190)

669 Mary Lee DeVilbiss. "The Approval-Built Collection in the Medium-Sized Academic Library," *College and Research Libraries* 36:6 (November 1975), 487-492.

670 Thomas P. Fleming and Frederick G. Kilgour. "Moderately and Heavily Used Biomedical Journals," *Bulletin of the Medical Library Association* 52:1 (January 1964), 234-241.

671 Richard J. Hyman. "Medical Interlibrary Loan Patterns," *Bulletin of the Medical Library Association* 53:2 (April 1965), 215-224.

672 L. Miles Raisig, Meredith Smith, Renata Cuff and Frederick G. Kilgour. "How Biomedical Investigators Use Library Books," *Bulletin of the Medical Library Association* 54:2 (April 1966), 104-107.

673 Helen Crawford. "Centralization vs. Decentralization in Medical School Libraries," *Bulletin of the Medical Library Association* 54:2 (April 1966), 199-205.

674 Peter Stangl and Frederick G. Kilgour. "Analysis of Recorded Biomedical Book and Journal Use in the Yale Medical Library," *Bulletin of the Medical Library Association* 55:3 (July 1967), 290-300.

675 Peter Stangl and Frederick G. Kilgour. "Analysis of Recorded Biomedical Book and Journal Use in the Yale Medical Library," *Bulletin of the Medical Library Association* 55:3 (July 1967), 301-315.

676 Gwendolyn S. Cruzat. "Keeping Up with Biomedical Meetings," *Bulletin of the Medical Library Association* 56:2 (April 1968), 132-137.

677 Joan B. Woods, Sam Pieper and Shervert H. Frazier. "Basic Psychiatric Literature: I. Books," *Bulletin of the Medical Library Association* 56:3 (July 1968), 295-309.

678 Joan B. Woods, Sam Pieper and Shervert H. Frazier. "Basic Psychiatric Literature: II. Articles and Article Sources," *Bulletin of the Medical Library Association* 56:4 (October 1968), 404-427.

679 Reva Pachefsky. "Survey of the Card Catalog in Medical Libraries," *Bulletin of the Medical Library Association* 57:1 (January 1969), 10-20.

680 Janet Barlup. "Mechanization of Library Procedures in the Medium-sized Medical Library: VII. Relevancy of Cited Articles in Citation Indexing," *Bulletin of the Medical Library Association* 57:3 (July 1969), 260-263.

681 Wilhelm Moll. "Basic Journal List for Small Hospital Libraries," *Bulletin of the Medical Library Association* 57:3 (July 1969), 267-271.

682 Lois Ann Colainni and Robert F. Lewis. "Reference Services in U.S. Medical School Libraries," *Bulletin of the Medical Library Association* 57:3 (July 1969), 272-274.

683 Vern M. Pings and Joyce E. Malin. "Access to the Scholarly Record of Medicine by the Osteopathic Physicians of Southeastern Michigan," *Bulletin of the Medical Library Association* 58:1 (January 1970), 18-22.

684 D.J. Goode, J.K. Penry and J.F. Caponio. "Comparative Analysis of *Epilepsy Abstracts* and a MEDLARS Bibliography," *Bulletin of the Medical Library Association* 58:1 (January 1970), 44-50.

685 Robert Oseasohn. "Borrower Use of a Modern Medical Library by Practicing Physicians," *Bulletin of the Medical Library Association* 59:1 (January 1970), 58-59.

686 Joan M.B. Smith. "A Periodical Use Study at Children's Hospital of Michigan," *Bulletin of the Medical Library Association* 58:1 (January 1970), 65-67.

687 Jean K. Miller. "Mechanization of Library Procedures in the Medium-sized Medical Library: XI. Two Methods of Providing Selective Dissemination of Information to Medical Scientists," *Bulletin of the Medical Library Association* 58:3 (July 1970), 378-397.

688 Stella S. Gomes. "The Nature and the Use and Users of the Midwest Regional Medical Library," *Bulletin of the Medical Library Association* 58:4 (October 1970), 559-577.

689 Donald A. Windsor. "Publications on a Drug before the First Report of Its Administration to Man," *Bulletin of the Medical Library Association* 59:3 (July 1971), 433-437.

690 Charles L. Bowden and Virginia M. Bowden. "A Survey of Information Sources Used by Psychiatrists," *Bulletin of the Medical Library Association* 59:4 (October 1971), 603-608.

691 Ruth E. Fenske. "Mechanization of Library Procedures in the Medium-sized Medical Library: XIV. Correlations between National Library of Medicine Classification Numbers and MeSH Headings," *Bulletin of the Medical Library Association* 60:2 (April 1972), 319-324.

692 Anne Brearley Piternick. "Measurement of Journal Availability in a Biomedical Library," *Bulletin of the Medical Library Association* 60:4 (October 1972), 534-542.

693 Isabel Spiegel and Janet Crager. "Comparison of SUNY and MEDLINE Searches," *Bulletin of the Medical Library Association* 61:2 (April 1973), 205-209.

694 Fred W. Roper. "Special Programs in Medical Library Education, 1957-1971: Part II: Analysis of the Programs," *Bulletin of the Medical Library Association* 61:4 (October 1973), 387-395.(6, 58)

695 Norma Jean Lodico. "Physician's Referral Letter Bibliographic Service: A New Method of Disseminating Medical Information," *Bulletin of the Medical Library Association* 61:4 (October 1973), 422-432.

696 Wilhelm Moll. "MEDLINE Evaluation Study," *Bulletin of the Medical Library Association* 62:1 (January 1974), 1-5.

697 Pamela Tibbetts. "A Method for Estimating the In-House Use of the Periodical Collection in the University of Minnesota Bio-Medical Library," *Bulletin of the Medical Library Association* 62:1 (January 1974), 37-48.

698 Joan Ash. "Library Use of Public Health Materials: Description and Analysis," *Bulletin of the Medical Library Association* 62:2 (April 1974), 95-104.

699 Ching-Chih Chen. "Current Status of Biomedical Book Reviewing: Part I. Key Biomedical Reviewing Journals with Quantitative Significance," *Bulletin of the Medical Library Association* 62:2 (April 1974), 105-112.

700 Ching-Chih Chen. "Current Status of Biomedical Book Reviewing: Part II. Time Lag in Biomedical Book Reviewing," *Bulletin of the Medical Library Association* 62:2 (April 1974), 113-119.

701 George Scheerer and Lois E. Hines. "Classification Systems Used in Medical Libraries," *Bulletin of the Medical Library Association* 62:3 (July 1974), 272-280.

702 Jo Ann Bell. "The Academic Health Sciences Library and Serial Selection," *Bulletin of the Medical Library Association* 62:3 (July 1974), 281-290.

703 Ching-Chih Chen. "Current Status of Biomedical Book Reviewing: Part III. Duplication Patterns in Biomedical Book Reviewing," *Bulletin of the Medical Library Association* 62:3 (July 1974), 296-301.

704 Ching-Chih Chen. "Current Status of Biomedical Book Reviewing: Part IV. Major American and British Biomedical Book Publishers," *Bulletin of the Medical Library Association* 62:3 (July 1974), 302-308.

705 M. Sandra Wood and Robert S. Seeds. "Development of SDI Services from a Manual Current Awareness Service to SDILINE," *Bulletin of the Medical Library Association* 62:4 (October 1974), 374-384.

706 Margaret Butkovich and Robert M. Braude. "Cost-Performance of Cataloging and Card Production in a Medical Center Library," *Bulletin of the Medical Library Association* 63:1 (January 1975), 29-34.

707 Donald A. Windsor. "Science-Speciality Literatures: Their Legendary-Contemporary Parity, Based on the Transmission of Information between Generations," *Bulletin of the Medical Library Association* 63:2 (April 1975), 209-215.

708 Helen J. Brown, Jean K. Miller and Diane M. Pinchoff. "Study of the Information Dissemination Service—Health Sciences Library, State University of New York at Buffalo," *Bulletin of the Medical Library Association* 63:3 (July 1975), 259-271.

709 Rachel K. Goldstein and Dorothy R. Hill. "The Status of Women in the Administration of Health Science Libraries," *Bulletin of the Medical Library Association* 63:4 (October 1975), 386-395. **(132, 133, 138, 140, 141, 145, 146, 150, 151, 176)**

710 Janet G. Schnall and Joan W. Wilson. "Evaluation of a Clinical Medical Librarianship Program at a University Health Sciences Library," *Bulletin of the Medical Library Association* (July 1976), 278-283.

711 Anne B. Piternick. "Effects of Binding Policy and Other Factors on the Availability of Journal Issues," *Bulletin of the Medical Library Association* 64:3 (July 1976), 284-292.

712 Richard B. Fredericksen and Helen N. Michael. "Subject Cataloging Practices in North American Medical School Libraries," *Bulletin of the Medical Library Association* 64:4 (October 1976), 356-366.

713 Paul M. McIlvaine and Malcolm H. Brantz. "Audiovisual Materials: A Survey of Bibliographic Controls in Distributors' Catalogs," *Bulletin of the Medical Library Association* 65:1 (January 1977), 17-21.

714 Bette Greenberg, Robert Breedlove and Wendy Berger. "MEDLINE Demand Profiles: An Analysis of Requests for Clinical and Research Information," *Bulletin of the Medical Library Association* 65:1 (January 1977), 22-28.

715 Renata Tagliacozzo. "Estimating the Satisfaction of Information Users," *Bulletin of the Medical Library Association* 65:2 (April 1977), 243-249.

716 Ruth W. Wender, Ester L. Fruehauf, Marilyn S. Vent and Constant D. Wilson. "Determination of Continuing Medical Education Needs of Clinicians from a Literature Search Study: Part I. The Study," *Bulletin of the Medical Library Association* 65:3 (July 1977), 330-337.

717 Ruth W. Wender, Ester L. Fruehauf, Marilyn S. Vent and Constant D. Wilson. "Determination of Continuing Medical Education Needs of Clinicians from a Literature Search Study: Part II. Questionnaire Results," *Bulletin of the Medical Library Association* 65:3 (July 1977), 338-341.

718 Donald J. Morton. "Analysis of Interlibrary Requests by Hospital Libraries for Photocopied Journal Articles," *Bulletin of the Medical Library Association* 65:4 (October 1977), 425-432,

719 Patrick W. Brennen and W. Patrick Davey. "Citation Analysis in the Literature of Tropical Medicine," *Bulletin of the Medical Library Association* 66:1 (January 1978), 24-30.

720 Theresa C. Strasser. "The Information Needs of Practicing Physicians in Northeastern New York State," *Bulletin of the Medical Library Association* 66:2 (April 1978), 200-209.

721 Inci A. Bowman, Elizabeth K. Eaton and J. Maurice Mahan. "Are Health Science Faculty Interested in Medical History? An Evaluative Case Study," *Bulletin of the Medical Library Association* 66:2 (April 1978), 228-231.

722 Maurice C. Leatherbury and Richard A. Lyders. "Friends of the Library Groups in Health Sciences Libraries," *Bulletin of the Medical Library Association* 66:3 (July 1978), 315-318.

723 Bette Greenberg, Sara Battison, Madeleine Kolisch and Martha Leredu. "Evaluation of a Clinical Medical Librarian Program at the Yale Medical Library," *Bulletin of the Medical Library Association* 66:3 (July 1978), 319-326.

724 Gloria Werner. "Use of On-Line Bibliographic Retrieval Services in Health Sciences Libraries in the United States and Canada," *Bulletin of the Medical Library Association* 67:1 (January 1979), 1-14.

725 B. Tommie Usdin. "Core Lists of Medical Journals: A Comparison," *Bulletin of the Medical Library Association* 67:2 (April 1979), 212-217.

726 John A. Timour. "Brief Communications: Use of Selected Abstracting and Indexing Journals in Biomedical Resource Libraries," *Bulletin of the Medical Library Association* 67:3 (July 1979), 330-335.

727 Rachel K. Goldstein and Dorothy R. Hill. "The Status of Women in the Administration of Health Sciences Libraries: A Five-Year Follow-Up Study, 1972-1977," *Bulletin of the Medical Library Association* 68:1 (January 1980), 6-15. (**138, 139, 141, 142, 143, 145, 146**)

728 Richard T. West and Maureen J. Malone. "Communicating the Results of NLM Grant-supported Library Projects," *Bulletin of the Medical Library Association* 68:1 (January 1980), 33-39. (**189**)

729 James A. Thompson and Michael R. Kronenfeld. "The Effect of Inflation on the Cost of Journals on the Brandon List," *Bulletin of the Medical Library Association* 68:1 (January 1980), 47-52.

730 Carol C. Spencer. "Random Time Sampling with Self-observation for Library Cost Studies: Unit Costs of Reference Questions," *Bulletin of the Medical Library Association* 68:1 (January 1980), 53-57.

731 Justine Roberts. "Circulation versus Photocopy: Quid pro Quo?" *Bulletin of the Medical Library Association* 68:3 (July 1980), 274-277.

732 Dick R. Miller and Joseph E. Jensen. "Dual Pricing of Health Sciences Periodicals: A Survey," *Bulletin of the Medical Library Association* 68:4 (October 1980), 336-347.

733 Jacqueline D. Bastille. "A Simple Objective Method for Determining a Dynamic Journal Collection," *Bulletin of the Medical Library Association* 68:4 (October 1980), 357-366.

734 Mary H. Mueller. "An Examination of Characteristics Related to Success of Friends Groups in Medical School Rare Book Libraries," *Bulletin of the Medical Library Association* 69:1 (January 1981), 9-13.

735 Scott Davis, Lincoln Polissar and Joan W. Wilson. "Continuing Education in Cancer for the Community Physician: Design and Evaluation of a Regional

Table of Contents Service," *Bulletin of the Medical Library Association* 69:1 (January 1981), 14-20.

736 Gary D. Byrd. "Copyright compliance in Health Sciences Libraries: A Status Report Two Years after the Implementation of PL 94-553," *Bulletin of the Medical Library Association* 69:2 (April 1981), 224-230.

737 Ester L. Baldinger, Jennifer P.S. Nakeff-Plaat and Margaret S. Cummings. "An Experimental Study of the Feasibility of Substituting Chemical Abstracts Online for the Printed Copy in a Medium-Sized Medical Library," *Bulletin of the Medical Library Association* 69:2 (April 1981), 247-251.

738 Doris R.F. Dunn. "Dissemination of the Published Results of an Important Clinical Trial: An Analysis of the Citing Literature," *Bulletin of the Medical Library Association* 69:3 (July 1981), 301-306.

739 Cynthia H. Goldstein. "A Study of Weeding Policies in Eleven TALON Resource Libraries," *Bulletin of the Medical Library Association* 69:3 (July 1981), 311-316.

740 K. Suzanne Johnson and E. Guy Coffee. "Veterinary Medical School Libraries in the United States and Canada, 1977-78," *Bulletin of the Medical Library Association* 70:1 (January 1982), 10-20. **(101, 112, 117)**

741 Suzanne F. Grefsheim, Robert H. Larson, Shelley A. Bader and Nina W. Matheson. "Automation of Internal Library Operations in Academic Health Sciences Libraries: A State of the Art Report," *Bulletin of the Medical Library Association* 70:2 (April 1982), 191-200.

742 Elizabeth R. Lenz and Carolyn F. Walz. "Nursing Educators' Satisfaction with Library Facilities," *Bulletin of the Medical Library Association* 70:2 (April 1982), 201-206.

743 Ruth Traister Morris, Edwin A. Holtum and David S. Curry. "Being There: The Effect of the User's Presence on MEDLINE Search Results," *Bulletin of the Medical Library Association* 70:3 (July 1982), 298-304.

744 James K. Cooper, Diane Cooper and Timothy P. Johnson. "Medical Library Support in Rural Areas," *Bulletin of the Medical Library Association* 71:1 (January 1983), 13-15.

745 Susan Crawford. "Health Science Libraries in the United States: I. Overview of the Post-World War II Years," *Bulletin of the Medical Library Association* 71:1 (January 1983), 16-20.

746 Susan Crawford and Alan M. Rees. "Health Sciences Libraries in the United States: II. Medical School Libraries, 1960-1980," *Bulletin of the Medical Library Association* 71:1 (January 1983), 21-29.

747 Susan Crawford. "Health Science Libraries in the United States: III. Hospital Health Science Libraries, 1969-1979," *Bulletin of the Medical Library Association* 71:1 (January 1983), 30-36. **(104)**

748 Mark E. Funk and Carolyn Anne Reid. "Indexing Consistency in MED-LINE," *Bulletin of the Medical Library Association* 71:2 (April 1983), 176-183.

749 Michael R. Kronenfeld and Sarah H. Gable. "Real Inflation of Journal Prices: Medical Journals, U.S. Journals and Brandon List Journals," *Bulletin of the Medical Library Association* 71:4 (October 1983), 375-379.

750 Jane McCarthy. "Survey of Audiovisual Standards and Practices in Health Sciences Libraries," *Bulletin of the Medical Library Association* 71:4 (October 1983), 391-395.

751 Rajia C. Tobia and David A. Kronick. "A Clinical Information Consultation Service at a Teaching Hospital," *Bulletin of the Medical Library Association* 71:4 (October 1983), 396-399.

752 Elizabeth R. Ashin. "Library Service to Dental Practitioners," *Bulletin of the Medical Library Association* 71:4 (October 1983), 400-402.

753 Peter P. Olevnik. "Non-Formalized Point-of-Use Library Instruction: A Survey," *Catholic Library World* 50:5 (December 1978), 218-220.

754 Susan A. Stussy. "Automation in Catholic College Libraries," *Catholic Library World* 53:3 (October 1981), 109-111.

755 R.M. Longyear. "Article Citations and 'Obsolescence' in Musicological Journals," *Notes* 33:3 (March 1977), 563-571.

756 Ann Basart. "Criteria for Weeding Books in a University Music Library," *Notes* 36:4 (June 1980), 819-836.

757 Richard P. Smiraglia and Arsen R. Papakhian. "Music in the OCLC Online Union Catalog: A Review," *Notes* 38:2 (December 1981), 257-274.

758 William Gray Potter. "When Names Collide: Conflict in the Catalog and AACR 2," *Library Resources and Technical Services* 24:1 (Winter 1980), 3-16.

759 Rose Mary Magrill and Constance Rinehart. "Selection for Preservation: A Service Study," *Library Resources and Technical Services* 24:1 (Winter 1980), 44-57.

760 Sally Braden, John D. Hall and Helen H. Britton. "Utilization of Personnel and Bibliographic Resources for Cataloging by OCLC Participating Libraries," *Library Resources and Technical Services* 24:2 (Spring 1980), 135-154.

761 Cynthia C. Ryans. "Cataloging Administrators' Views on Cataloging Education," *Library Resources and Technical Services* 24:4 (Fall 1980), 343-351. **(8, 9, 158)**

762 Thomas Schadlich. "Changing from Sears to LC Subject Headings," *Library Resources and Technical Services* 24:4 (Fall 1980), 361-363.

763 Elizabeth L. Tate. "For Our 25th Anniversary...," *Library Resources and Technical Services* 25:1 (January/March 1981), 3-7.(**40, 41, 190, 195, 197**)

764 Barbara Moore. "Patterns in the Use of OCLC by Academic Library Cataloging Departments," *Library Resources and Technical Services* 25:1 (January/March 1981), 30-39.

765 Judith J. Johnson and Clair S. Josel. "Quality Control and the OCLC Data Base: A Report on Error Reporting," *Library Resources and Technical Services* 25:1 (January/March 1981), 40-47.

766 Edward T. O'Neill and Rao Aluri. "Library of Congress Subject Heading Patterns in OCLC Monographic Records," *Library Resources and Technical Services* 25:1 (January/March 1981), 63-80.

767 Elizabeth H. Groot. "A Comparison of Library Tools for Monograph Verification," *Library Resources and Technical Services* 25:2 (April/June 1981), 149-161.

768 Elizabeth G. Mikita. "Monographs in Microform: Issues in Cataloging and Bibliographic Control," *Library Resources and Technical Services* 25:4 (October/December 1981), 352-361.

769 Lee R. Nemchek. "Problems of Cataloging and Classification in Theater Librarianship," *Library Resources and Technical Services* 25:4 (October/December 1981), 374-385.

770 John Hostage. "AACR 2, OCLC, and the Card Catalog in the Medium-Sized Library," *Library Resources and Technical Services* 26:1 (January/March 1982), 12-20.

771 Robert H. Hassell. "Revising the Dewey Music Schedules: Tradition vs. Innovation," *Library Resources and Technical Services* 26:2 (April/June 1982), 192-203.

772 Patricia Dwyer Wanninger. "Is the OCLC Database Too Large? A Study of the Effect of Duplicate Records in the OCLC System," *Library Resources and Technical Services* 26:4 (October/December 1982), 353-361.

773 Stephen R. Salmon. "Characteristics of Online Public Catalogs," *Library Resources and Technical Services* 27:1 (January/March 1983), 36-67.

774 Thomas E. Nisonger. "A Test of Two Citation Checking Techniques for Evaluating Political Science Collections in University Libraries," *Library Resources and Technical Services* 27:2 (April/June 1983), 163-176.

775 John Rutledge and Willy Owen. "Changes in the Quality of Paper in French Books, 1860-1914: A Study of Selected Holdings of the Wilson Library, University of North Carolina," *Library Resources and Technical Services* (April/June 1983), 177-187.

776   Jim Williams and Nancy Romero. "A Comparison of the OCLC Database and *New Serial Titles* as an Information Resource for Serials," *Library Resources and Technical Services* 27:2 (April/June 1983), 177-187.

777   Mary E. Clack and Sally F. Williams. "Using Locally and Nationally Produced Periodical Price Indexes in Budget Preparation," *Library Resources and Technical Services* 27:4 (October/December 1983), 345-356.

778   Victoria Cheponis Lessard and Jack Hall. "Vocational Technical Collection Building: Does it Exist?" *Collection Building* 4:2 (1982), 6-18.

779   Virginia Witucke. "The Reviewing of Children's Science Books," *Collection Building* 4:2 (1982) 19-30.

780   Margaret F. Stieg. "The Information Needs of Historians," *College and Research Libraries* 42:6 (November 1981), 549-560.

781   Howard D. White. "Library Censorship and the Permissive Minority," *Library Quarterly* 51:2 (1981), 192-207.

782   Judith Serebnick. "Book Reviews and the Selection of Potentially Controversial Books in Public Libraries," *Library Quarterly* 51:4 (1981), 390-409.

783   Richard W. Scamell and Bette Ann Stead. "A Study of Age and Tenure as it Pertains to Job Satisfaction," *Journal of Library Administration* 1:1 (Spring 1980), 3-18.

784   Robert M. Hayes. "Citation Statistics as a Measure of Faculty Research Productivity," *Journal of Education for Librarianship* 23:3 (Winter 1983), 151-172. (**42, 43, 44, 66**)

785   William Skeh Wong and David S. Zubatsky. "The First-Time Appointed Academic Library Director 1970-1980: A Profile," *Journal of Library Administration* 4:1 (Spring 1983), 41-70. (**65, 140, 165, 181, 187, 192**)

786   James Rice, Jr. "An Assessment of Student Preferences for Method of Library Orientation," *Journal of Library Administration* 4:1 (Spring 1983), 87-93.

787   Frank William Goudy. "Affirmative Action and Library Science Degrees: A Statistical Overview, 1973-74 through 1980-81," *Journal of Library Administration* 4:3 (Fall 1983), 51-60. (**22, 23, 48, 49, 51, 52, 56, 57, 58**)

788   Thomas G. English. "Librarian Status in the Eighty-Nine U.S. Academic Institutions of the Association of Research Libraries: 1982," *College and Research Libraries* 44:3 (May 1983), 199-211. (**115, 116, 122, 125, 205**)

789   Nathan M. Smith and Veneese C. Nelson. "Burnout: A Survey of Academic Reference Librarians," *College and Research Libraries* 44:3 (May 1983), 245-250.

790 Floris W. Wood. "Reviewing Book Review Indexes," *Reference Services Review* (April/June 1980), 47-52.

791 Herbert Goldhor. "Public Library Circulation up 3%; Spending Jumps 11%," *American Libraries* 14:8 (September 1983), 534.

792 Laura N. Gasaway and Steve Margeton. "Continuing Education for Law Librarianship," *Law Library Journal* 70:1 (February 1977), 39-52.

793 Michael L. Renshawe. "The Condition of the Law Librarian in 1976," *Law Library Review* 69:4 (November 1976), 626-640. **(80, 81, 89, 95, 101, 111, 116, 128, 134, 141, 153, 176, 177, 178)**

794 Susanne Patterson Wahba. "Women in Libraries," *Law Library* Journal 69:2 (May 1976), 223-231.

795 Jean Finch and Lauri R. Flynn. "An Update on Faculty Libraries," *Law Library Journal* 73:1 (Winter 1980), 99-106.

796 Robert D. Swisher, Peggy C. Smith and Calvin J. Boyer. "Educational Change Among ACRL Academic Librarians," *Library Research* (*Library and Information Science Research* since Spring 1983) 5:2 (Summer 1983), 195-205.

797 Michael D. Cooper. "Economies of Scale in Academic Libraries," *Library Research* (*Library and Information Science Research* after Spring 1983) 5:2 (Summer 1983), 207-219.

798 Virgil Diodato. "Faculty Workload: A Case Study," *Journal of Education for Librarianship* 23:4 (Spring 1983), 286-295. **(94)**

799 Jerry D. Saye. "Continuing Education and Library School Faculty," *Journal of Education for Librarianship* 24:1 (Summer 1983), 3-16. **(143, 144)**

800 Maurice P. Marchant and Carolyn F. Wilson. "Developing Joint Graduate Programs for Librarians," *Journal of Education for Librarianship* 24:1 (Summer 1983), 30-37.

801 Barbara L. Stein and Herman L. Totten. "Cognitive Styles: Similarities Among Students," *Journal of Education for Librarianship* 24:1 (Summer 1983), 38-43. **(45)**

802 Marilyn J. Markham, Keith H. Stirling and Nathan M. Smith. "Librarian Self-Disclosure and Patron Satisfaction in the Reference Interview," *RQ* 22:4 (Summer 1983), 369-374. **(32, 33)**

803 June L. Engle and Elizabeth Futas. "Sexism in Adult Encyclopedias," *RQ* 23:1 (Fall 1983), 29-39. **(10, 11, 91, 92)**

804 David F. Kohl. "Circulation Professionals: Management Information Needs and Attitudes," *RQ* 23:1 (Fall 1983), 81-86. **(69, 71)**

805 Kevin Carey. "Problems and Patterns of Periodical Literature Searching at an Urban University Research Library," *RQ* 23:2 (Winter 1983), 211-218.

806 Beverly P. Lynch and Jo Ann Verdin. "Job Satisfaction in Libraries: Relationships of the Work Itself, Age, Sex, Occupational Group, Tenure, Supervisory Level, Career Commitment and Library Department," *Library Quarterly* 53:4 (October 1983), 434-447.

807 Louise W. Diodato and Virgil P. Diodato. "The Use of Gifts in a Medium Sized Academic Library," *Collection Management* 5:1/2 (Spring/Summer 1983), 53-71.

AUTHOR INDEX
TO BIBLIOGRAPHY OF ARTICLES

Note: The index is arranged alphabetically, word by word. All characters or groups of characters separated by spaces, dashes, hyphens, diagonal slashes or periods are treated as separate words. Acronyms not separated by spaces or punctuation are alphabetized as though they are single words, while initials separated by spaces or punctuation are treated as if each letter is a complete word. Personal names beginning with capital Mc, M' and Mac are all listed under Mac as though the full form were used, and St. is alphabetized as if spelled out.

ABOUT THE AUTHORS

DAVID F. KOHL is currently Undergraduate Librarian and Assistant Director for Undergraduate Libraries and Instructional Services at the University of Illinois-Urbana, with the rank of Associate Professor. Dr. Kohl did his graduate work at the University of Chicago. He has taught library administration at the University of Illinois Graduate School of Library and Information Science and has published numerous articles and monographs on library management and automation. His wide range of service in library management includes active participation in the ARL/OMS Library Consultant Program, the Washington State University's Managing for Productivity Program, and the Assessment Center Program for Potential Managers, sponsored jointly by the University of Washington Graduate Library School and the Washington State Library.

KATHLEEN M. HEIM has been Dean of the School of Library and Information Science at Louisiana State University since 1983. She was previously on the faculty of the Graduate School of Library and Information Science at the University of Illinois. Dr. Heim currently chairs the American Library Association's Advisory Committee to the Office for the Library Personnel Resources and edits the Association's official journal of reference and adult services, *RQ*. In addition to presenting many papers at national and state conferences, Heim has written several articles on career development issues for librarians and gender considerations for the profession. Her current research in observation of the centennial of library education is on the role of faculties in national policy making.